THE COMPLETE GUIDE TO FLIPPING PROPERTIES
2nd Edition

Steve Berges

BICENTENNIAL
1807
WILEY
2007
BICENTENNIAL

John Wiley & Sons, Inc.

Published by John Wiley & Sons, Inc., Hoboken, New Jersey
Published simultaneously in Canada

Wiley Bicentennial Logo: Richard J. Pacifico

For general information on our other products and services or for technical support, please contact our Customer Care Department within the United States at (800) 762-2974, outside the United States at (317) 572-3993 or fax (317) 572-4002.

Wiley also publishes its books in a variety of electronic formats. Some content that appears in print may not be available in electronic books. For more information about Wiley products, visit our web site at www.wiley.com.

ISBN 978-0-470-14677-4

Printed in the United States of America
10 9 8 7 6 5 4 3 2 1

CONTENTS

Acknowledgments   vii

Chapter 1   **Fundamental Principles of Investing in Real Estate**   1
     Background   2
     Real Estate—A Sound Investment   3
     Leverage—The OPM Principle   5
     Economic Housing Outlook for the Next Decade   6

PART I   **WHAT EVERY INVESTOR NEEDS TO KNOW ABOUT FLIPPING PROPERTIES**

Chapter 2   **Flipping Properties Defined**   11
     Three Primary Classes of Flippers   13
       Scouts   13
       Dealers   14
       Retailers   16
     Using Options to Flip Properties   17
     Clearly Defined Objectives   18
       Entry Strategy   20
       Post-Entry Strategy   20
       Exit Strategy   21

Chapter 3   **The Value Play Strategy**   23
     Buy-and-Hold Strategy   24
     The Value Play Strategy   25
     The Value Play Selection Process   26
       Property Location   29
       Price Range   30
       Physical Condition   31

Chapter 4   **Ten Ways to Locate Properties**   39
     Real Estate Agents   39
     Classified Advertising   42
     Real Estate Publications   44
     Local and National Web Sites   44
     Real Estate Investment Clubs   45
     Bank REOs   47

■ Contents ■

	Marketing	*48*
	For Sale By Owners (FSBOs)	*51*
	Vacant Properties	*52*
	Foreclosures	*53*

PART II   HOW TO VALUE, ANALYZE, AND NEGOTIATE FOR MAXIMUM PROFIT

Chapter 5	**Valuation Methodologies**	*57*
	How to Know How Much Is too Much	*57*
	Valuation Methodologies	*58*
	Replacement Cost Approach	*58*
	Income Capitalization Approach	*60*
	Sales Comparison Approach	*61*
Chapter 6	**Financial Analysis**	*63*
	The Texas Two-Step	*63*
	Multiply Your Efforts by 22	*70*
	From Residential to Commercial	*77*
Chapter 7	**Seven Steps of Successful Negotiations**	*91*
	The Psychology of Negotiating	*91*
	Comprehensive Knowledge of Market	*93*
	Degree of Seller's Motivation	*94*
	Back Door Exits	*98*
	Concessions	*99*
	The Red Herring Technique	*100*
	The Money Talks Approach	*101*

PART III   INVESTING STRATEGIES FOR THE SMART INVESTOR

Chapter 8	**Financing and Closing Considerations**	*105*
	Conventional Mortgages	*105*
	Mortgage Brokers	*107*
	Local Banks	*107*
	Lines of Credit	*108*
	Owner Financing	*110*
	Partnerships	*111*
	Your Business Plan	*112*
	What Every Borrower Should Know about Credit Scores	*113*
	Underwriting Guidelines	*115*
	The Closing Process	*117*
Chapter 9	**Assemble a Winning Team of Professionals**	*121*
	Scouts and Dealers	*121*
	Office Manager	*123*

■ Contents ■

	Property Rehab Manager	*123*
	Local Lender or Mortgage Broker	*124*
	Real Estate Attorney	*124*
	Title Company	*125*
	Real Estate Agents	*126*
Chapter 10	**Three Keys to Maximizing Your Potential**	**129**
	Post-Entry Planning	*129*
	Doing It Yourself versus Hiring It Out	*131*
	Increase Your Property's Marketability	*134*
PART IV	**IT'S A NEW DAY IN REAL ESTATE**	
Chapter 11	**Radio Program: Weeks 1 and 2**	**141**
	Investment Week #1	*141*
	Investment Week #2	*145*
Chapter 12	**Radio Program: Weeks 3 and 4**	**151**
	Investment Week #3	*151*
	Investment Week #4	*155*
Chapter 13	**Radio Program: Weeks 5 and 6**	**161**
	Investment Week #5	*161*
	Investment Week #6	*166*
Chapter 14	**Radio Program: Weeks 7 and 8**	**173**
	Investment Week #7	*173*
	Investment Week #8	*177*
PART V	**CASE STUDY ANALYSIS AND EPILOGUE**	
Chapter 15	**Case Study Analysis: How *You* Can Go from Zero to $20K in 90 Days or Less!**	**187**
	Case Study: From $0 to $20K	*187*
	The Value Play Rehab Analyzer	*188*
	Purchase Assumptions	*194*
	Primary and Secondary Financing Assumptions	*194*
	Estimate for Improvements	*195*
	Comparable Home Sales	*195*
	Comp Averages	*195*
	Subject Property	*196*
Chapter 16	**The Three Principles of Power**	**201**
	The Principle of Vision	*204*
	The Principle of Passion	*208*
	The Principle of Autonomy	*209*

■ Contents ■

Chapter 17	**(Bonus!) S.M.A.R.T. Goals**	**213**
Appendix A	**Property Inspection Checklist**	**221**
Appendix B	**Owner and Subcontractor Agreement**	**233**
Appendix C	**Sample Real Estate Forms**	**237**
Appendix D	**Sample Personal Financial Statement**	**254**
Appendix E	**thevalueplay.com**	**257**
Appendix F	**symphony-homes.com**	**258**
Glossary		**259**
Index		*279*

ACKNOWLEDGMENTS

Much of my life has been profoundly influenced by not one, but two, loving fathers. The first father is the father of my spirit. He is my Heavenly Father. It is with deep humility and eternal gratitude that I acknowledge His hand in all that is good and virtuous in my life. The second father is the father of my body. He is my earthly father. It is with intense love and great respect that I acknowledge his hand in all that is pure and decent in my life.

The principle of parenthood, and more particularly, fatherhood, is an eternal principle. It is a pattern that was established in our premortal existence, continues in our earthly existence, and shall endure throughout our post-mortal existence. It is with all the sincerity of my heart that I pray I may continue the righteous and loving pattern of fatherhood previously established to the beloved children who have been entrusted into my care—Philip, Samuel, and Benjamin.

Chapter 1

Fundamental Principles of Investing in Real Estate

$\mathbb{B}$uying and selling real estate can be one of the most profitable and lucrative investment activities an individual can participate in. There are many approaches to investing in real estate, most of which are centered around various time horizons. On one end of the investment spectrum is the buy-and-hold strategy where an investor might purchase a property and hold it for many years, and on the other end is the buy-and-sell strategy where an investor might hold the property for only a few months, weeks, or even days. It is the latter of these two strategies that I focus on in this book.

While readers of this book are likely to have broad and diverse backgrounds, you do share one thing in common, that being your interest in real estate and in particular, your interest in flipping properties. I will attempt to be as thorough as possible, since some of you are likely to have little to no experience, while others of you are seasoned professionals searching for that edge. This being the case, those of you who have a great deal of experience may find some of the material to be a bit basic. It is vital, however, that I lay the proper foundation for those who are not as experienced. Many of you have most likely purchased single family houses at one time or another and have at least a minimal degree of rental property experience.

In the next chapter, the concept of flipping properties along with specific types of flipping is more fully discussed. Then in Chapter 3, we examine the notion of a term I coined in a previous book, *The Complete Guide to Buying and Selling Apartment Buildings*, which I refer to as "the value play." I love using the value play strategy because it is the quickest and surest way to build wealth that I know of when the subject is real estate. In Chapter 4, we explore several methods you can begin using immediately to locate prospective investment properties, and in Chapter 5, we study in depth the most common methods of determining value and examine the most appropriate one for use in your analysis. A proper understanding of the valuation process will greatly facilitate the building up of your real estate portfolio. Then in Chapter 6, we examine more fully the practical application of the valuation methods described in Chapter 5 by using various financial analysis models that were created to analyze potential purchase opportunities.

Chapter 7 will help you more fully understand the rules of engagement as they apply to buying and selling properties as we examine the seven steps of successful negotiating. Then in Chapter 8, we study the advantages and disadvantages of many of the methods of financing. We also take a look at the key elements of writing a professional business plan, as well as credit scores, underwriting guidelines, and the closing process. In Chapter 9, we discuss how you can assemble a winning team of professionals to help you maximize your potential. In Chapter 10, we examine the merits of three keys that will better enable you to maximize your potential as a real estate investor.

In Chapters 11 through 14, I have included a section taken from our weekly radio program, "It's a New Day in Real Estate," that features a special eight-week investor series. Chapter 15 provides a detailed case study analysis of how to take a house from start to finish through the flipping process. Chapter 16 discusses what I refer to as the three principles of power. These three principles are not just limited to helping you succeed in real estate, but when properly applied, will benefit you in many aspects of your life and will lead to an increase in your level of fulfillment and happiness. Finally, I have included a special bonus chapter titled S.M.A.R.T. Goals. This chapter provides key information that will allow you to accelerate your progress toward achieving financial success by helping you plan and set goals.

BACKGROUND

A convergence of events from my own life experiences over the last 20-plus years has provided me with unique insight into the real estate market. There are three primary components that have contributed to my experience. First and foremost, like many of you, I have bought and sold a number of both single family and multifamily properties over the years, and I am a current and active investor.

Second, my experience as a financial analyst at one of the largest banks in Texas has provided me with a comprehensive understanding of cash flow analysis. Working in the mergers and acquisitions group for the bank, I reviewed virtually every line item of financial statements of related income and expenses for potential acquisition candidates of numerous banks that we may have had an interest in at any given time. I spent several hours a day using a fairly complex and sophisticated model to determine the proper value, given a specific set of assumptions, that these banks had. Since leaving the bank some years ago, I have developed my own proprietary model that I now use to facilitate the valuation process for single family, multifamily, and development opportunities. The beauty of understanding cash flow analysis is that once you grasp the concept, it can be applied to anything that generates some type of cash flow, whether it be banks, single family houses, manufacturing businesses, or retail outlets. The type of business is not important, provided you understand the key assumptions that relate to the specific industry you are evaluating. Finally, my experience as a commercial mortgage broker has provided me with an inside look at the lending process, and more specifically, what the lenders' underwriting departments typically require to get a loan approved.

I believe the culmination of my own skill sets and life experiences will be of great advantage to you as you seek to enlarge your personal real estate portfolio. I should mention one additional characteristic of mine, which I attribute more to my personality than to any other factor. It is my inability to be satisfied with any single real estate purchase or acquisition. In other words, the traditional process of buying and holding a property, quite frankly, bores me. Who in his right mind wants to buy a piece of real estate and then just sit on it for 10 or 20 years? I know, I know, a lot of people do, including some of you, I'm sure. For me, however, I can't sit still long enough to hold an investment that long. I am more of a trader of sorts, and as that applies to real estate, a flipper. My personality is much better suited to buying, creating value, selling, and then doing it all over again. It is the thrill of the hunt that I most enjoy. It is finding that next deal, and then exploring every possible way to maximize the value of it. In all honesty, I really don't even care for the work and the repairs that are often required to add value to the property. I prefer to delegate as much of that part of the process as possible to those whose skills are more closely suited to those types of activities.

REAL ESTATE—A SOUND INVESTMENT

The concept of buying and selling real estate properties, or flipping, is indisputably one of the surest means for the accumulation of wealth. Although the strategy involving flipping is itself short-term in nature, let me emphatically state that this book is *not* a get-rich-quick book. I am not aware of any so-called get-rich-quick books that were worth the price paid for them. Garnering a sizable real estate portfolio is a process that can take anywhere from a few years to many years. The patient and diligent investor who applies a well defined and systematic approach over time will enjoy a high probability of earning above-average returns for his efforts. As a real estate investor, the fruit you enjoy, however, is directly related to the amount of effort put forth on your part. One is unquestionably a function of the other.

Just as a beautiful and healthy tree requires sunlight, food, and water for proper nourishment, so does the process of building wealth. Leave your fortune to chance, and chances are you will have no fortune to leave. To build wealth, you must plant the proper seeds, and then nourish them with food and water over time. An occasional pruning will also be required. Almost before you realize it, a strong and magnificent tree will begin to take shape right before your very eyes. Although the grand and noble oak tree exhibits towering beauty and strength above the surface of the earth, it is the tree's root system, which extends deep beneath the surface, unseen by human eyes, that gives it force and stability, allowing it to withstand the mighty forces of nature. Like the oak tree, you too, must be well rooted in fundamentally sound principles of real estate before your branches can grow. As you apply the principles you learn from this book, you will eventually be able to enjoy a sweet comfort from the shade that your branches will provide. Although the winds of adversity may descend upon you with great vigor, if you are prepared, they shall not prevail.

To be successful in real estate does not happen by chance. You must have a well-defined plan outlining your specific objectives. Determine exactly what it is you want out of your real estate investment activities and identify your time horizon for accomplishing your goals. Be realistic as well as specific with your objectives. You must begin with the end in mind. In other words, you must know where it is you are going before you can begin the journey to your destination. Otherwise, if you don't know where you are going, how will you know when you get there? I recently traveled to New York City for a business meeting on Wall Street, not far from the New York Stock Exchange. Since I had never been to New York before, the first thing I did was to map out a plan for my trip. I began with the end in mind. The end, the 22nd floor of 67 Wall Street, New York City, New York, was my specific objective. Since I knew that was my destination, it was simple enough to map out a precise plan on how to get there from my point of origin. Inasmuch as I was well prepared when the day for the trip arrived, I was able to travel directly to the city and arrive well ahead of my scheduled time. Only you can determine your destination in life. If you don't have one, then you'll end up exactly where you intended to go, which is nowhere.

You must carefully analyze each property you consider for investment. You cannot afford to shoot from the hip. Proper analysis requires more than a simple review of the property's physical condition and location. To be successful in this business, you must use a comprehensive approach. This book is intended as a guide with which you can develop a format for a complete analysis of each property you consider for flipping. This format, when properly applied, will provide you with a significant competitive edge for the simple reason that most investors do not have a system in place. They may have bits and pieces of a system that they use from time to time, but that is usually the extent of it. By following the guidelines in this book, you will no longer arbitrarily buy and hold or buy and sell, but rather, you will truly understand the keys to successful real estate investing. By the time you are finished reading this book, you will know when to pass on a deal and when not to, and even more importantly, you will know *why*. You will have a better understanding of the principles of valuation and how to apply them to your specific market. Proper understanding of this single principle can be the difference between success and failure. Use the tools at your disposal to make prudent business decisions, and real estate will prove to be one of the best and most sound investments you will ever make.

LEVERAGE—THE OPM PRINCIPLE

Most likely you are already familiar with the OPM principle, which stands for "other people's money." Your objective is to control as much real estate as possible while using as little of your own capital as possible, and this means that you have to use other people's money. The name of the game in this business is leverage. The more of it you have, the more property you can control. Borrowed money can come from many sources, including traditional sources such as a bank, a family member, a business partner, or even the seller by carrying back a note in the form of a second mortgage.

Other popular sources of borrowing include a HELOC, more commonly known as a home equity line of credit. Another source of borrowing includes using a line of credit against credit cards. I don't know about you, but I get several offers a week from various credit card companies, often times offering $10,000 or more in available credit. In a favorable interest rate environment, there is nothing at all wrong with using these cards as a source of financing for your investments. Be careful, though! Don't get caught in the credit card trap by maxing out your cards on consumer goods. You also want to be sure that you have structured the purchase of your property in such a manner that will allow you to service the debt on it, whatever the source of that debt is. Debt is a wonderful tool, but like any tool, you must exercise caution and respect when using it. Otherwise you can quickly find yourself in trouble. You must be in control of your debt and must manage it wisely. Do not allow your debt to control you.

Whatever the source of your funding, the idea is to use as little of your own money as possible because that is what your returns are based upon. Your return on investment, or cash on cash return, is derived from the simple ratio of the net cash left over after all expenses have been paid over the amount of your original investment plus any out-of-pocket improvements or expenses that require an additional owner's contribution. So in a very simple example, if you paid all cash for a $100,000 house that generated $6,000 of income, your return on investment is 6 percent. You may as well leave your money in the bank and save yourself the time and energy that investing in real estate will require. On the other hand, if you invested only $10,000 in the deal and borrowed, or leveraged, the remaining $90,000, assuming the same $6,000 of income, your return on investment now jumps to 60 percent. That's how the concept of leverage works. It allows you to take a little bit of your own money and maximize the return on it.

There are a number of popular books about how to apply no-money-down techniques. Many of them are well written and have sound principles. While I am a firm believer in the use of other people's money, in my opinion these methods carry the concept of leverage to an extreme. That's not to say they don't work. I'm sure in many cases they do. By relying solely on these techniques, however, you are restricting yourself to a much more limited pool of available properties to choose from. Let's face it. You are in the real estate business to make money, and time is money. Why spend all of your time trying to find a no-money-down deal when there are far more houses that can easily be purchased with 5 to 10 percent down? I realize that some of you may not have even that to start with and if that is the case, then you may have to search for that nothing-down deal. I would encourage you to build as large a base of capital as possible so that you can quickly and easily purchase some of the more attractive opportunities as they become available. For every one or two nothing-down deals that are available, there are at least a hundred deals that can be purchased with 10 percent down. The pool of investment properties available to choose from is much larger at this level. In the end, more choices means greater opportunity, which can potentially mean much more money, and that's what you're in the real estate business for, right?

ECONOMIC HOUSING OUTLOOK FOR THE NEXT DECADE

I recently attended the American Housing Conference in Chicago. Although the theme of the conference was centered around mergers, acquisitions, and valuation methods, Dr. David Berson, Vice President and Chief Economist for Fannie Mae, was there to present the *Long-Term Economic, Housing and Mortgage Outlook to 2010*. In his presentation, Dr. Berson noted several key points with respect to a favorable outlook for the housing industry as a whole over the next decade.

Table 1.1 Historical and Projected Economic and Housing Activity

	1980s	1990s	2000s
Real GDP growth	3.2%	3.2%	3.4–3.5%
30-year FRM rates	12.3%	7.9%	7.2–7.5%
Housing starts	1.48 million	1.41 million	1.64–1.68 million
New home sales	0.61 million	0.73 million	0.91–0.93 million
Existing home sales	2.98 million	4.21 million	5.50–5.64 million
Mortgage originations	$325.5 billion	$934.6 billion	$1,599.4–$1,808.1 billion

Sources: Commerce Department, Federal Reserve Board, HUD, National Association of Realtors, Fannie Mae Economic Projections.

Dr. Berson's forecast called for average real GDP growth of 3.4 to 3.5 percent, versus 3.2 percent during the 1990s (see Table 1.1). His forecast also expected fixed rate mortgages to be 7.2 to 7.5 percent, versus 7.9 percent during the 1990s. Furthermore, census data for 2010 projected a total population of 315 million, representing an increase of an additional 35 million residents (see Exhibit 1.1). Lastly, the national average of unsold homes is at historically low levels, providing for a tight supply-and-demand relationship

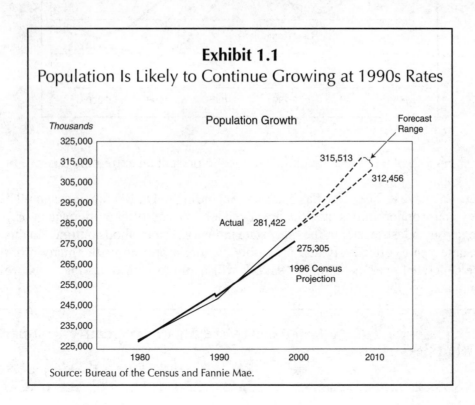

Exhibit 1.1
Population Is Likely to Continue Growing at 1990s Rates
Source: Bureau of the Census and Fannie Mae.

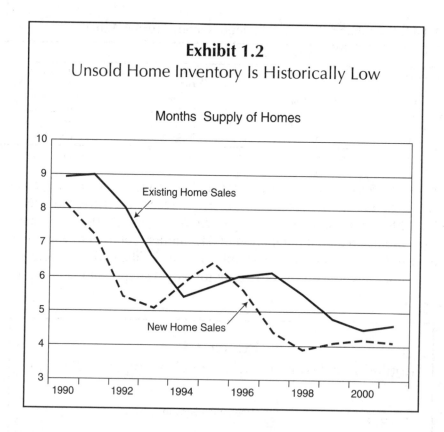

Exhibit 1.2
Unsold Home Inventory Is Historically Low

Months Supply of Homes

(see Exhibit 1.2). All of these factors combined to present an extremely positive outlook for real estate investors.

There you have it. The stage has been set. According to Dr. Berson, you should be able to enjoy many opportunities over the next decade to successfully participate in one of the most exciting industries of all, the real estate industry. The methods outlined in this book will enable you to effectively and profitably capture a portion of the many profits that will be generated over the coming years. It will be up to you to use the tools provided herein to achieve the level of success you desire.

> **What lies behind us, and what lies before us, are tiny matters compared to what lies within us.**
>
> —*Ralph Waldo Emerson*

PART I

What Every Investor Needs to Know About Flipping Properties

Chapter 2

Flipping Properties Defined

While there are a number of strategies and techniques used to invest in real estate, there is one thing they all share in common—the element of time. Most investors have some idea of the length of the holding period for properties they intend to acquire. Time can have a significant impact on the growth rate of your real estate portfolio. Time affects such things as the tax rate applied to your gain or loss. The long-term capital gains tax rate has historically been more favorable than the short-term tax rate. Time is also the variable in the rate of inventory turnover. Large retailers are willing to accept lower profit margins on items they merchandise in exchange for a higher inventory turnover rate. Would you rather earn 20 percent on each item, or house, you sell and have a turnover rate of one, or would you rather earn 8 percent on each item you sell and have a turnover rate of three? Let's do the math.

$$\text{Turnover Ratio} = \frac{\text{Turnover}}{\text{Years}} = \frac{1}{1} \times 20\% = 20\% = \text{Total Return}$$

or

$$\text{Turnover Ratio} = \frac{\text{Turnover}}{\text{Years}} = \frac{3}{1} \times 8\% = 24\% = \text{Total Return}$$

This simple example clearly illustrates that an investor can accept a lower rate of return on each property bought and sold and earn a higher overall rate of return, provided that the frequency, or turnover rate, is increased. I should mention that this example does not, of course, take into consideration transaction costs. These costs may or may not be significant, depending on your specific situation, but they must be factored in when analyzing a potential purchase.

Long-term investors may purchase real estate properties and keep them in the family for generations. They will typically hold them for a minimum of five years. Long-term investors seek gains through capital appreciation by simply holding and maintaining their investments while making improvements on an as-needed basis. They often seek to minimize the associated debt and maximize the cash flow. Long-term investors are quite often not fully leveraged. They generally prefer the positive cash flow over being excessively leveraged. When the property is finally sold, the more favorable long-term capital gains tax rates will apply. Also, long-term investors may or may not elect to take advantage of deferring the tax liability indefinitely through a provision outlined in the Internal Revenue Code referred to as a 1031 exchange.

Intermediate-term investors most often hold their properties for at least two years, but not more than five years. This class of investors typically seeks gains through a combination of increases in property values resulting from overall price appreciation in real estate, as well as by making modest improvements to the property. Reducing debt to increase cash flow is not as high a priority for intermediate-term investors as it is for their long-term counterparts. This class of investors also tends to be more highly leveraged. Finally, since intermediate-term investors hold their investment properties for a minimum of two years, they are able to take advantage of the lower and more favorable capital gains tax rate.

Short-term investors are defined as those who buy and sell real estate for a shorter duration. They typically hold their investments less than two years. This class of investors most often seeks gains through direct improvements to the property. The shorter holding period does not allow enough time for gains through increases in the overall market. The short-term investor seeks to profit by using the higher inventory turnover strategy, and may be willing to accept smaller returns, but with greater frequency, realizing the overall rate of return can be considerably higher than the long-term approach. Since current tax codes penalize short-term investors by imposing higher tax rates on short-term capital gains, they must factor this into their analysis before ever purchasing a property.

The short-term investor can be further subdivided into different classes. Those investors with an extremely short-term time horizon are known as flippers and are the subject of this book. A flipper's primary objective is to locate properties that are undervalued for any number of reasons, add some measure of value to the property, and then quickly resell it for a profit. Flippers may hold a property for a few months, weeks, or even a few days. In some cases, they may not even actually hold title to the property and may never take possession. This is perfectly legal and can be done through options. The use of options will be more fully discussed as we explore the different classes of flippers.

Exhibit 2.1
Three Primary Classes
of Flippers

1. Scouts

2. Dealers

3. Retailers

THREE PRIMARY CLASSES OF FLIPPERS

There are three primary classes of flippers. (See Exhibit 2.1.) They are the scout, the dealer, and the retailer. Each class has its own unique characteristics and serves a valuable function in the world of real estate investing.

Scouts

Scouts serve an important role in the process of flipping, and can be very useful to the other two types of flippers, the dealer and the retailer. A scout does exactly what the name suggests—he scouts for investment opportunities. Scouts were used many years ago during the Civil War, as well as other wars, by the United States army. They were sent out in advance of the troops to gather information about what might lie ahead. The scouts then faithfully and diligently reported back to their captain the key facts gathered during their journey. Important decisions were then made on the basis of the information gathered by the scout. A good scout was worth his weight in gold. The military today uses a much more sophisticated type of scout. They rely on technology such as radar and satellite imagery to report the enemy's position, as well as other vital information. The process itself is much the same though, with key information being provided to those empowered to make decisions.

Just as the scouts in the military report vital information to those who have the power to act upon it, so do real estate scouts report key facts regarding potential investment opportunities to dealers and retailers. A good scout will gather as much of the relevant data as possible so that the investors can make well-informed decisions. Scouts provide pertinent information such as:

- the general condition of the house or property and its location
- the general condition of the neighborhood
- the price the seller is asking
- the terms the seller is seeking
- the seller's reason for selling
- the seller's time frame for selling and her degree of urgency
- comparable sales for other homes in the neighborhood, if possible

Armed with this information, the investor is in a much better position to make a decision about whether or not to buy. The dealer or retailer can quickly analyze the data and proceed with a purchase according to the results of their analysis.

A scout does not purchase or take legal title to the property. He leaves that part of the process to those he reports to. Since a scout does not take legal possession, he typically will not be entitled to participate in the profits. This is not always so, as when the individual performing the duties of the scout may belong to a partnership in which the profits are shared. Most often, though, scouts are paid a referral, or finder's fee. Just as a real estate agent does not earn a commission unless a sale is made, neither does a scout earn a referral fee unless a deal is consummated. Scouts compensated on this basis will work extra hard to bring you only the best deals. Scouts can be very valuable to investors because they help them make the best and most effective use of their time.

Dealers

Much like the scout, dealers also play an important role in bringing opportunities to investors. They often act as a wholesaler for retailers and other investors looking to buy property at below-market prices. Dealers are often licensed real estate agents and make their money from the commission and sometimes a slight markup in the price of the property. They know that the markup must be minimal so as to leave enough profit in the deal to remain attractive to other investors to whom they will sell. Dealers are also in a position to earn money from both sides of the transaction. They are usually both the listing agent as well as the selling agent. Furthermore, if a dealer sells to a retailer, many times after the retailer has made the required improvements, she will turn around and list the property for sale with the dealer again. This provides the dealer with a perfectly legitimate opportunity to double dip with his inventory of listings.

Dealers usually have an extensive network of contacts with whom they work to provide them with inventory to sell. I know several dealers, for example, who have established relationships with various banks' real estate–owned, or REO, departments. These are properties that have been foreclosed upon by local banks and remain on the bank's books. The banks are not in the real estate business; they are in the lending business. They have no desire to retain REOs on their books because they represent loans that have gone uncollected, or bad debts. Banks prefer to sell these assets and recoup any losses possible. Many times, they will sell the property at the book value of the bad debt, or even below. This practice is not at all uncommon, as most every bank in the country has REOs in its portfolio.

An example of how the real estate–owned process works is as follows:

1. Investor A, a novice real estate investor, purchases a rental house for $100,000, puts down $20,000, and borrows the balance of $80,000 from Local Bank B.
2. After three years of ownership, Investor A discovers that the real estate rental business is more difficult than she thought and stops making her payments to Local Bank B.
3. Approximately six months lapse before Local Bank B is able to repossess the rental house, which it doesn't want and will gladly sell.
4. Local Bank B calls Dealer C for help to get the bad debt off its books, knowing that Dealer C has a large pool of investors he works with who will gladly consider picking up an investment at well below market value.
5. Dealer C contacts Retailer D who in turn negotiates a deal with Local Bank B to take it off the bank's hands at a discounted price of $65,000.

Local Bank B is happy because it has converted a nonperforming loan into one that is now performing and collecting interest. Dealer C is happy because he earned a commission from the sale of the property. Retailer D is happy because he bought a house at well below market value and will profit handsomely at the time of resale.

Much like the scout, the dealer specializing in REOs does not take title in most cases to the real estate. There is no need to, since his primary role is to act as an agent representing sellers who desire to dispose of unwanted assets. Buying real estate–owned properties directly from banks would create unnecessary transaction costs for the dealer and greatly increase the amount of time expended. The most efficient manner is to act as an agent for the banks, thereby allowing the bank to sell directly to the retailer or investor. The dealer can make up in volume what he may give up in profit margin.

While some dealers specialize in REOs, other dealers focus on the foreclosure market. Buying and selling foreclosures requires that an individual have a working knowledge of that market. While there are a number of good books written on the subject, many investors do not have the expertise or the time to find undervalued foreclosures. Furthermore, they are unfamiliar with the auction or bidding process and may lack the resources to purchase properties in this manner. A dealer who understands the mechanics of buying foreclosed properties can easily make a market by wholesaling to her network of retailers. Dealers participating in foreclosures will most likely take title to the property.

Retailers

The concept of retailing involves buying houses, fixing them up by making various improvements, and then reselling them. As the name suggests, the retailer purchases properties at wholesale and subsequently sells at retail. He represents the end of the food chain for flippers. The scout and the dealer serve a vital function in bringing opportunities to the retailer, who will then usually flip the property to a more permanent type of buyer, whether it be another investor who wants to hold it as a rental unit, or a home owner who will be moving in to the home to use as a primary residence.

Unlike the scout and the dealer, the retailer most often takes title to the property. He will typically hold it anywhere from 30 to 90 days while making any necessary improvements to the property, and then make it available for sale to a more permanent type of buyer. The retailer must also have more capital available to work with than the scout or dealer. He will need whatever funds are required for the down payment, as well as additional funds for property improvements. In addition, the retailer must have adequate capital to sustain the property during whatever holding period may be required. The retailer can plan and hope to have the house sold within 30 days after making all the improvements, but in reality it may, in fact, take up to six months, and in some cases, even longer. Holding costs during this period include the interest on the debt used to acquire the property, taxes, insurance, and utilities. Since the retailer usually takes title to the property and has more capital at stake, his level of risk relative to the scout and dealer is significantly higher.

Of the three primary classes of flippers, it is the retailer who stands to gain the most financially. The relationship between risk and reward is in most cases directly correlated. This means that the greater the risk an investor is willing to assume, the greater the reward can potentially be. This application holds true among all three primary classes of flippers. The scout assumes virtually no risk and his reward is most often limited to a referral fee. The dealer assumes a greater degree of risk than does the scout, and stands to gain substantially more than the scout. The retailer's risk is significantly greater than that of the scout and the dealer. She most often takes title to the property, has a longer holding period, and invests more capital. It is the retailer, therefore, who stands to enjoy the greatest reward from flipping properties. In Chapter 3, we will more fully explore the concept of retailing *the value play* way.

USING OPTIONS TO FLIP PROPERTIES

An *option* is a legal instrument that gives you the right to buy at a predetermined price. This is done millions of times a day in the stock market. For example, investors can buy a call option on MSFT with a strike price of, let's say, $55. As with all options, time, or *t*, is one of the variables that determine the value of an option using the Black Scholes model. The investor has the right to exercise her option at her discretion within a specified period of time. It is possible that the outcome will be favorable, and it is also possible that the option will expire and become worthless. So it is with real estate. Investors may enjoy the legal right to buy a piece of property at a predetermined price through the use of options, and then turn around and sell their interest in the property without ever taking title to it.

Some of my real estate investment activities include the use of options for the development of new residential construction in single family communities. While my musical background is limited to playing the trombone and some piano in middle school and high school, I have a great love and appreciation for music and truly admire individuals who have mastered those talents. By now you are probably wondering what that has to do with residential construction! The name of the company my partner and I formed is

Symphony Homes (www.symphony-homes.com). Within this entity, we use options to acquire rights to property to build on without ever taking legal title. We do, however, have a recordable interest. We just don't take title, at least not initially.

Just recently, I optioned 28 lots in Phase I of a particular community. This gave Symphony Homes a legal interest in the property and the right to acquire all 28 lots at a predetermined price. When we get a purchase agreement to build a new home for a client on one of our lots, we then exercise our option on that lot and take legal title to it. The advantage of using an option in this case is twofold. The first is that if we have difficulty selling new homes to prospective buyers, we are not stuck with the burden and cost of ownership. The only thing we have at risk is our option money. The second reason is that if we were to actually purchase the lots, the sale would trigger an increase in taxes due to a new and much higher assessed value. As the new owners, we would then be obligated to assume the tax liability.

So you see, options can be one of many valuable tools available to the real estate investor who is interested in mastering the art of flipping. Options enable you to gain control of property with very little money down, thereby allowing you to maximize the use of leverage. I recommend, however, that they be used with prudence. Remember that time is one of the variables and when t expires, so does your option. Analyze the market as it applies to your particular investment opportunity carefully before committing your resources to determine that you have a high probability of a favorable outcome.

CLEARLY DEFINED OBJECTIVES

As an investor who is serious about being successful in the real estate industry, you will need to establish clearly defined objectives. You will need to determine whether you are going to be a long-term, intermediate-term, or short-term investor. If you are going to engage in the practice of flipping, will you be a scout, a dealer, or a retailer? Perhaps your real estate investment activities will include a combination of these strategies. The real estate business is like any other business with respect to defining your objectives. You must have a business plan in place. Taking the time to do so will help you stay the course. If you don't know where you are going, how will you know when you get there?

Think of an aircraft about to embark on an intercontinental flight to Europe. The pilot will use an established flight plan to chart his course. His navigator will input key coordinates into the aircraft's navigation system. Once in flight, the crew will rely primarily on the plane's instruments to arrive safely at their exact destination at a place on the earth thousands of miles away from their point of origin. Now try to imagine the crew making this same trip with no flight plan whatsoever. By doing so, they would greatly jeopardize their ability to reach their destination safely. The crew would also place in danger the very people who have hired them to fly to Europe, the passengers.

Like the pilot, you as a real estate investor must also rely on an established flight plan. That flight plan will be your plan of attack, your clearly defined objectives, your business plan. And like the pilot of an aircraft who must occasionally adjust his course, so will you, too, occasionally have to adjust your course. You cannot afford to undertake a journey in your real estate profession without having some idea of where you want to go. Many people go through their entire lives in a rather random and indiscriminate fashion with no sense of direction; hence, they end up precisely where they set out to go, which is nowhere.

The process of proper planning in this business is critical to your success. Yes, you may have to think a little bit and it will require some effort on your part to formalize your plans, but I can assure you that any time spent developing a plan will greatly contribute to your success. By mapping out your strategy in advance, like the pilot who directs his aircraft across the vast expanse of the earth, you will eventually reach your destination. You may run into a few storms along the way, but like the aircraft, you will ultimately reach your destination safely.

Three primary components that must be considered when defining your objectives are your entry, post-entry, and exit strategies. Let's take our pilot as an example. His entry strategy would include the preparation of his flight plan, crew, and aircraft. The captain would take every precaution to ensure that all was in order before departing on the journey. In fact, pilots and their crews (ground crew included) use what is referred to as a preflight check list before each and every flight to make sure that not a single item is overlooked. The check list takes into consideration everything the pilot will need in order to have a safe flight, including fuel requirements, weight limitations, and maintenance status. The pilot must also be certain that the weather is conducive to the flight. The pilot's post-entry strategy begins as soon as he starts the engines. He and the crew are now fully engaged in the process of flying the aircraft and must focus completely on flying the plane to its destination in the safest and most efficient manner possible. The crew may be able to fly directly to their destination if all goes as planned; however, in the event that their radar indicates turbulence ahead, they may be required to alter their course. It is better for them to adjust their post-entry strategy by flying around the turbulent weather than to run the risk of flying directly through it. Upon the successful navigation to the crew's intended destination, they then implement their exit strategy, which includes landing the aircraft at its predetermined destination and unloading the cargo.

ENTRY STRATEGY

To define your entry strategy you will need to start by determining what type of property you are looking for, the price range you are considering, and the holding period. Are you going to buy a single family house, fix it up, and turn around and sell it, or are you going buy a more expensive small apartment building to hold for a number of years? Are you going to use flipping techniques as part of your investment strategy? If so, you must decide whether you are going to act in the capacity of a scout, dealer, retailer, or some combination of the three. How do you intend to finance your purchase? You must, of course, take into consideration the investment capital you have to work with. It may be that although you don't initially have the adequate resources required for retailing, that you start as a scout or a dealer while progressively building up your capital base. The important thing to remember about having a well-defined entry strategy, regardless of what that may entail, is that like the pilot, you have a predetermined plan based upon specific criteria established by you. Since you have already determined all the factors such as price range, location, financing, and holding period, you will not waste any time examining opportunities that do not match your criteria.

POST-ENTRY STRATEGY

While the post-entry strategy begins the moment you close on the property, you should have already established your specific objectives long before the closing. You cannot wait until after you purchase the property to decide what you are going to do with it. You absolutely must know that before ever spending a single dollar. Your post-entry agenda should include things such as property improvements, rental increases and management changes if applicable, and lease or sell preparations as required. If you know, for example, that your strategy is to be a retailer and flip properties, the time to procure estimates for the needed improvements is during the inspection period while the property is under contract, not after it closes. As a prudent investor, you know almost exactly how much it will take to repair the property and make it ready for resale. If you are contracting the work out, then your contractors should already be scheduled and should be ready to start the work the day after your closing. Don't let a week go by, and then decide to get the painter out. Have your painter ready to go as soon as you close! Since you want your investment operations to run as efficiently as possible, it is imperative that you develop as much of your post-entry strategy in advance as possible.

EXIT STRATEGY

Your exit strategy is probably the most important of the three components. You should specifically define your intentions before you even purchase a property. Whether you are going to hold it for a short term or long term, you must determine in advance how you will eventually unwind your position in the property. If you are a short-term investor and are going to flip the property, you want to be certain the market is conducive to your planned activities. In other words, is there sufficient demand, and are interest rates going up, down, or are they stable? If you are going to hold the property for a number of years, these factors are not as critical. If you elect to maintain your interest in the property and choose not to sell, an alternative to consider is refinancing. This will allow you to unlock some of the equity that has accumulated over the years to invest in additional properties. An advantage of accessing your equity in this manner is that you avoid paying any capital gains taxes. As a flipper, however, you will not be as concerned about long-term holding periods, since your objective is to dispose of the property as quickly as possible. You should determine in advance, however, your method of disposal. Do you plan to sell the property yourself, or list it with a real estate sales agent? Regardless of the methods you choose, the criteria for your exit strategy should be established long before you invest any resources.

Just as the pilot and his crew use a comprehensive flight plan to successfully fly their aircraft, so must you, too, use a comprehensive business plan to be successful in your real estate activities. From start to finish, it is important to plan as much of your strategy as possible in advance. It is in that manner that when you are alerted on your radar screen to unforeseen circumstances ahead, you will be able to adjust your course as necessary and complete your journey to have a safe and successful landing in your real estate career.

> I would sooner have the approval of my own conscience and know that I had done my duty than to have the praise of all the world and not have the approval of my own conscience. A man's conscience, when he is living as he should, is the finest monitor and the best judge in all the world.
>
> —*Heber J. Grant*

Chapter 3

The Value Play Strategy

In my experience of working with other investors and previous clients, I have often heard comments like, "Yes, Mr. Berges, I prefer the buy-and-hold approach to investing in real estate. My idea is to buy a property, pay it off, and live off the income." Sound familiar? While this method of building a real estate portfolio is a valid one, it is in my estimation certainly not the best method. If you have another source of income that is fairly substantial and therefore allows you to make investments in real estate on a periodic basis, then this may be the method for you, or at least one that you are the most comfortable with. This approach, however, precludes you from maximizing the utility of your investment resources.

In *The Complete Guide to Buying and Selling Apartment Buildings*, I described an aggressive real estate acquisition campaign for apartment buildings based on a term I coined, which I refer to as *the value play*. The value play strategy as it relates to apartment buildings is very similar to the concept of the retailer who flips single family properties. The primary difference is that the concept is applied to income-producing properties on a much larger scale. The fundamental premise of this strategy is based on finding an undervalued apartment building, large or small, creating value through one or more of many mechanisms, and reselling, or flipping, the property. The value play strategy is undeniably one of the quickest and surest methods available to investors to create and build wealth.

Many real estate books embrace the buy-and-hold strategy of building long-term wealth. Proponents of this approach claim that for an individual to retire with a leisurely lifestyle, all she has to do is buy one property a year for, let's say 10 years, rent the units out and pay down the debt. At the end of 25 years, all of the debt will be paid off and the investor can live off the rents. It may be that this strategy works fine for many, and for some, this may be all they are comfortable with, but as I will demonstrate, the investor who maximizes her efforts through the use of the value play concept, especially as it applies to the retailer, will end up with far more wealth than one who implements a simple buy-and-hold strategy.

The financial implications of value-added measures can be quite significant for the retailer. The examples in Tables 3.1 and 3.2 illustrate just how powerful the value play strategy can be. Investor A implements a simple buy-and-hold strategy of acquiring one property a year for 10 years and holds all 10 properties through year 25. He chooses not to sell any of them, but ensures that all mortgages are fully paid by the end of the 25-year period. Investor B implements the value play methodology over the same 25-year period. She, on the other hand, buys and sells two value play properties for each one sold in the prior period for 10 years, with the exception of the last year. In year 10, she retains all properties purchased, which she will keep and maintain through year 25. Like Investor A, she will ensure that the mortgage is fully paid by year 25. Take a minute to review the following assumptions and then carefully study Tables 3.1 and 3.2.

BUY-AND-HOLD STRATEGY

Investor A Assumptions
- ☐ Investor A saves enough to purchase one house each year for 10 years.
- ☐ Each house he buys costs $75,000.
- ☐ He obtains a 90 percent loan on each house, which means he makes a down payment on the property of 10 percent, or $7,500.
- ☐ Investor A holds each property purchased over the 10-year period all the way through year 25 and does not sell any of them.
- ☐ He arranges his mortgage payments to be paid down to zero by year 25. So in year 1, he gets a 25-year loan, in year 2, he gets a 24-year loan, and so on. Finally, in year 10, Investor A gets a 15-year loan so that all loan balances will be zero in year 25, enabling him to live off the income as planned.
- ☐ All properties purchased appreciate in value at an annual growth rate of 4 percent, so that by the end of year 25, the 10 units purchased have a cumulative value of $1,621,674.
- ☐ The rental income on a house purchased for $75,000 in year 1 is assumed to be $800 per month, or $9,600 for the year. The rental income grows at an annual growth

rate of 4 percent, so that by year 10, the income per unit has grown to $13,664, and by year 25, the rental income per unit has grown to $25,592, or $255,920 combined income for all 10 units owned.

THE VALUE PLAY STRATEGY

Investor B Assumptions

- ☐ Investor B starts with $15,000 of equity.
- ☐ Each house she buys costs $75,000. She is able to use the $15,000 of equity for both the down payment and minor improvements that will be required.
- ☐ She buys and sells two value play properties for each one she sells, in effect doubling the number of houses bought and sold each year for years 1–10. All properties purchased in year 10 are retained in her real estate portfolio.
- ☐ Investor B creates value of 20 percent on each property purchased.
- ☐ She arranges her mortgage financing so that all loan balances will be zero by year 25, thereby enabling her to live off the income.
- ☐ All properties purchased and retained in her real estate portfolio appreciate in value at an annual growth rate of 4 percent, so that by the end of year 25, the 512 units purchased have a cumulative value of $69,156,231.
- ☐ The rental income on a house purchased for $75,000 in year 1 is assumed to be $800 per month, or $9,600 for the year. The rental income grows at an annual growth rate of 4 percent, so that by year 10, the income per unit has grown to $13,664, and by year 25 the rental income per unit has grown to $25,592, or $13,103,119 combined income for all 512 units owned.

After reviewing Tables 3.1 and 3.2, I think you will agree that the difference between the two investment strategies is quite significant. Using the assumptions as outlined in the table, Investor A's buy-and-hold strategy has netted him an equity in the combined properties of $1,621,674. In addition, he will enjoy an annual income of $225,920. That actually sounds pretty good, doesn't it? All he has to do is buy one property a year for 10 years and hold them for 25 years and he can retire with a very comfortable income. Investor A's buy-and-hold strategy sounds good, that is, until you compare his value with Investor B's. Investor B, using the value play strategy, has managed to accumulate a sizable fortune of $69,156,231. Furthermore, she will enjoy a very comfortable annual rental income of $13,103,119. What a fantastic difference between the two! To fully take advantage of the value play methodology, you must have a well-defined plan that is strictly adhered to, and you must be willing to execute it, that is, to take action. This kind of wealth accumulation is possible only through the systematic application of a well-designed plan.

It could be argued that the assumption of 20 percent appreciation is not reasonable, but I can tell you from my own experience that not only is it reasonable, it is conservative. A 22-unit property I purchased, for example, was subsequently sold within a year for a price that represented approximately 80 percent more than what I paid for it. Creating value in single family houses is actually much easier to do than in apartment buildings, and you should have no trouble earning 20 percent or more on your real estate transactions.

It should be noted that Tables 3.1 and 3.2 are, of course, hypothetical tables. The example is used to demonstrate the full potential of an investor who diligently applies the value play strategy, given certain assumptions, over a period of many years. The volume of units bought and sold in Years 1–8 is entirely feasible and quite manageable. In the latter years, where many more properties are acquired, the value created of 20 percent or more is still achievable; the sheer volume, however, will be more difficult to achieve. To buy and sell that many properties in a single year requires a team of investors working together with each one performing a unique set of functions. If we were to take Table 2 and reduce Assumption #3 for Investor B from 20 percent down to 15 percent, the resulting value at the end of year 25 would be $20,792,360. That still represents a value of wealth equating to roughly 13 times greater than the wealth created by Investor A. Clearly the value play strategy warrants every investor's consideration.

THE VALUE PLAY SELECTION PROCESS

As you recall, the retailer is in the business of buying real estate at wholesale or below and subsequently reselling it at retail. The principal mechanism that enables the retailer to do this is the process of creating value through any number of methods. Since multifamily properties such as apartment buildings derive their value primarily from the income they generate, there are many ways to enhance the revenues while simultaneously reducing expenses to improve the overall Net Operating Income, or N.O.I. The price an investor is willing to pay for an apartment building is almost always a function of the N.O.I. divided by a given capitalization rate for similar income-producing properties. The following

Table 3.1 Investor Strategies

						Investor A Buy-and-Hold Strategy					Combined
Year	Unit 1	Unit 2	Unit 3	Unit 4	Unit 5	Unit 6	Unit 7	Unit 8	Unit 9	Unit 10	Values
1	75,000										75,000
2	78,000	75,000									153,000
3	81,120	78,000	75,000								234,120
4	84,365	81,120	78,000	75,000							318,485
5	87,739	84,365	81,120	78,000	75,000						406,224
6	91,249	87,739	84,365	81,120	78,000	75,000					497,473
7	94,899	91,249	87,739	84,365	81,120	78,000	75,000				592,372
8	98,695	94,899	91,249	87,739	84,365	81,120	78,000	75,000			691,067
9	102,643	98,695	94,899	91,249	87,739	84,365	81,120	78,000	75,000		793,710
10	106,748	102,643	98,695	94,899	91,249	87,739	84,365	81,120	78,000	75,000	900,458
11	111,018	106,748	102,643	98,695	94,899	91,249	87,739	84,365	81,120	78,000	936,476
12	115,459	111,018	106,748	102,643	98,695	94,899	91,249	87,739	84,365	81,120	973,935
13	120,077	115,459	111,018	106,748	102,643	98,695	94,899	91,249	87,739	84,365	1,012,893
14	124,881	120,077	115,459	111,018	106,748	102,643	98,695	94,899	91,249	87,739	1,053,409
15	129,876	124,881	120,077	115,459	111,018	106,748	102,643	98,695	94,899	91,249	1,095,545
16	135,071	129,876	124,881	120,077	115,459	111,018	106,748	102,643	98,695	94,899	1,139,367
17	140,474	135,071	129,876	124,881	120,077	115,459	111,018	106,748	102,643	98,695	1,184,941
18	146,093	140,474	135,071	129,876	124,881	120,077	115,459	111,018	106,748	102,643	1,232,339
19	151,936	146,093	140,474	135,071	129,876	124,881	120,077	115,459	111,018	106,748	1,281,633
20	158,014	151,936	146,093	140,474	135,071	129,876	124,881	120,077	115,459	111,018	1,332,898
21	164,334	158,014	151,936	146,093	140,474	135,071	129,876	124,881	120,077	115,459	1,386,214
22	170,908	164,334	158,014	151,936	146,093	140,474	135,071	129,876	124,881	120,077	1,441,662
23	177,744	170,908	164,334	158,014	151,936	146,093	140,474	135,071	129,876	124,881	1,499,329
24	184,854	177,744	170,908	164,334	158,014	151,936	146,093	140,474	135,071	129,876	1,559,302
25	192,248	184,854	177,744	170,908	164,334	158,014	151,936	146,093	140,474	135,071	1,621,674
Income	9,600	9,984	10,383	10,799	11,231	11,680	12,147	12,633	13,138	13,664	255,920

Assumptions for investor A
1. Saves enough to purchase one house per year for 10 years by putting down $7,500, or 10%, on each house
2. Holds each property through year 25
3. Arranges mortgage payments so all units are owned free and clear by year 25
4. Assumes annual growth rate of 4 percent
5. Assumes rental income of $800 per month in year 1 that grows at the annual rate of 4%

Table 3.2 Investor Strategies

						Investor B The Value Play Strategy					
Year	Units 1	Units 2	Units 4	Units 8	Units 16	Units 32	Units 64	Units 128	Units 256	Units 512	Combined Values
1	75,000										75,000
2	20%	150,000									150,000
3	15,000	20%	300,000								300,000
4	15,000	30,000	20%	600,000							600,000
5	30,000	30,000	60,000	20%	1,200,000						1,200,000
6	20%	60,000	60,000	120,000	20%	2,400,000					2,400,000
7	150,000	20%	120,000	120,000	240,000	20%	4,800,000				4,800,000
8		300,000	20%	240,000	240,000	480,000	20%	9,600,000			9,600,000
9			600,000	20%	480,000	480,000	960,000	20%	19,200,000		19,200,000
10				1,200,000	20%	960,000	960,000	1,920,000	20%	38,400,000	38,400,000
11					2,400,000	20%	1,920,000	1,920,000	3,840,000	39,936,000	39,936,000
12						4,800,000	20%	3,840,000	3,840,000	41,533,440	41,533,440
13							9,600,000	20%	7,680,000	43,194,778	43,194,778
14								19,200,000	20%	44,922,569	44,922,569
15									38,400,000	46,719,471	46,719,471
16 Example									48,588,250	48,588,250	
17 Purchase Price			75,000						50,531,780	50,531,780	
18 Value Created Percent			20%					52,553,052	52,553,052		
19 Value Created Dollars			15,000					54,655,174	54,655,174		
20 Original Equity			15,000					56,841,381		56,841,381	
21 Accumulated Equity			30,000					59,115,036	59,115,036		
22 LTV Ratio			20%						61,479,637	61,479,637	
23 Next Purchase(s)			150,000						63,938,823	63,938,823	
24									66,496,376	66,496,376	
25									69,156,231	69,156,231	
Income	0	0	0	0	0	0	0	0	0	13,664	13,103,119

Assumptions for investor B
1. Starts with initial $15,000 equity
2. Buys and sells two value play properties for each one sold, but holds all properties purchased in years 10 through 25
3. Creates value on each deal of 20 percent
4. Maximizes leverage on each new property purchased using a loan-to-value ratio of 80 percent (or 20 percent down on each deal)
5. Assumes annual growth rate of 4 percent
6. Assumes no rental income except in years 10 through 25

illustrates a simplified example of how this valuation formula works.

$$\text{Property Value} = \frac{\text{Net Operating Income}}{\text{Capitalization Rate}} = \frac{\$100,000}{.10} = \$1,000,000$$

For the retailer dealing with single family houses, however, income is not as important, because the resale value is based more upon market comparables than the income it generates. This means that the buying public will evaluate the house you have for sale based on what is currently available in your immediate market. Buyers will compare and contrast your property to many others and will ultimately select the one that best fits their needs. Their buying decision will be based upon factors such as the property's location, its condition, the price it is being offered at, its proximity to major streets and shopping areas, and the quality of schools in the area. In addition, there are many personal factors that affect the buying decision, such as how close they will be to work, church, and Grandma and Grandpa's house. Some of the factors that affect a buyer's decision-making process fall outside the realm of your control because not all buyers are searching for the exact set of conditions that may compel them to choose one house over another.

Three factors that you as the retailer do have some control over, however, include the property's location, its price range, and its physical condition. Although a prospective buyer's needs will vary, you can still make sound investment decisions based on market generalizations. You must recognize that the products you have available to sell cannot, and will not, be all things to all people. Nevertheless, you can make certain assumptions on the basis of objective data, which will greatly improve the chances of your success.

PROPERTY LOCATION

As an investor who is in the business of flipping properties, you are not interested in carrying your inventory any longer than necessary. That means you should carefully study your area to determine which vicinities are selling with the shortest average number of days on the market. If you have lived in a particular area for a while, you are likely to already know which areas of town are hot and which are not. You do not have to rely solely on your intuition, however, as almost any real estate agent will have access to the local Multiple Listing Service, or M.L.S., in your area. They can provide you with objective data to support your analysis. Most real estate agents will gladly furnish this information to you free of charge. They are in the business of earning commissions by representing buyers and sellers and to do this, they must also agree to provide them with information that will enable them to make a well-informed decision. The sales agent knows that if she can give you the facts you need which will support your decision to buy, then that will bring her one step closer to earning a commission.

The type of location best suited for a retailer seeking to flip properties is a neighborhood that is typically between 10 and 30 years old. These neighborhoods represent where the average middle class citizen lives. Neighborhoods newer than 10 years old tend to have larger and more expensive homes where fewer retailing opportunities exist. Neighborhoods older than 30 years old are often run down and in declining areas of town. This is not always the case, of course, as I have seen some areas more than 40 years old that continue to be well maintained and where pride of ownership exists. The 30-year age rule is a generalization where the propensity for homes and neighborhoods older than that tend to be declining in value, or may require a longer holding period.

The ideal location is one in which the majority of homes are well maintained and is not suffering from functional obsolescence. The area is established, has good schools nearby, and continues to have homes that sell in a shorter-than-average number of days compared to surrounding communities. Characteristics of this kind of neighborhood often include mature landscaping, pristine lawns, and homes that are well cared for. What you are looking for is a home in a community such as this that is in obvious need of repair. The grass is often overgrown, the house looks run down (and usually is), and the neighbors shake their heads in disgust as they pass by. Believe me, they are waiting for someone just like you to come along and fix up that eyesore in their neighborhood! (See Exhibit 3.1.)

PRICE RANGE

Most opportunities for flipping properties are at the lower to middle end of the price range. The lower end of the price range is, of course, relative to your area. In California and New York, it may be $250,000, while in Texas $75,000 to $100,000 represents the lower end of the price range.

There are three primary reasons for concentrating your efforts in this price range. The first reason is that there tends to be many more opportunities available. Homes selling in this price range tend to be older and are frequently in greater disrepair than newer and more expensive homes. The second reason to focus on the lower to middle end of the price range is that there is a larger pool of buyers available to purchase these types of homes. Many prospective buyers in the lower price range are younger couples who may be first-time buyers, or working class people who are simply looking for affordable housing. The higher up the price scale you go, the smaller the pool of buyers. Finally,

Exhibit 3.1

Property Location Checklist

☑ The neighborhood is between 10 and 30 years old.

☑ The majority of the homes are well cared for and not run down.

☑ Mature landscaping and pristine lawns are the norm.

☑ No junk cars parked in the driveway or in front of the house.

☑ Boats are properly stored (if allowed).

☑ The neighborhood is free of trash and debris.

☑ Low crime rate in the area.

☑ Close proximity to schools, churches, and shopping.

☑ The neighborhood should not be located in a declining area of town.

☑ Home sales should be moderate to strong.

homes in this price range are easier for you as the investor to afford. Why tie up your capital in larger, more expensive homes that are harder to resell when you can buy smaller, more affordable homes? Also, if you have a limited amount of investment capital to work with, financing will be easier to obtain on less expensive homes.

PHYSICAL CONDITION

A property's physical condition can range from extremely poor, as in condemned, to very good. Your focus should be on those properties that fall somewhere in between.

Investing in houses that fall into this category will prove to be the most profitable, as you will be able to minimize the amount of capital required for improvements, thereby allowing you to maximize your return on investment. Another key consideration is the time involved in making the more extensive repairs. The turnaround time for houses that require only minor repairs is much shorter than it is for those that require major repairs. A thorough understanding of knowing what to look for is key to your success in this business. Ideally, you want to locate properties that look a lot worse than they really are. In other words, you are looking for houses that are in need of cosmetic-type repairs such as new paint, landscaping, and perhaps a good, thorough cleaning. Cosmetic repairs are quick and easy to make and are often the least expensive type of repair.

While properties in extremely poor condition can frequently be purchased at bargain basement prices, they will typically require much more money for improvements. When it comes to houses, cheaper is not necessarily better. The initial price may be much less than other homes in the area, but the time and resources required for property improvements will often outweigh any advantage gained from the purchase price. Houses that fall into this category are usually in need of major repairs, which can be quite expensive.

The following inspection items represent a partial list of things to look for in your assessment of a property's physical condition. For a more comprehensive checklist, please see Appendix A, Property Inspection Checklist.

A bad foundation is one such problem that can be very costly to repair. If the house is built on a concrete slab where major settling has occurred, the house will have to be leveled. Leveling a house may not only be very costly, it can also be time consuming. Furthermore, houses with foundation problems are likely to have other structural damage caused by the settling. A close inspection of the interior walls will almost always show evidence of settling, as the drywall will crack and separate. It is common to see hairline cracks in walls, especially around the seams, so don't be alarmed if you see small cracks such as these. If, on the other hand, you see large cracks running down the wall, you can almost bet the house has a foundation problem.

If the house was not built on a slab, but was built with a basement type foundation instead, you must be particularly aware of moisture problems. This is fairly common, especially in older homes. Look for cracks in the basement walls, which may have evidence of leaking around them, such as staining or mildew. Leaks in the walls can also create a buildup of mold in the basement area, an issue that is becoming a major liability for some homeowners. It is not at all unusual to observe hairline cracks in the basement floor or even in the walls. In fact, I don't believe I've ever seen one without some kind of small cracks. You don't need to be overly concerned about these types of cracks, as they are usually just surface cracks, which do not go all the way through the floor or the wall. Just as houses built on slabs with foundation problems can be very costly to repair, so can houses built on basements with similar problems. As a general rule, your best bet is to stay away from dealing with these types of issues.

Roofs also represent another area where major repairs may be required. The cost to repair a roof can vary widely with age and condition. Most composition shingles have a minimum life of 25 years, so if the existing shingles are less than 15 years old, it's a pretty safe bet that any repairs required will be minimal. After 15 years, the shingles can begin curling up, wearing to the point where leaks may begin to develop. Newer roofs can show signs of discoloration, but this is a problem that can be easily and inexpensively resolved by applying a chemical cleaning process. The discoloration is usually caused by a buildup of mildew that can be killed and removed with a solution of water and bleach, which is available at most hardware stores. If a new roof is needed, the cost to replace it may not be prohibitive. If, for example, a new layer of shingles can be applied over the existing layer, the cost and time involved is minimal. On the other hand, if two or three layers of shingles already exist, then a tear-off will almost certainly be necessary. This can effectively double the price of a new roof, as the labor required for the tear-off can be quite expensive because of the additional time that is needed. Furthermore, older homes that already have several layers of shingles on them may require additional work. The roof deck may be damaged as a result of water leaks that have occurred over time. If the house needs to be completely redecked, this will certainly drive up the cost.

Other repairs that may prove costly include replacing equipment, windows, and exterior surfaces, such as brick or siding. If the furnace and air conditioner are worn out, replacing them can quickly add up. New windows for the entire house can also be quite expensive. Replacing the siding or brick on a house can add thousands of dollars to the cost of your repairs. A close inspection of these items is essential for the success of your project. It may be that only minor repairs are needed, that only one or two windows need to be replaced, or that the exterior of the house just needs a fresh coat of paint. These types of improvements are easy to make, do not require much time, and most of all, do not require as much money to make the repairs.

The house's plumbing should also be carefully checked for proper operation. The plumbing can be checked by flushing toilets, inspecting underneath sink cabinets, and looking for leaky faucets. You will also want to check the age and condition of the home's hot water heater. Leaky faucets and hot water heaters are fairly easy to repair and/or replace and can be done quickly and inexpensively. With homes older than 20 years, you will want to make a special note to determine whether the roots from mature plants or trees are causing any blockage. Recurring problems in the same line are usually symptomatic of root damage. Some older sewage lines are made of a clay-like material and when trees are planted nearby, the roots can literally grow right through the sewer lines. When that happens, it creates a blockage within the line and causes the sewer system to back up. I bought a house a number of years ago that was 40 years old or so, which I held for rental purposes at the time. Sure enough, I had one line in particular that kept getting backed up. It cost me $75 every time the plumber came out to clear the line. As it turned out, the line was severely blocked with roots that had grown through it. I finally had the plumber dig up the line in the back yard, which was made of clay, and had him replace it with a new PVC line.

Sewer lines that run through a concrete slab type of foundation or through concrete driveways can get backed up as a result of settling. As the concrete settles, the sewer lines, which are usually PVC, will crack and break. The separation in the line does not allow the sewage to drain properly and can also cause the line to back up. In another house I bought, the driveway had a large crack in it because of settling. When I purchased the house, I wasn't really too concerned about the crack because I initially thought I would just patch the driveway with a little cement. As it turns out, the repair was much more costly. The concrete driveway had to be chiseled out with a jackhammer to replace the broken sewage line. Once the line was repaired, a new driveway then had to be poured. As an investor, you will want to minimize dealing with the more severe types of plumbing problems such as these. Leaky faucets and hot water heaters are generally easy to repair or replace. Broken sewer lines, on the other hand, are harder to detect and can be much more expensive to repair. A careful inspection of the plumbing system can potentially spare you thousands of dollars.

Finally, the home's electrical wiring should be checked for its proper working condition. A simple check of outlets and light switches can tell you a great deal about a house's electrical condition. If they are working properly, chances are the system is okay. Homes older than 30 to 40 years tend to have more problems, as breakers and switches may eventually wear out. In some homes, the wiring may be so old that it will have to be completely replaced. Installing an entirely new electrical system can be very expensive, due in part to the fact that much of the wiring is run behind the walls of a house. The new wiring will either have to be fished or pulled through openings from the attic or basement if there are any, or cuts will have to be made in the drywall that will afterward have to be repaired and repainted.

As you gain more experience and look at more and more properties, you will be able to quickly assess a house's physical condition and know within a short time whether or not it meets your investment criteria. If you lack experience or are not yet comfortable with the inspection process, you may want to hire a professional house inspection company.

These companies perform a very thorough inspection and give you a written report when they are finished. Their services commonly cost anywhere between $150 up to $500, depending on the area of the country you live in and the size of the house. I seldom use professional inspectors anymore because, more often than not, they end up telling me what I already knew from my own inspection. About the only time I do use them is if the house is way more than 30 years old. In fact, just last week I had an inspection performed on a house I have under contract that was built in 1903. The main reason I wanted an inspection in this particular case was to ensure that the wiring was up to code. As previously mentioned, replacing the entire wiring in a house can be very expensive. As it turned out, the electrical wiring did in fact meet current code requirements. The $335 I spent on the inspection was well worth it to me.

In summary, the ideal property will look like it's in a lot worse shape than it actually is. You should focus your efforts on finding houses that are in relatively good condition, but look like a dump. This is difficult for many people to do, and that is exactly why an astute investor such as yourself can profit handsomely from the retailing business. It's hard to look beyond that first impression of a house, especially if it's a negative one. Most people will keep right on driving. They won't even stop to look at such a house! They absolutely cannot see the hidden potential just waiting to be unlocked in properties like these. As an investor who is serious about flipping properties, you *must* be able to look beyond what you see on the surface. In fact, you will come to enjoy driving up to a house that appears to be run down and lacking in care because experience has taught you that these houses are actually diamonds in the rough. While most people see a lump of coal, you will come to recognize it as a diamond that just needs a little polishing. Ideally, you will be able to buy houses at coal-like prices and sell these highly polished gems at diamond-like prices.

This same concept can be applied on a larger scale. For example, I have used it in the apartment business as well as in the new home residential construction business. As a principal for Symphony Homes, I recently took over an entire community that was partially completed with new homes and successfully applied the value play strategy. The community was only about three years old, but the original builder apparently ran into financial difficulty, which caused the progress of new home construction to come to a standstill. As a result, the entrance way and all of the remaining vacant lots became neglected. Weeds and grass went uncut and grew as high as four to five feet. Many of the vacant lots were littered with debris left over from the previous builder. In short, the community was a real eyesore! The developer of the subdivision had tried unsuccessfully for more than six months to get another builder to come in and take over where the previous builder had left off. No one would touch it. In fact, you would probably be considered foolish to go in and take over something like that. Discussions with the city inspectors led me to believe that even they had written the community off.

My experience has taught me to look beyond what is visible on the surface. Let's take a closer look at the facts of this particular community.

First we'll look at the negatives:

■ The entrance into the community was overgrown with weeds.

■ The weeds were overgrown on all of the vacant lots.

■ Many of the lots were littered with debris left over from the previous builder.

■ The residents and city officials were in despair and had given up hope.

Now let's look at the positives:

■ Landscaping improvements to the entrance would be quick and easy to make.

■ Weeds can be easily cut and is an inexpensive and quick way to improve a property's appearance.

■ Debris is easy to remove.

■ The community was ideally situated immediately off a main road, which provided terrific visibility to passersby.

■ A brand new post office was located directly across the street, which meant that no less than once or twice a month, everyone in town would drive by the community and see the improvements being made along with all the new construction activity.

■ The community was located only half a mile from a major state road, which was heavily traveled, and only a mile or so from a major interstate highway. Both of these roads served as major traffic arteries for commuters and would be easily accessible from the community.

■ The homes in the community were only three years old or less, which meant that our new homes would fit in perfectly.

As it turned out, our company was able to negotiate a very favorable price and subsequently took over the remaining lots. As a condition for doing so, the developer agreed at his expense to have all of the vacant lots mowed, the debris removed, and the entrance way cleaned up immediately upon closing. Within one week, the community was cleaned up and a sense of pride was restored to the residents who lived there. In fact, the existing residents in the community treated us like knights in shining armor who had come to their rescue. They were so thankful that finally another builder had taken enough interest in their community to come in and make a positive difference. Their sincere expression of gratitude toward us meant a great deal and was certainly appreciated by the Symphony Homes team. Our ability to envision the hidden potential in that community has allowed us to enjoy a substantially higher profit margin on a per unit basis than we would otherwise have.

In summary, don't underestimate the power of the value play strategy. It is indisputably one of the most effective means available to you to create wealth and to enjoy a fuller and more rewarding life.

> **I believe life is constantly testing us for our level of commitment, and life's greatest rewards are reserved for those who demonstrate a never-ending commitment to act until they achieve. This level of resolve can move mountains, but it must be constant and consistent. As simplistic as this may sound, it is still the common denominator separating those who live their dreams from those who live in regret.**
>
> **—*Anthony Robbins***

Chapter 4

Ten Ways to Locate Properties

$\mathbb{F}$inding exactly the right property can sometimes prove to be challenging. The application of a comprehensive and all-inclusive approach will provide you with the greatest chances for success. You must be willing to exercise patience and diligence in your search. Doing so will enable you to minimize your risk and maximize the return of your hard-earned investment capital. The more selection options you have available to you, the better your odds are for locating the type of property most suited to your objectives. In my experience, brokers, classified ads, real estate publications, web sites, real estate investment clubs, and lenders have all proven to be useful at one time or another. Advertising, for sale by owners, vacant properties, and foreclosures can also generate good leads. (See Exhibit 4.1.)

REAL ESTATE AGENTS

Having several real estate agents scouting properties for you is one of the most effective ways to quickly and efficiently identify potential properties that can be flipped. I must stress that it is *critical to your success* to ensure the competency level of the brokerage team you put together. I have worked with many brokers and agents whose range of expertise and experience varies greatly. Most residential brokers focus primarily on the more traditional single family housing sales. They act in a fiduciary capacity to represent buyers and sellers who have a broad and diverse range of needs. The sales process typically goes something like this.

SALES AGENT: "Mr. Buyer, what type of home are you looking for?"
BUYER: "We're looking for a 3-bedroom, 2-bath ranch."

Exhibit 4.1
Ten Ways to Locate Properties

1. Real estate brokers and agents

2. Classified advertising

3. Real estate publications

4. Local and national web sites

5. Associations and real estate investment clubs

6. Bank R.E.O.s

7. Marketing

8. For Sale By Owners (FSBOs)

9. Vacant properties

10. Foreclosures

SALES AGENT: "Great! Have you been prequalified?"

BUYER: "Yes, Ms. Agent. Our loan officer has preapproved us for $150,000."

SALES AGENT: "That's terrific, Mr. Buyer! What area of town do you prefer?"

BUYER: "I work on the north side of town, so something within fifteen minutes or so would be ideal."

SALES AGENT: "That's wonderful! The M.L.S. shows there are twelve homes available in the area you prefer and eight of them are within your price range!"

The sales agent will then schedule time with the buyer and the sellers to visit as many of the homes as possible. If the buyer sees something he likes, the agent writes it up and presents the offer to the seller. There is often a counteroffer or two before a deal is consummated. The broker collects her commission upon closing and the buyer lives happily ever after . . . well, maybe.

While this is a simplified example of how the sales process works, the process for locating properties that can be flipped does share a few similarities with the more traditional role the sales agent plays. The sales agent will locate the types of properties you are looking for, present them to you, and if an opportunity that makes financial sense avails itself, you will make an offer that the agent will present. Significant information traditional sales agents are not used to providing are data specific to the market you are buying in. If requested, they may provide a few comparables, or comps as they are known, but you need lots of hard data to support your investment decision. Housing prices vary widely from city to city and from community to community. Prices are relative. For example, an identical house selling for $85,000 in one neighborhood might be worth $110,000 in another neighborhood. That's a difference of $25,000 for the exact same house. You must be provided with market data that will enable you to make sound investment decisions.

Unlike the traditional real estate sales agent, there are those agents who specialize in investment properties and nothing else. These are the dealers we discussed in Chapter 2. These are the people you want on your team! Dealers play an important role in bringing opportunities to investors. They often act as a wholesaler for retailers and other investors looking to buy property at below-market prices. Dealers are often licensed real estate agents and earn their money from commissions generated. These agents are generally experts in their industry who have migrated from single family residential sales for one reason or another, but usually because of a shared interest they have for investment-type properties. Their specialized knowledge can save you a great deal in time, energy, and money. While the traditional sales agent is not used to providing her clients with market data, the dealer knows exactly what you need. He understands the nature of the business of flipping properties and recognizes that you will need key market information for a proper financial analysis.

Dealers are well informed and are in direct contact with buyers and sellers every single day. They know which areas of town are hot and which are not. They also know when new properties are about to be made available for sale, so if they know what you are looking for, they can notify you immediately when a property that meets your criteria hits the market. Since dealers are plugged in to a network of relationships that provide them with inventory, they will be among the first to know when a new opportunity becomes available. An additional advantage dealers can offer is that they often have an extensive database of other investors, both buyers and sellers, whom they can contact, so even if a house is not officially listed for sale, the broker may know from a prior conversation that if the right buyer comes along with the right price, the owner would consider an offer.

Furthermore, dealers will often know how to use the MLS in ways that traditional real estate agents may not be aware of. For example, they can search the description fields of homes available for sale for key words like *handyman special* or *TLC needed*. Other key words include *needs work*, *as is*, and *motivated seller*. One additional term your dealer can search on is *VLB*, which means "vacant on lock box." This frequently indicates that the seller has already moved into another house for any number of reasons (transfer, new home, and so forth) and is now in the position of having to make two house payments every month. The house is likely to be in fairly good condition with only minimal repairs needed, but because the seller is making two payments, she may be willing to take considerably less than its true market value. I found myself in that very position several years ago. My wife and I bought a new house in Michigan that we were required to close on, even though we had not yet sold our home in Texas. After about six months of making payments on both houses, a buyer offered me much less than what similar houses in the neighborhood were selling for. I wasn't at all excited about taking less than what I thought the house was worth, but I was thankful for the opportunity to be relieved of the obligation to the mortgage company on the other residence. Meanwhile, the buyer got a great deal and I am certain that he could sell it today for much more than he paid for it then.

CLASSIFIED ADVERTISING

Almost all newspapers, large or small, carry a section in their classified advertising specifically for real estate that is available for sale. Many of these ads are placed by real estate agents and are designed to prompt you to call their office. Most homes listed for sale in the newspaper by agents are active listings and will typically be priced at full retail. You might notice some ads, however, that use key words like "motivated seller" or "must sell, owner transferring." These types of classified advertisements are worth following up on, and even if the home is no longer available or it does not meet your investment objectives, it still provides you with an opportunity to create a dialogue with a sales agent who might be able to find investment property that will meet your needs. The agent may even refer you to someone in her office who specializes in investment property, such as a dealer.

Many of the ads listed in the classified section are for sale by owners, or FSBOs. Again, you will want to look for any key words that may indicate that the owner is anxious to sell or that the property may be offered at a price below retail. Some of these keywords include *handyman special*, *needs work*, or *as is*. You should be prepared to take the time to call on as many of these properties as possible. You must also have the self-discipline to exercise restraint in your selection and analysis process. It is easy to get excited about an opportunity and to become emotionally engaged in the buying process. To be successful, you have to be able to remain impartial and objective in your analysis. Sooner or later, your patience will pay off and you will find that diamond in the rough.

Another way to use the classified advertising section is to place your own ad in the real estate wanted section. You don't need to spend a lot of money on these ads. A well-written small ad can be just as effective as a larger and more expensive ad. Your goal is to get people who are motivated and want to sell their house to call you. Your ad should be written to solicit these types of calls so that you are not bothered with individuals who are not likely to have the type of property for sale that you are seeking. The following are some sample ads you may want to consider using.

NEED QUICK CASH?

I BUY HOUSES!

FAST CLOSINGS! ALL CASH!

CALL **(800) 123–4567**

MOTIVATED SELLERS WANTED!

ANY CONDITION! FAST CLOSINGS!

WE BUY HOUSES!

CALL **(800) 123–4567**

VACANT AND HANDYMAN SPECIAL

PROPERTIES WANTED!

ANY AREA! ANY CONDITION!

(800) 123–4567

REAL ESTATE PUBLICATIONS

Almost all areas publish books or magazines periodically that are specifically designed for residential real estate sales. Some of these are local, while others are regional. The magazines can often be found in racks or newsstands located outside of real estate offices, convenience stores, and grocery stores. These real estate publications can be a very good source for locating potential deals. You will also find many real estate related advertisers in these publications that can be helpful, such as real estate agents, mortgage companies, appraisers, surveyors, title companies, real estate legal services, and insurance companies.

The majority of ads in these magazines are placed by real estate agents who will often advertise all their listings on one page. The ads usually feature a photo of the agent along with some compelling reason why you should contact him for your real estate needs. Although the bulk of the ads in real estate magazines are placed by agents and brokers, some do offer a "for sale by owner" section. While most of the sales agents with listings in these publications focus on the traditional retail housing segment, there are usually a number of agents who specialize in different niches within the real estate market. For example, some firms focus solely on commercial real estate, while others are vacant land specialists. Still others specialize in the wholesale market, such as dealers. As discussed in Chapter 2, dealers can be an excellent source for you. A good dealer can fax twenty or thirty wholesale listings to your office within minutes of your calling him. Don't overlook these easy-to-find real estate publications because they can provide you with lots of leads and lots of information vital to your success!

LOCAL AND NATIONAL WEB SITES

There are a number of web sites that offer all kinds of information about houses for sale. You can do a local search by keying in a phrase such as "homes for sale Dallas, Texas," for example. A search like this will usually generate results of 20 to 30, and even more, web sites with listings in your area. The most comprehensive and well-known web site related to single family properties for sale is hosted by the National Association of Realtors. You can find them on the web at www.realtor.com. Realtor.com boasts over two million listings for various types of properties, including single family homes, condominiums, townhouses, multifamily apartments, mobile homes, vacant land, farms, and rentals. The data derived for these listings come from the Multiple Listing Service, so it will not include any for sale by owner properties. The web site is available to the general public, so you don't have to be a real estate agent to have access to their listings. It is very much like a public MLS for properties made available to the general public, or anyone with a computer and access to the Internet. You can also search by property type, state, city, zip code, price range, minimum and maximum square feet, age of home, number of floors, as well as several other criteria. Most listings provide a descriptive overview of the property, photos, and offering information. Exhibit 4.2 illustrates how very specific you can be by using the search criteria available on Realtor.com.

Other good Internet sources include your local newspapers. Almost all major newspapers now list their entire classifieds section on web sites. The information is often updated daily. This is usually determined by how often the paper is published. For example, if it is a daily paper, it is most likely to be updated daily. A weekly paper would be updated weekly. An advantage the newspaper web sites offer over a site such as Realtor.com is that in addition to providing ads placed by real estate agents, there are also many ads placed by individuals, or for sale by owners. In fact, other than placing a sign out in the front yard, this is really about the only way an individual can market her property. Newspaper classifieds are not nearly as comprehensive as a site like Realtor.com, but they do provide you with a good mix of properties for sale by both real estate agents and individual home owners.

These are only two of many examples available on the Internet to locate investment opportunities. The best way for you to locate properties in your own area is to use a search engine like Yahoo, Google, or MSN to do a search specific to your area.

REAL ESTATE INVESTMENT CLUBS

Most cities have a number of real estate investment–related associations and clubs. These clubs provide an excellent opportunity for you to network with others who share similar interests. Members often include investors like yourself, real estate brokers, tax and real estate attorneys, architectural engineers, appraisers, and other real estate professionals. Club and association members will usually meet on a periodic basis, such as monthly, to discuss current events and share information. They will also frequently feature guest speakers who provide insight into a given area of expertise. You can find real estate associations in your area by looking in the Yellow Pages or by doing a search on the Internet for "real estate investment clubs." One site that I have used is called Real Estate Promo.com and is located at www.realestatepromo.com. Click on the "Investment Clubs" link to find a club near you. They have clubs listed in almost all 50 states, so you should be able to find something near you. A similar site is offered by a company called Creative

Exhibit 4.2
Web Site of Realtor.com

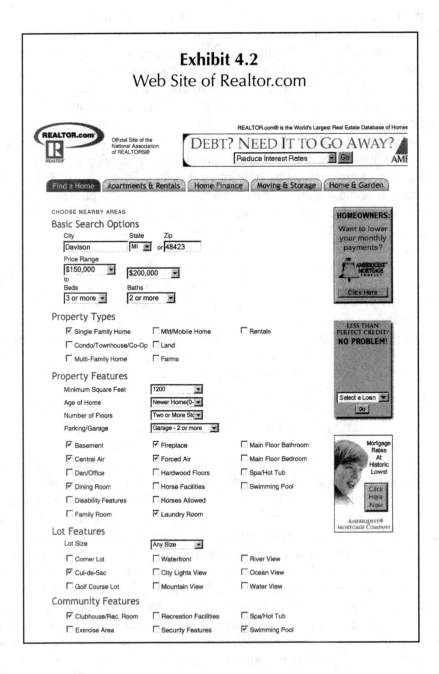

Exhibit 4.2 (*Continued*)

☐ Golf ☐ Senior Community ☑ Tennis

FREE MATERIAL LIST FOR YOUR DREAM HOME

Financial Options

☐ Lease Option Considered

☐ Trade Considered

MLS ID Search

MLS ID

(You'll need to fill in the City and State fields at the top of the page to complete an MLS search.)

Show Properties

Site Map | Corporate News & Info | Contact Us | Advertise With Us | Join our staff
Terms of Use and Privacy Policy.

© 1995-2002 NATIONAL ASSOCIATION OF REALTORS® and Homestore, Inc. All rights reserved. Equal Housing Opportunity REALTOR.com® is the official site of the National Association of REALTORS® and is operated by Homestore, Inc.

REALTOR® -- A registered collective membership mark that identifies a real estate professional who is a member of the National Association of REALT subscribes to its strict Code of Ethics. Inquiries regarding the Code of Ethics should be directed to the board in which a REALTOR® holds member

Real Estate Online. Their web site is www.real-estate-online.com. Go to the home page and click on "Real Estate Clubs" to find an investment association in your area.

BANK REOs

Smaller local or regional banks can also be a good source for locating properties. Lenders, of course, are not in the business of managing real estate, nor do they want to be. The very nature of their business, however, demands that they assume risk with each and every loan extended to borrowers. Unfortunately for the banks, sometimes those borrowers default and when they do, the lender forecloses on the property and the real estate is transferred into the lender's "real estate–owned," or REO, portfolio.

Most people don't event know that REOs exist. Banks certainly don't promote the fact that they have real estate that has been foreclosed on and is now listed on their books as a nonperforming loan. After all, their customers come to them for banking services, not real estate services. Although almost all banks have REOs, very few, if any will publicize that information. Small local banks will usually have one individual who is responsible for the real estate–owned portfolio, while regional banks may have several people, or even a whole department, responsible for its REOs. Banks divest these properties through a network of private investors who have expressed an interest in them, and also through real estate agents, such as dealers who specialize in wholesale property. The network of private investors can include anyone. If you are interested in acquiring properties in this manner, then you will need to be prepared to do some initial legwork to establish the proper contacts. There is no limit to the number of banks you can contact. I recommend establishing relationships with 8 to 10 banks in your area to provide you with as large of a pool of houses for sale as possible.

Lenders are often quite flexible in the terms and conditions they are willing to offer, which may result in an opportunity for you to reach an agreement that is acceptable to both of you. The basis for the lender's initial asking price will likely be determined by the hard costs the bank has into it, or its book value. While the bank will no doubt make every effort to minimize its losses, if they are anxious to get the property off their books, there's a good chance they will be willing to negotiate in your favor by agreeing to write down a portion of the loan. You should take time to physically inspect the property, determine the costs required for repairs, carrying costs, and transactions costs and make your offer to the bank based on your analysis. In other words, determine the maximum amount you can have into the deal and still make money on it based on a rate of return that is acceptable to you. If the deal doesn't make sense for you as an investor, you're better off letting the bank keep it. After all, there are many more banks with just as many REO properties available that are likely to meet your investment criteria.

MARKETING

As you graduate from buying and selling real estate on a part-time basis to a full-time business, you will want to give serious consideration to promoting your company and the services you offer. Just as any other business owner budgets a certain portion of her expected revenues for marketing purposes, so will you, too, want to allocate a portion of your resources to promoting your real estate investment company. The more people who know that you are in business to buy and sell houses, the more opportunities you will have presented to you.

There are numerous ways to market your business and just as many books written about how to do so. Since this is not a marketing book, I will mention just a few of the many ways you can promote your company. Some of these include advertising in newspapers and magazines, implementing a direct mail campaign, using signs, and doing a broadcast fax.

As previously mentioned, you can place small ads in the classified section of the newspaper, which can be highly effective. As your company grows, however, you will want to consider placing larger display ads in real estate publications as well as in newspapers.

You can use the same newspapers and magazines to advertise in as you do to search for properties for sale. It should be easy enough for you to make your ad stand out from all of the others because you are in the business of buying houses at wholesale while most of all the other advertisers are buying and selling houses at retail. The sample ad shown here is just one of many ideas you can use to promote your company. The focus of this ad is to generate referrals by offering a $500 reward for each and every referral received. You should be sure to qualify your offer, however, by stating that the referral must result in the signing of a purchase agreement by both the buyer and the seller. (See Exhibit 4.3.)

Another very effective method of promoting your company is to implement a direct mail campaign. Since the cost of printing and postage can quickly add up, your direct mail piece should be targeted to the people who can best help you—real estate agents. You can get a list of names and addresses for the agents in your area by purchasing a list from a reputable company, or if you have the time, by simply using your local telephone book to build your own list. Much of the content used in your display ads in newspapers and real estate publications can also be used in your direct mail piece. The literature that you mail can be in the form of a letter in which you introduce yourself and the services you offer, a flyer containing the same information, sales literature, or any combination of the three. I suggest that you also include at least two or three of your business cards. While the recipients of your mailing may discard the enclosed letter or flyer, they will most likely save your business cards, and if you send more than one, there's a good chance they may pass one along to a business associate in the office.

Signs are also a cost effective way of marketing your company. Smaller signs such as those approximately 18" × 24" and made out of corrugated plastic are fairly inexpensive to buy. You can buy them with wire frame stands, which makes them easy to place in high traffic locations. I recommend not putting too much information on your signs. Just stick to the basics, such as "I buy houses," your company name, and a telephone number. I've seen some real estate signs that are so overloaded with information that it's difficult to make anything out on them, especially when you are driving by and may have only a few seconds to glance at the sign. Fill the sign with large letters and keep it simple. I would also suggest using a color that works well both in the winter and in the summer. For example, white signs with blue lettering look great in the summer; however, in the winter the white sign will blend in with the snow and will be barely visible. Likewise, a green sign with white lettering looks great in the wintertime because the colors are sharply contrasting. Once again, though, in the winter, the green sign blends in with grassy roadsides and surrounding foliage. I suggest using colors that work well year-round, such as a red or blue sign with white letters.

Exhibit 4.3
Example of a Promotional Ad

WANTED!

Handyman Specials!

Fixer-Uppers!

$500

REWARD!!!

To collect your reward of $500 in cold, hard cash, simply refer a seller to us with a house that is in need of repairs! $500 will be paid for each and every referral! Sellers must sign a purchase agreement to qualify!

Submit 3 or more referrals to us by December 31 and receive a $2,500 Christmas bonus!
Sellers must sign a purchase agreement by December 31 to qualify!

People to consider — friends, family, neighbors, doctors, dentists, teachers, co-workers, business owners...

Symphony Homes

Call (810) 603-3077 or log on to www.symphony-homes.com for details!

As your company grows and you have more money available in your advertising budget, you may also want to consider using billboards. These signs can be very effective, especially in areas of town where the traffic count is known to be high. It is also helpful if the posted speed limit is 40 mph or less. That way the passersby have more time to read the information on the signs. As with the smaller roadside signs, don't put too much information on billboards. Drivers usually have only a few seconds to read your message, so keep it simple.

Finally, you may want to consider faxing your message to as many recipients as possible. Your primary target market should be real estate offices. There are a number of good fax programs that allow you to generate what is known as a broadcast fax directly from your computer. These programs are easy to use and easy to set up. A broadcast fax, also known as a blast fax, allows you to send a document to multiple recipients. The fax program allows you to set up telephone directories, so, for example, you could set up a directory named County Real Estate and enter the fax numbers of all the real estate agents in it. When you get ready to send your letter, flyer, or other document from your computer, the fax program allows you to select the entire directory. All you have to do is click on it, push Send and the computer will do the rest. It will spend the next two to three hours dialing every number in your directory and sending the fax. If you live in an area where the calls are all local, then all the fax costs you is a little bit of your time. One cautionary note I will add is that not everyone wants to receive faxes they consider to be advertisements. As a general rule, the real estate community will be receptive to your message; be respectful, however, of those who do not wish to receive faxes and promptly remove them from your list.

FOR SALE BY OWNERS (FSBOs)

Individuals who prefer to sell their own house are frequently referred to as *for sale by owners*, or FSBOs. This group of homeowners represents an important segment of the potential properties that are available to you, so be sure to give them the attention they deserve. They can be located by looking through the real estate section of your local newspaper or by driving through neighborhoods and looking for FSBO signs. FSBOs typically maintain the attitude that they can sell their house on their own without any professional help from the real estate community, thereby enabling them to save thousands of dollars on the cost of the commission. What they fail to realize, unfortunately, is that although they may save money on the commission, they may lose more money on the overall transaction than if they had listed with an agent. This results from their lack of experience and lack of knowledge of local market prices.

FSBOs all have an idea of how much they think their house is worth, but in reality, their houses are usually priced too high or too low. For example, some owners have lived in their homes for 20 years or more and have no idea that they have appreciated as much as they have. Other home owners, on the other hand, have heard that a neighbor down the street sold her house for X, therefore their house must be worth Y. In truth, neither seller really knows what the true market value of their home is. Guess what? That's good news for you as an investor. Since you will be intimately familiar with market values in the neighborhoods you will be prospecting, you will know immediately from your initial telephone conversation with them whether or not the price of the house fits your investment criteria. If you find a seller who is willing to sell his home at a price 10 or 15 percent below what you believe the market value to be, that can certainly work to your advantage. For those of you who may think this is taking advantage of the seller, I disagree. You have no moral obligation to tell a seller that his house may be worth more than what is being asked for. The FSBO has set the asking price at a value they believe to be fair for any number of reasons. As a buyer willing to meet his terms, you have become an important component of a relationship that is amenable to both parties. Finally, for sale by owners are often flexible on terms, so they may be able to provide you with a more favorable and creative deal structure, one which permits you to minimize your cash outlay in the property.

VACANT PROPERTIES

As you drive hrough neighborhoods in your search for investment opportunities, be sure to pay special attention to those houses that may appear vacant. Vacant houses are more of a liability than an asset for their owners, so they are often available at bargain prices. For any number of reasons, the seller has moved out and is no longer around to care for the house. It may be that he just went through a divorce, had a new house built, or was transferred to another area. Whatever the reason, the end result is the same. If the owner is to prevent the house from going into foreclosure, he must not only make the payments on his new house, but must also keep up the payments on the old one, too. After just a few months of making double house payments, sellers of vacant properties become very motivated. In some cases, they are happy just to get somebody to relieve them of their monthly obligation, regardless of any equity they may have built up in the house.

Obvious signs of empty houses include overgrown weeds and shrubs, newspapers in the driveway, and a general rundown appearance. Sometimes these houses have only recently been vacated, while other times they have been sitting empty for several months. They may have a FSBO sign or a real estate firm's sign in the front yard. If so, this makes your job of finding the owner much easier. If there is no sign out front, you may have to do a little research. Usually a telephone call to the local taxing authority can provide you with the information you need. The clerks who work in the tax offices and who are responsible for maintaining the tax rolls can quickly and easily provide you with the current owner's name and the address of where the tax bill is mailed to. With the name and address, you can call information to obtain a phone number for the owner. If the number is unlisted, you can express your interest in the property through the mail, since you at least have the owner's address. Be sure to provide her with your telephone number so that if the owner is interested in selling her house to you, she can call you with as little effort as possible.

FORECLOSURES

While vacant properties can be an excellent source of finding investment opportunities, properties that sit vacant for too long often become foreclosed properties. This, too, can be another great source for finding potential deals. Buying and selling foreclosures requires an individual to have a working knowledge of that market. While there are a number of good books written on the subject, many investors do not have the expertise or the time to find undervalued foreclosures. Furthermore, they are unfamiliar with the auction or bidding process and may lack the resources to purchase properties in this manner. An investor who understands the process of buying foreclosed properties can potentially make substantial profits. Buying foreclosures, however, is not as easy as many would have you believe. In many markets, the bidding process is very competitive, and therefore difficult to buy at an attractive price. The investor participating in this market must have specialized knowledge, patience, and enough investment capital to be successful.

The best approach to identifying the right property best suited to your specific needs will include using as many of these tools as possible. The most important thing to remember is to *be patient*. You will find the right property at the right price with the right terms. As the employer of your capital, your task is to have your employees (your capital) working as hard for you as possible. That means your investment must offer an acceptable rate of return to you. Only you can determine what is acceptable. It is best to establish what is an acceptable rate of return early in the process so you don't make the mistake of lowering your standard because you think you have found a property that is okay. Determine what your investment criteria and objectives are, implement them as an initial filtering device, and when the time comes, be prepared to execute your acquisition strategy.

> The heights by great men reached and kept,
> Were not attained by sudden flight,
> But they, while their companions slept,
> Were toiling upward in the night.
> —*Henry Wadsworth Longfellow*

PART II

How to Value, Analyze, and Negotiate for Maximum Profit

Chapter 5

Valuation Methodologies

$\mathbb{N}$ow that you understand the concept of flipping properties, how to create value, and what types of properties to look for, the next step is to learn how to analyze potential value play opportunities to determine whether or not they meet your investment criteria. This chapter is probably the most critical chapter in the entire book. The key to your success in buying and selling single family houses is to have a thorough and comprehensive understanding of value. Proper valuation is the basis for all investment decisions, whether it be commodities, real estate, or an investment in the stocks of various companies. You absolutely must be able to understand how value is derived in order to make rational and balanced investment decisions. Without these essential skill sets, you will find yourself at a tremendous disadvantage.

Before you even make an offer on a prospective investment property, you will want to know beforehand the potential value that can be created from it. Creating value in single family houses can be accomplished in any one of several ways. Your review of a prospective flipping opportunity will consist of examining the variable components of the property that affect its value, or, in other words, anything at all about the property that can be changed to add value. For flipping or rehab properties, this would primarily include, for example, the physical condition of the property, but not its location. While the property's location is certainly important, it is not a variable that can be changed to add value.

HOW TO KNOW HOW MUCH IS TOO MUCH

In this chapter, you will learn how to determine whether a house a seller is asking $50,000 for is really in fact worth that asking price. How do you know? It may in reality be worth only $40,000, or it could actually be underpriced and may be worth $65,000. The bottom line is, you need to know and understand the difference for yourself and not rely solely on what the sales agent or seller is telling you. In my experience, I have met many agents who believe their client's property is worth more than it really is. I have also met inexperienced investors over and over attempt to justify the value the agent is asking. Somehow they think if they could only buy the property, they are going to be able to unlock all that extra value that really doesn't exist. The truth is, however, they will have overpaid for the property. Paying too much for a rehab property is the quickest way I know of to put you out of business.

VALUATION METHODOLOGIES

There are three traditional approaches used to determine the value of a property. They are the sales comparison approach, the cost approach, and the income capitalization approach. Each approach has its place and serves a unique function in determining value. Depending on the type of property being appraised, the majority of the weight may be given to one particular approach because the other two methods may not be relevant. (See Exhibit 5.1.)

REPLACEMENT COST APPROACH

In an appraisal report conducted by Butler Burgher, Inc., a well-known appraisal firm based in Houston, Texas, the replacement cost approach is defined as follows:

> The cost approach is based on the premise that the value of a property can be indicated by the current cost to construct a reproduction or replacement for the improvements minus the amount of depreciation evident in the structures from all causes plus the value of the land and entrepreneurial profit. This approach to value is particularly useful for appraising new or nearly new improvements.

The replacement cost approach is usually not used to value investment properties such as single family houses. It is most appropriately used when estimating the actual costs associated with replacing all of the physical assets. For example, if a house were partially

Exhibit 5.1
Three Traditional Valuation
Approaches

1. Replacement Cost Approach

2. Income Approach

3. Sales Comparison Approach

or completely ruined by fire, the value established from the cost approach would be useful in helping to determine exactly how much an insurance company would pay for the resulting damages. Depending on the type of policy you have in place, the insurance company may pay for only the remaining useful life of the item damaged. For example, if the roof on the house was 20 years old and became damaged as a result of high winds, the insurance company may not pay 100 percent of the cost for a brand new roof. If the estimated life of the shingles was 25 years, the company may reimburse you only for the remaining useful life, which in this case would be only 20 percent.

$$\text{Remaining Useful Life} = 1 - \frac{20}{25} = 20\%$$

When buying insurance for your investment properties, you will want to be sure to determine what exactly your policy covers and what it does not cover.

INCOME CAPITALIZATION APPROACH

I again refer to the appraisal firm of Butler Burgher to define the income capitalization approach, or income approach, as it is also known.

> The income capitalization approach is based on the principle of antici-pation, which recognizes the present value of the future income benefits to be derived from ownership of real property. The income approach is most applicable to properties that are considered for investment purposes, and is considered very reliable when adequate income/expense data are available. Since income-producing real estate is most often purchased by investors, this approach is valid and is generally considered the most ap-plicable.
>
> The income capitalization approach is a process of estimating the value of real property based upon the principle that value is directly related to the present value of all future net income attributable to the property. The value of the real property is therefore derived by capitalizing net income, either by direct capitalization or a discounted cash flow analysis. Regardless of the capitalization technique employed, one must attempt to estimate a rea-sonable net operating income based upon the best available market data. The derivation of this estimate requires the appraiser to 1) project potential gross income (PGI) based upon an analysis of the subject rent roll and a comparison of the subject to competing properties, 2) project income loss from vacancy and collections based on the subject's occupancy history and upon supply and demand relationships in the subject's market. . . . 3) derive effective gross income (EGI) by subtracting the vacancy and collection in-come loss from PGI, 4) project the operating expenses associated with the production of the income stream by analysis of the subject's operating his-tory and comparison of the subject to similar competing properties, and 5) derive net operating income (NOI) by subtracting the operating expenses from EGI.

The technical description Butler Burgher uses here to define the income approach may initially appear somewhat complex to those of you who may not be very familiar with the methodologies used for the analysis of financial statements. The income approach can be broken down to its most basic and fundamental level by examining a simple financial instrument such as a certificate of deposit. For example, assuming a market interest rate of 5 percent, how much would you be willing to pay for an annuity yielding $10,000 per year? The answer is easily solved by computing the ratio of the two values as follows:

$$\text{Present Value} = \frac{\text{Income}}{\text{Rate}} = \frac{\$10,000}{.05} = \$200,000$$

In other words, if you purchased a certificate of deposit for $200,000 that yielded 5 percent annually, you could expect to have an income stream of $10,000. It doesn't matter if the income continues indefinitely, or perpetually. The present value remains the same and will continue to generate an income stream of $10,000 as long as you continue to hold the $200,000 certificate of deposit. If, at some point in your real estate career, you decide to invest in income-producing properties such as apartments, strip centers, or office buildings, I urge you to thoroughly acquaint yourself with the income capitalization approach and to become proficient in its application. In *The Complete Guide to Buying and Selling Apartment Buildings*, I expound upon these principles in depth and provide many examples of this particular valuation approach.

SALES COMPARISON APPROACH

Once again, I rely on Butler Burgher to define the third valuation approach, which is the sales comparison approach. Butler Burgher states:

> The sales comparison approach is founded upon the principle of substitution, which holds that the cost to acquire an equally desirable substitute property without undue delay ordinarily sets the upper limit of value. At any given time, prices paid for comparable properties are construed by many to reflect the value of the property appraised. The validity of a value indication derived by this approach is heavily dependent upon the availability of data on recent sales of properties similar in location, size, and utility to the appraised property.
>
> The sales comparison approach is premised upon the principle of substitution—a valuation principle that states that a prudent purchaser would pay no more for real property than the cost of acquiring an equally desirable substitute on the open market. The principle of substitution presumes that the purchaser will consider the alternatives available ..., that they (sic) will act rationally or prudently on the basis of this information

about those alternatives, and that time is not a significant factor. Substitution may assume the form of the purchase of an existing property with the same utility, or of acquiring an investment which will produce an income stream of the same size with the same risk as that involved in the property in question.... The actions of typical buyers and sellers are reflected in the comparison approach.

In essence, the sales comparison approach examines like properties and adjusts value on the basis of similarities and differences. This method is used most often in valuing single family houses. Let's say, for example, you decide to sell your house. To help you determine what price you should list your house for, your sales agent will pull up all of the current listings in your neighborhood, as well as recent sales, and calculate a range of prices based on the average sales price per square foot. Then she will consider factors such as the overall condition and the various amenities of your house. Does it have a fireplace, or a swimming pool? Do you have a two-car garage or a three-car garage? And so goes the process, adding and subtracting until a final value is determined. The use of sales comps, as they are called, is the most important factor to consider for the overall analysis of determining the value of single family properties. It is very much like shopping for a new car. You will consider all the alternatives that each manufacturer has to offer, compare each and every feature, and match them to your specific needs. As an investor in value play opportunities, you will rely heavily on the sales comps in your particular market. It is the basis that all buyers looking at your house will use to make their purchase decisions.

In summary, each of the traditional valuation methods serves a unique function by estimating value using one of three different approaches. In some cases, all three approaches may be used with varying weights applied to each one. Butler Burgher affirms, "The appraisal process is concluded by a reconciliation of the approaches. This aspect of the process gives consideration to the type and reliability of market data used, the applicability of each approach to the type of property appraised and the type of value sought."

> **This is the mark of a really admirable man: steadfastness in the face of trouble.**
>
> *—Ludwig van Beethoven*

Chapter 6

Financial Analysis

Now that you have a good understanding of the three primary valuation approaches, let's look at some examples of how to apply them. In particular, we'll examine more closely how to use the comparable sales approach in estimating the potential resale value of various properties. Then we'll look at an example in which a multifamily property is converted into individual single family units. Finally, we'll examine the conversion of a single family house to one of an income-producing commercial use and evaluate its effect on the property's value.

THE TEXAS TWO-STEP

I bought my very first investment property more than 20 years ago. I was living in Texas at the time. I actually bought two houses at the same time from an older gentleman who had owned the houses for years and had maintained them as rental units. The houses were located in the same neighborhood and were right around the corner from each other. They were about 40 years old and in need of minor repairs such as paint and cleanup. All of the real estate books I had read at the time advocated the traditional buy-and-hold approach, so my intentions were to do exactly that—buy the two houses and hold them, much the same as the gentleman from whom I was buying them had done. I decided I would spend a little bit of money fixing them up and then rent them out.

The seller owned the two houses free and clear, which meant that he had no underlying obligations, such as mortgages, on them. Since he was retiring, he did not want to sell them for all cash, but instead preferred to receive regular monthly payments. He was more than glad to carry the financing, which worked out well for me. That meant I wouldn't have to bother with getting a mortgage from a more traditional lending source, such as a bank. We agreed on a sales price of $20,000 apiece for the two houses. Exhibit 6.1 shows how the deal was structured.

A few weeks later, we closed on both houses simultaneously and before I knew it, I was in the real estate business! Since I was young and full of energy at the time, I decided to take on the painting and cleanup myself. I spent the next month painting the exteriors of both houses, cutting down the weeds, mowing the grass, and giving them a good thorough cleaning. It didn't take long after that to locate tenants and rent the houses out. Since these were my first two rental houses, I didn't have any property management experience. The only training I had came from a couple of books I had read.

After a few months of being in the rental business, I was beginning to have second thoughts about my new career in real estate. Actually, the tenants weren't that bad. It just seemed to me that this so-called buy-and-hold approach was going to be a long and painstaking process. At the rate I was going, it would be a long time before I could even

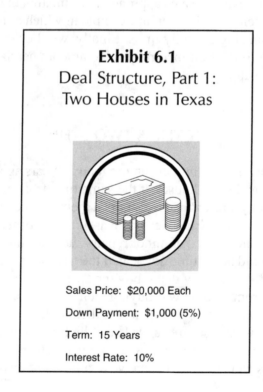

Exhibit 6.1
Deal Structure, Part 1:
Two Houses in Texas

Sales Price: $20,000 Each

Down Payment: $1,000 (5%)

Term: 15 Years

Interest Rate: 10%

begin to think about retirement. After about a year, I began to consider the idea of selling the houses to the tenants who lived there and thought about how I could structure the sale in a manner that would be agreeable to them. I decided to carry the note myself, or provide owner financing, as it is sometimes referred to, just as I was doing with the fellow from whom I had originally bought the houses. I agreed to let the tenants apply a portion of the rent they had been paying. Take a look at Exhibit 6.2 to see how the deal was structured.

Now take a minute to study Exhibit 6.3 —Property Analysis Worksheet for Two Houses in Texas. The worksheet you see is a proprietary model I developed which I use to quickly and easily analyze potential value play investment opportunities. I call it the *Value Play Rehab Analyzer*. Once I have gathered the necessary data, I can input the information into the model, and in less than five minutes, know with a reasonable degree of accuracy on the basis of my investment criteria whether or not a deal makes sense. All I have to do is key in the information and the model makes all of the calculations.

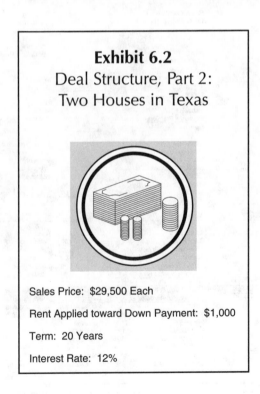

Exhibit 6.2
Deal Structure, Part 2:
Two Houses in Texas

Sales Price: $29,500 Each

Rent Applied toward Down Payment: $1,000

Term: 20 Years

Interest Rate: 12%

Exhibit 6.3
Property Analysis Worksheet: The Value Play Rehab Analyzer

Purchase Assumptions

Project Name:	Two Houses In Texas
Address:	123 South State St.
City, State, Zip:	Baytown, TX 77520
Contact:	Mr. Retired Gentleman
Telephone:	(800) 555-1234

Land	2,500
Building/House	17,500
Closing Costs	500
Other Related Costs	0
Total Purchase Price	20,500

Financing Assumptions - Primary

Primary Mortgage or Loan:

Total Purchase	100.00%	20,500
Down Payment	7.32%	1,500
Balance to Finc	92.68%	19,000

	Annual	Monthly
Interest Rate	10.000%	0.833%
Amort Period	15	180
Payment	2,450	204
Interest Only	1,900	158

Financing Assumptions - Secondary

Secondary Financing/Line of Credit:

Total Imprvmnts	100.00%	1,085
Down Payment	100.00%	1,085
Balance to Finc	0.00%	0

	Annual	Monthly
Interest Rate	8.000%	0.667%
Amort Period	15	180
Payment	0	0
Interest Only	0	0

Estimate for Improvements

Appliances		Flooring		Lighting	0
Dishwasher	0	Carpet	0	Masonry	0
Disposal	0	Ceramic Tile	0	Other	0
Microwave	0	Hardwood	0	Other	0
Range	0	Vinyl	0	Other	0
Refrigerator	0	Subtotal	0	Painting: Exterior	450
Subtotal	0			Painting: Interior	0
		Foundation	0	Permits	0
Architectural Drawings	0	Framing	0	Subtotal	450
Cabinets	0	Garage	0		
Caulking	25	Gas & Electric Hookup	0	Plumbing	
Subtotal	25	Glass: Mirrors, showers	0	Commodes	0
		Gutters	0	Drain Lines	0
Cement Work		Subtotal	0	Faucets	0
Basement Floor	0			Fixtures	0
Driveway	0	HVAC		Hot Water Heater	0
Garage Floor	0	Air Conditioner	0	Showers	0
Porches	0	Duct Work	0	Tubs	0
Sidewalks	0	Filters	10	Water Lines	0
Subtotal	0	Furnace	0	Subtotal	0
		Subtotal	10		
Cleaning	225			Roofing	0
Counter Tops	0	Insulation	0	Siding	0
Decorating	0	Insurance Premiums	250	Site Planning & Engineering	0
Doors	0	Subtotal	250	Steel	0
Drywall	75			Trim	0
Electrical	0	Landscaping		Utility: Gas & Electric	0
Engineering	0	Irrigation System	0	Utility: Water & Sewer	0
Equipment Rental	0	Lot Clearing	0	Warranty	0
Excavation Work	0	Mowing Services	35	Windows	0
Fences	0	Sod	0	Subtotal	0
Fireplace	0	Trees, Plants, & Shrubs	15		
Subtotal	300	Subtotal	50	Total Cost of Improvements	1,085

Comp #1

Address:	
Sales Price	0.00
Adjustments to Price	0.00
Adjusted Price	0.00
Square Feet	1.00
Price Per Square Foot	0.00

Comp #2

Address:	
Sales Price	0.00
Adjustments to Price	0.00
Adjusted Price	0.00
Square Footage	1.00
Price Per Square Foot	0.00

Comp #3

Address:	
Sales Price	0.00
Adjustments to Price	0.00
Adjusted Price	0.00
Square Feet	1.00
Price Per Square Foot	0.00

Comp Averages

Sales Price	0.00
Adjustments to Price	0.00
Adjusted Price	0.00
Square Feet	1.00
Price Per Square Foot	0.00
Turn Comps Off/On	OFF
Est Price/Sq Ft If Turned OFF	39.33

WWW.THEVALUEPLAY.COM - COPYRIGHT PROTECTED 1998

Subject Property 123 South State St.

Square Feet	750.00
Price/Sq Ft	27.33
Improvements/Sq Ft	1.45
Total Price/Sq Ft	28.78
Estimated Time To Complete Project	0.00

Description	Best Case	Most Likely	Worst Case 4.25
Est Sales Price	32,688	29,500	26,313
Purchase Price	20,500	20,500	20,500
Improvements	1,085	1,085	1,085
Interest Charges	0	0	0
Taxes	0	0	0
Closing Costs	350	350	350
Total Costs	21,935	21,935	21,935
Profit Margin	10,753	7,565	4,378
Return On Inv	415.96%	292.65%	169.34%

Under the Purchase Assumptions section, the basic property information is listed, including a project name, address, and pricing information. The value of the land does not really matter as long as the price of the land plus the price of the house is equal to the total purchase price. There are two sections for Financing Assumptions—one for primary financing and another for secondary financing. The primary financing section is used for the main source of lending, which can be in the form of a loan from a mortgage company, bank, or private individual, as this example illustrates. The secondary financing section is used for any additional loans you may secure. For lower cost improvements such as the one in this example, you may use all cash. On the other hand, if the cost of the improvements is greater than the amount of capital you want to use, then this is the section to use. Rates and terms are typically different for a line of credit, such as a home equity line or a credit card, than they are for a regular mortgage, so having two sections for financing allows you to more accurately determine your carrying costs.

Under the Estimate for Improvements section, there is quite a bit of detail that allows you to estimate the costs for virtually everything in a house. Estimating these costs accurately is, of course, vitally important for the proper analysis of an investment rehab opportunity. The more experience you have, the easier estimating costs will become. At first, you may need to procure bids or estimates from contractors to help you determine how much the required improvements will cost. As you gain experience, however, you'll be able to estimate many of the costs on your own. The Total Cost of Improvements was minimal in this example and came to only $1,085.

The next section of the model allows you to enter information for comparable home sales. This information is needed to help you make accurate projections of the estimated resale value of your investment property. Any sales agent can provide you with comparable sales data for your area. There is also a provision in this section to allow you to make adjustments to the sales price of the comps. This provision permits you to make a direct comparison. For example, if the home you are buying has a two-car garage and the comparable home sale has a three-car garage, you will need to revise the price downward in the Adjustments to Comps section. This is exactly how real estate agents and appraisers compute the market value of a house. They start with an average price per square foot of several similar houses and make compensating adjustments to estimate value.

The Comp Averages section simply takes an average of the three comps sales prices to come up with an average sales price. This number is then divided by the average price per square foot. The result is a weighted average price per square foot. This section also has a provision that allows you to turn the comps section off or keep it on. As you become familiar with a specific market or neighborhood, you are likely to already know what the average sales price per square foot is, so you may not always need to key in sales comp data. Instead, you can turn the comps section off and plug in your own estimate. In this example, I had only one comparable sale and that was the house I lived in. I paid $40,000 for a 1,000-square-foot house located in the same neighborhood just a few blocks away. I reasoned that since I paid $40 per square foot for my house and had just had a recent appraisal on it, then I should be able to get close to $40 per square foot for the houses I was selling. I liked the number, $29,500, because it was less than $30,000 and sounded more affordable. So in the example in Exhibit 6.3, the comparable sales section is turned off.

The average sales price per square foot is then fed into the Subject Property section. All of the information keyed into the rest of the model is summarized in this section. You must know the square footage of the house you are buying so that you can make an accurate comparison. The purchase price per square foot is automatically calculated, as is the total cost of the improvements per square foot. The two numbers are then added together to give you the total cost of the project. In this example, the Total Cost of Improvements of $1,085 was added to the Total Purchase Price of $20,500. The resulting sum was then divided by 750 square feet to give me a Total Price per Square Foot of $28.78. Below that is a provision that allows you to estimate the total time for completion and resale in months. In other words, it calculates the carrying costs for interest, a factor that many less experienced investors do not consider. In the example here, the number of months is set to zero since the house was occupied as a rental.

The Adjustment to Comps section is used to create the Estimated Sales Price for three different sales scenarios—Best Case, Most Likely, and Worst Case. In this example, $4.25 per square foot is used. For the Best Case Sales Price, the model adds $4.25 to the Price per Square Foot cell in the Comp Averages section, and then multiplies the sum of the two by the square feet of the subject property. Exhibit 6.4 shows how it works.

Exhibit 6.4
Best Case Sale Price

(Avg. Price/Sq Ft + Adj to Comps) x Subject Property Sq Ft

= Best Case Sales Price

($39.333 + $4.250) x 750 = $32,688

Exhibit 6.5
Most Likely Sales Price

Avg. Price/Sq Ft x Subject Property Sq Ft

= Most Likely Sales Price

$39.333 x 750 = $29,500

The Most Likely Sales Price calculation in the model neither adds nor subtracts the value of $4.25 to the Price per Square Foot cell in the Comp Averages section. It is simply the product of the Average Price per Square Foot and the Square Feet. Take a moment to examine Exhibit 6.5.

For the Worst Case Sales Price, the model subtracts $4.25 from the Price per Square Foot cell in the Comp Averages section, and then multiplies the difference of the two by the square feet of the subject property. Take a minute to review Exhibit 6.6.

The purpose of creating three different scenarios in the model is to provide us with a range for the estimated sales price. This allows you to evaluate the very minimum you might expect on the low end of the price range, and the very most you might expect on the high end of the price range. Take a moment to refer back to Exhibit 6.3. The Purchase Price, Improvements, Interest Charges, Taxes, and Closing Costs remain constant across all three scenarios since these values are not affected by the Adjustment to Comps variable of $4.25. The Profit Margin is the dollar amount that you can expect from your investment after all costs have been accounted for. The Return on Investment is calculated as the

---

Exhibit 6.6
Worst Case Sales Price

(Avg. Price/Sq Ft – Adj to Comps) x Subject Property Sq Ft

= Worst Case Sales Price

($39.333 – $4.250) x 750 = $26,313

Exhibit 6.7

Return on Investment

$$\frac{\text{Profit Margin}}{\text{Primary Down Payment} + \text{Secondary Down Payment}} = \text{R.O.I.}$$

$$\$7,565/(\$1,500 + \$1,085) = 292.65\%$$

ratio of the Profit Margin divided by the total cash you have invested in the property. It is calculated in Exhibit 6.7 for the Most Likely scenario as follows:

My very first investment in the two houses in Texas proved to be a classic example of just how effective the value play strategy can work. I was able to find two houses priced below market that needed minimal repairs from a seller who was willing to carry the note and who also only required $1,000 down on each house. With a little bit of sweat equity on my part, I was able to substantially improve the two houses, rent them out, and later sell them for a respectable profit of $7,565 each. As calculated in Exhibit 6.7, this represented a return of 292.65% on my invested capital. Not bad for a rookie.

Since I had not yet developed the Value Play Rehab Analyzer, the output depicted in Exhibit 6.3 was not available to me at that time. Although I had done my homework with respect to market prices and believed that I was purchasing the two houses at a good price, I did not have the foresight to look ahead and determine exactly how much profit could be unlocked from this investment. Selling the houses for a profit early in the game really came as an afterthought. I'm sure you'll agree that there is great value in having a dynamic model such as the one illustrated here. By keying in the basic assumptions, you can very easily change a few variables, which allows you to quickly identify any upside potential. Additional information regarding the availability of the model used in this example and the ones following are provided for your benefit in Appendix C.

MULTIPLY YOUR EFFORTS BY 22

Now let's look at another example. Those of you who have read *The Complete Guide to Buying and Selling Apartment Buildings* may recognize this as one of the examples I used in that book. The example is one of a multifamily property I acquired that falls into both the income-producing property category as well as the rehab, or flipping, category. For those readers who have been involved in a condominium conversion, you will understand why. With a condo conversion, you are taking an income property such as an apartment building and converting it to non-income producing units that are to be sold on an individual basis. You are removing the income aspect from the property and converting it to a different use; therefore, the valuation method changes from the income capitalization approach to the market comparables approach. The reason I am using the example here is to illustrate how the value play concept can be applied on a larger scale.

Several years ago, I came across a 22-unit multifamily property that at first glance appeared to be very reasonably priced. The seller was asking $350,000. The 22 units consisted of eleven duplex buildings that were neatly lined up side by side. Also included in the sale was an empty lot, which was located adjacent to the units. The apartments enjoyed an occupancy of more than 95 percent, with very little turnover. A drive by the property revealed that the buildings had not seen any new paint since their construction approximately 17 years earlier. The lawn was not kept up and was in dire need of attention. Shrubs and hedges lined each building, but had not been trimmed for years. There were trees planted in between each driveway that offered nice shade for the tenants, but they, too, were overgrown. Each unit had its own private cedar fenced yard, but like the worn paint, the fences also appeared to be in poor condition. So far, this was shaping up to be the kind of deal I liked. Paint, landscaping, and fencing are all fairly inexpensive improvements and could be made quickly.

While the $350,000 asking price sounded very reasonable, I needed something to compare it to so as to give me an idea of the potential value that could be created once they were cleaned up. As I drove around the neighborhood, I came across an entire street just a few blocks away lined with duplexes very similar to the ones I was looking at. One of them had a For Sale sign out front, so I jotted down the number and returned to my office to inquire about the property. I visited with the seller at length and, as it turned out, he represented the owner who had at one time owned all 36 duplex buildings on the street, which was a total of 72 units. The owner had initially maintained them as rentals, but over the last three years, began selling them off to individuals who lived in them, or to other investors who rented them out. Out of his original inventory of 72 units, he had sold 68 and now had only four left. His asking price was $39,000 per unit or $77,000 for two units. This information was critical in that it told me two important things. First, the owner had sold 68 units over a three-year period. This meant there was a market for these properties. Second, the price of $77,000 per building had been established and could be used as valuable comps for appraisal purposes. Since both properties had two bedrooms and two baths and were comparable in size, I knew immediately what the potential upside was. The 22 units I was looking at suddenly began to look very attractive, as the seller was asking only $31,818 per building.

The seller of the 22-unit building I was interested in was a partner in a surveying and engineering company that kept him quite busy. He was not in the apartment business, nor did he care to be. He ended up taking over the duplexes quite by chance. The seller had helped design the project years earlier for an out-of-state investor who eventually came back to him for help in managing the property. As it turned out, the seller ended up taking over the units altogether.

The seller employed an elderly couple full-time who occupied one of the units rent-free in exchange for collecting the rents in addition to performing some light maintenance. The seller also paid the couple a salary. His objective was to completely minimize his involvement in dealing with tenants, upkeep, and pretty much anything to do with the property. In short, the seller was a bona fide *don't wanter*. Fortunately for me, he was not aware of the underlying value that could be unlocked from his property, and even if he were, I don't think he would have been inclined to undergo the process required to create that value. I sincerely believe that all he was interested in was getting rid of what was a source of stress for him.

After brief negotiations with the seller through my real estate broker, I put the duplexes under contract for an agreed-upon price of $333,000. This included all 22 units as well as the vacant tract of land adjacent to them. One unique attribute of this transaction was that all 11 duplex buildings were separately platted and surveyed. This meant that as long as the right type of financing was in place going into the deal, the buildings could all be sold separately or parceled out in any number of ways. For example, an individual could purchase one unit (half or one side of a duplex), two units (all of a duplex), or any combination of units he wanted. Proper financing on this type of purchase was a key factor. Most lenders financing multifamily apartments will place a single loan on the entire property and use all of it as collateral. Then when it comes time to sell, it is either all or none. In other words, you cannot sell off individual units or buildings because the entire purchase is being used to secure the loan or mortgage. After numerous phone calls, I finally found a local bank that was willing to work with me and structure the purchase in a manner that would facilitate my objectives. The loan was set up so that each time I sold a unit, building, or group of buildings, a portion of the loan was paid off and the respective collateral was released to the new lender. As previously mentioned, this transaction was very similar to a condominium conversion, with similar financing being required. See Exhibit 6.8 to see how the sale was structured.

As soon as I had the duplexes under contract, I performed the usual due diligence. This included an examination of the seller's record of income collected, and expenses such

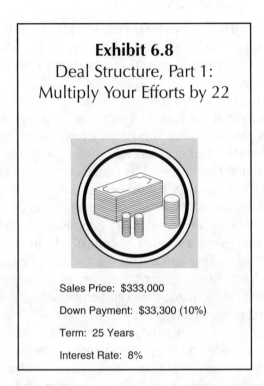

Exhibit 6.8
Deal Structure, Part 1:
Multiply Your Efforts by 22

Sales Price: $333,000

Down Payment: $33,300 (10%)

Term: 25 Years

Interest Rate: 8%

as taxes, utilities, and repairs. The next step was a thorough physical inspection of each unit inside and out. After carefully examining the property, I was able to assess more precisely the amount of repairs needed to bring the duplexes up to a level I thought was appropriate. The drive-by of the property I did before entering into the contract proved to be representative of the interiors as well. Just like the exterior, the needed interior repairs were largely cosmetic. There was the usual wear and tear—carpets, leaky faucets, and paint, but nothing of major importance.

After I was satisfied with the due diligence, the next step was to order the required third party reports. This particular lender required a survey, an appraisal, an inspection, and a Phase I environmental report. All reports came in satisfactory. An added bonus was the appraised value, which was determined to be $520,000 with the property in its "as is" or existing condition. I was, of course, pleased with the report because it served to validate my beliefs about the upside potential that existed in this deal.

After all reports were sent to the lender, a final review of the loan package was completed and subsequently approved. The seller and I closed a few days later. It was truly a win/win/win situation for all the parties involved. The seller was relieved of his headache, I had just purchased a superb value play opportunity, and the banker had made a sound loan. Now the real fun was about to begin. It was time to get to work and unlock the hidden value in this little gem!

I have already described at length the entry strategy implemented to acquire the 22 units. Now let's take a look at the post-entry process. During the period I had the duplexes under contract, I procured several estimates from contractors on all of the work I wanted performed. Before the deal ever closed, I had most of the contractors lined up to begin working the week after the closing. The tenants were notified that the property was under new management and that they would begin seeing some much needed improvements. The flurry of activity actually created some excitement among them and they were genuinely enthusiastic that someone was finally taking an interest in their community.

The property was a real eyesore when I bought it. My intent was to clean it up and make it as aesthetically appealing as I could for the least amount of money possible. As an investor, my goal was to maximize the utility of each and every dollar spent on the project. Over the next 60–90 days, the contractors stayed busy getting the property cleaned up. The very first people I had go in was a professional landscaping crew. You'd be amazed at what a difference simply mowing down the weeds can make. They didn't stop there, though. They trimmed all the hedges, edged along the sidewalks, and cleaned up the grounds. I also had the landscaping crew bring in several truckloads of fresh mulch to place all around the bushes and hedges. By signing an annual contract with them, they assumed responsibility for all mowing, hedging, and edging on a weekly basis and at a very reasonable rate. There were large, beautiful trees planted in between each of the driveways, but they were so overgrown, they too had become an eyesore. A tree trimming service promptly alleviated that problem. Within a single day, they had all of the trees trimmed and most of the branches hauled away.

While the landscapers and tree trimmers were busy with their work, I had also engaged the services of a painting crew. The painters did an excellent job of painting the exteriors of all eleven buildings. They used a combination of four different color schemes so as to give each building its own unique look while still maintaining a standard of uniformity throughout the community. The painters had the most work to do and consequently, their job took the longest. As previously mentioned, all eleven buildings were side by side. Each one had a fence running down the middle to separate them. This gave each tenant a small private yard with a gate that could be locked for privacy. Most of the fences were run-down and the gates going in to the yards were barely functional. I had another crew replace all of the worn-out fencing with brand new cedar fencing. Each unit also got a new entry gate for the backyards. Meanwhile, I hired a sign maker to build signs for the two entryways into the community. There were no signs up at all when I acquired the duplexes, so there was no way for prospective tenants or buyers to call for information. The sign maker built two professional signs out of two-inch thick redwood and installed one at each entryway where the name of the community and the telephone number were prominently displayed.

Since the community was family oriented, I thought a nice amenity to offer the tenants would be a playground where they could bring their children. As it was, there was not any playground equipment close by. I had determined the vacant lot included in the purchase, which was immediately adjacent to the buildings, would be the perfect place for such a playground. I started off by having a concrete crew come in and pour a large 20-foot by 30-foot slab of concrete complete with goal posts. This gave the tenants a new basketball court. I also had a company that made professional playground equipment install a swing set, monkey bars, and two ride-on animals that were mounted on springs and anchored in concrete. For the parents, new vinyl coated park benches were installed. By the time all of the work had been completed, the 22 units looked like new and the tenants lived in a complex that they could truly take pride in.

I knew before I ever bought the duplexes that my exit strategy would be to either sell or refinance the property within twelve months from the time of purchase. The market research I did before I had even purchased the duplexes proved to be right on target. Since I had just spent a considerable amount of time and money improving the overall condition of the property, I now had a very attractive community to offer to prospective families.

To unlock the newly created value in the duplexes, I considered several approaches. The first was to sell the units either individually or as a package deal to an investor. My original intent was to sell the units individually for $77,000 per building or $38,500 per unit just as the other seller with the 72 units that were similar to mine had done. With this in mind, I decided to set up one unit as an office that would also double as a model. The initial response from my existing tenants as well as others was quite favorable. Within the first ninety days, I had commitments for seventeen of the units. What I was not prepared for was the poor credit quality that most of them had. I was working through a mortgage company that could provide financing for A, B, or C quality paper, but the majority of those who expressed an interest couldn't even come up with the necessary down payment, which was minimal. I could have put together some creative seller carryback financing of my own, but I was not really interested in doing so at the time. Out of those original seventeen who were interested, only one made it all the way to closing.

Exhibit 6.9
Deal Structure, Part 2:
Multiply Your Efforts by 22

Sales Price of All 22 Units: $736,318

Down Payment: $22,000 (3%)

Term: Varied

Interest Rate: Varied

Shortly afterward, I decided to advertise the units in the classifieds section of the newspaper. I offered them as a package deal to investors. The ad generated quite a bit of interest. I had the remaining 21 units under contract with one investor who assured me he could close the deal in 30 days. As it turned out, he couldn't and the deal fell out of contract. I then received a call from two investors who were partners. They told me they were interested in all remaining 21 units and wanted to meet me at the property. I agreed to meet with them, but didn't have to take them too seriously because I had already had a number of prospective buyers come by and "kick the tires." I initially met with one of the two partners and later met with the second one. As it turned out, the two investors were eager to put a deal together.

I knew that each building would easily appraise for a minimum of $77,000 since I had an entire neighborhood of comps right down the street. Inasmuch as the investors agreed to buy all remaining 21 units in a package deal, I agreed to what was an attractive discount for them, but also left plenty of profit for me. Here's how the deal played out. I agreed to sell each building at a net discounted price of $66,364. Since the buyers were receiving a discount of a little over $10,000 per building, they agreed to pay all closing costs. Over the next six to eight months, the buyers followed through and purchased all remaining 21 units from me. It took that long because they used several lenders for their financing. They could have gotten a commercial loan to cover all 21 units, but they would have had to put down 15 to 20 percent. Instead, they placed several single family housing loans on the property, which provided 90 percent financing instead of the 80 percent a commercial lender would have offered them. Furthermore, since the properties appraised for well over the contract price, the buyers did not have to come up with the full 10 percent down payment. This is because the 90 percent financing was based on the appraised value and not the net sales price. The buyers had to use several lenders because the lenders' underwriting guidelines did not permit them to lend on more than a maximum of four units to any one individual. Although their decision to use this type of financing prolonged the sale, they did follow through and within a year of purchasing the property myself, I had all 22 units sold. Take a look at Exhibit 6.9 to see how the deal was structured.

On the one hand, my willingness to take less than the appraised value meant that I would leave a lot of money on the table. On the other hand, however, it allowed me to offer a very attractive deal to two willing buyers who could purchase the property with very little money down and have built-in equity on the day of closing. Take a moment to study Exhibit 6.10.

After reviewing Exhibit 6.10, you can see that this is another powerful example of the potential of the value play strategy. This strategy can obviously be quite effective. In this case, my out-of-pocket capital would have been about $100,000; however, since the bank financed 75 percent of the cost of improvements, I only ended up using about $50,000 of my own money. The total increase in value to the property was almost 80 percent (($736,318 – $410,000)/$410,000). By using some very basic techniques that are fundamental to the value play strategy, I was able to effectively increase the value of the property by over twice the original sales price that I had paid. Although I may have left money on the table for the two investors, there was still plenty left in it for me. In about a year's time, I netted over $326,000 from the deal. While it is true that I could have held out for another buyer who may have been willing to pay full price, I place a lot of faith in the old adage that a bird in the hand is worth two in the bush.

FROM RESIDENTIAL TO COMMERCIAL

In this last example, we'll take a look at a conversion process that is exactly the opposite of the previous example. In the case of the 22 duplex units, the property was converted

Exhibit 6.10
Property Analysis Worksheet: The Value Play Rehab Analyzer

Purchase Assumptions		
Project Name:	Multiply Your Efforts By 22	
Address:	123 South State St.	
City, State, Zip:	Houston, TX 77520	
Contact:	Mr. I Don't Want Her	
Telephone:	(800) 555-9876	
Land		50,000
Building/House		283,000
Closing Costs		10,000
Other Related Costs		7,000
Total Purchase Price		350,000

Financing Assumptions - Primary			
Primary Mortgage or Loan:			
Total Purchase	100.00%		350,000
Down Payment	10.00%		35,000
Balance to Finance	90.00%		315,000
		Annual	Monthly
Interest Rate		8.000%	0.667%
Amort Period		25	300
Payment		29,175	2,431
Interest Only		25,200	2,100

Financing Assumptions - Secondary			
Secondary Financing/Line of Credit:			
Total Improvments	100.00%		60,000
Down Payment	25.00%		15,000
Balance to Finance	75.00%		45,000
		Annual	Monthly
Interest Rate		8.000%	0.667%
Amort Period		25	300
Payment		4,168	347
Interest Only		3,600	300

Estimate for Improvements

Appliances		Flooring		Lighting		0
Dishwasher	1,000	Carpet	4,200	Masonry		0
Disposal	250	Ceramic Tile	0	Other — Playground Equipment		15,000
Microwave	0	Hardwood	0	Other — Signage		5,000
Range	500	Vinyl	1,450	Other		0
Refrigerator	0	Subtotal	5,650	Painting: Exterior		12,000
Subtotal	1,750			Painting: Interior		0
		Foundation	0	Permits		0
Architectural Drawings	0	Framing	0	Subtotal		32,000
Cabinets	0	Garage	0			
Caulking	0	Gas & Electric Hookup	0	Plumbing		
Subtotal	0	Glass: Mirrors, showers	0	Commodes		0
		Gutters	0	Drain Lines		0
Cement Work		Subtotal	0	Faucets		0
Basement Floor	0			Fixtures		0
Driveway	1,200	HVAC		Hot Water Heater		0
Garage Floor	0	Air Conditioner	1,800	Showers		0
Porches	0	Duct Work	0	Tubs		0
Sidewalks	0	Filters	50	Water Lines		0
Subtotal	1,200	Furnace	700	Subtotal		0
		Subtotal	2,550			
Cleaning	800			Roofing		0
Counter Tops	0	Insulation	0	Siding		0
Decorating	0	Insurance Premiums	0	Site Planning & Engineering		0
Doors	450	Subtotal	0	Steel		0
Drywall	0			Trim		0
Electrical	0	Landscaping		Utility: Gas & Electric		0
Engineering	0	Irrigation System	0	Utility: Water & Sewer		0
Equipment Rental	600	Lot Clearing	350	Warranty		0
Excavation Work	0	Mowing Services	400	Windows		0
Fences	7,000	Sod	0	Subtotal		0
Fireplace	0	Trees, Plants, & Shrubs	7,250			
Subtotal	8,850	Subtotal	8,000	Total Cost of Improvements		60,000

Comp #1		
Address:		
Sales Price	Per duplex bldg	77,000.00
Adjustments to Price		0.00
Adjusted Price		77,000.00
Square Feet		2,000.00
Price Per Square Foot		38.50

Comp #2		
Address:		
Sales Price	Per duplex bldg	77,500.00
Adjustments to Price		0.00
Adjusted Price		77,500.00
Square Footage		2,000.00
Price Per Square Foot		38.75

Comp #3		
Address:		
Sales Price	Per duplex bldg	78,000.00
Adjustments to Price		0.00
Adjusted Price		78,000.00
Square Feet		2,000.00
Price Per Square Foot		39.00

Comp Averages	
Sales Price	77,500.00
Adjustments to Price	0.00
Adjusted Price	77,500.00
Square Feet	2,000.00
Price Per Square Foot	38.75
Turn Comps Off/On	OFF
Est Price/Sq Ft If Turned OFF	33.47

WWW.THEVALUEPLAY.COM - COPYRIGHT PROTECTED 1998

Subject Property 123 South State St.		Description	Adjustment to Comps		5.28
			Best Case	Most Likely	Worst Case
		Est Sales Price	852,500	736,318	620,136
Square Feet	22,000.00	Purchase Price	350,000	350,000	350,000
Price/Sq Ft	15.91	Improvements	60,000	60,000	60,000
Improvements/Sq Ft	2.73	Interest Charges	0	0	0
Total Price/Sq Ft	18.64	Taxes	0	0	0
		Closing Costs	0	0	0
		Total Costs	410,000	410,000	410,000
Estimated Time To		Profit Margin	442,500	326,318	210,136
Complete Project	0.00	Return On Inv	885.00%	652.64%	420.27%

from one of an income-producing property to that of a single family residential. Even though two investors ended up buying the majority of the units, it was still valued through the use of a market comparison approach instead of an income approach. In this example, we will study the conversion of a single family residence to one of a commercial income-producing property and examine the differences in the two valuation approaches.

The house in this example is one that I currently have under contract to purchase. It is located in the downtown area of a small but growing community with a population of about 42,000 residents. The street it is located on is actually a state highway that runs right through the heart of the city. It is considered to be a high traffic location with an average daily traffic count of about 22,000 vehicles. When the house was originally built back in 1903, it was probably inconceivable at the time that the street running in front of the house would eventually become a state highway. The house is a very charming two story with approximately 2,400 square feet of living space. There is also a large basement that can be used for storage. It has been fairly well maintained over the years, although some work is needed. The inside of the house is full of charm and character reminiscent of days of old. It has a beautiful hand-crafted wooden stairway leading to the upstairs, along with many other features characteristic of that era.

For literally the last one hundred years, the house has been occupied as a residence. The current owner has lived there since 1980, and even since then, there has been significant growth in the area. The owner had been trying to sell the house for close to a year with the assistance of a real estate agent with very little success. With new communities sprawling up all around, who wants to live on a busy state highway? Not many people, that's for sure. You can just about rule out any family with small children. Being that close to a busy road would be much too dangerous for little ones. Rule out the seniors, too. They prefer quiet communities with sidewalks and streetlights. Who does that leave? No one, really, except maybe a guy like me looking for cheap office space.

The house is actually in an ideal location for an office building. The high traffic location is particularly appealing in that it will enable our company, Symphony Homes, to greatly increase its brand identity and name recognition in that market. Approximately 22,000 motorists will pass by our brightly lit sign each and every day for 365 days a year, and as they do, they will become more and more familiar with our name. Eventually, many of them will come to us seeking the services we offer. With 2,400 square feet, the building is large enough to meet our current needs. In addition, it is a much cheaper alternative to leasing office or retail space in the same area, and certainly much cheaper than purchasing office or retail space.

As previously mentioned, this is why understanding the differences among the three market valuation approaches is so important. If you can grasp the underlying logic and understand the fundamental principles of each method, you can use them to your advantage to create value. In its current state of use as a single family house, the most appropriate valuation method is to use the comparable sales approach. This is the method that will be used when the appraiser comes out to appraise the property. He will examine other like properties and make adjustments as necessary, and from this, will compute a value that is most appropriate for this property in its current state of use. When the house is converted to an income-producing office building, its usage will change from one of residential to one of commercial. At that time, the value of the building will no longer be based upon comparable sales of similar houses. Instead, it will be based on the income generated from the rents, in which case the income capitalization approach will be the most appropriate method of valuing the property.

My objective going into this transaction is, as always, to apply the OPM principle, that is, to use as much of other people's money as possible and as little of my own money as possible. Since the house is literally a century old, it is in need of some

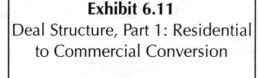

Exhibit 6.11
Deal Structure, Part 1: Residential to Commercial Conversion

Sales Price: $188,000

Down Payment: $18,800 (10%)

Term: 30 Years

Interest Rate: 6.5%

Cash Back at Closing: $40,000

repair work. There will also be additional costs involved to convert the property from residential use to commercial use. The owner and I agreed on a sales price of $188,000 with a repair and improvement allowance of $40,000, making the effective sales price $148,000. Since I will borrow 90 percent of the sales price, my down payment will be only 10 percent, or $18,000. At closing, I will receive an allowance for the necessary repairs and improvements in the amount of $40,000. Take a look at Exhibit 6.11 to see how the deal was structured.

Structuring the transaction in this manner will allow me to limit the amount of out-of-pocket cash to only 10 percent of the total deal value, including the improvements. This is a creative and effective way to pull cash out of a deal at closing, especially when you have an immediate use for the cash, such as for property improvements. To use this financing strategy, there are two caveats you should be aware of. The first is that the house has to appraise for a high enough value in its existing condition. In this example, the house must appraise for the sales price of $188,000 before any repairs or improvements are made. That means there must be existing comparable sales the appraiser can use to support that value. We are already aware of several comps that will support the sales price. The second caveat is that you must have a lender who is willing to work with you in allowing the credit at closing. While most lenders will allow the buyer to receive some type of credit, they generally limit it to anywhere from 3 to 5 percent of the sales price. I usually have the most success using a mortgage broker when trying to structure a deal like this rather than going directly to a lender. Many small, community banks, however, will work with you as long as they understand what you are trying to do. In addition, they may require the funds credited at closing to be placed in an escrow account and paid only after the work has been completed. Take a moment to examine Exhibit 6.12.

In the Purchase Assumptions box, I used $152,000 ($33,000 + $115,000 + $3,650 + $350) for the purchase price since that is the net effective sales price of the house. The loan terms for the purchase price are reflected in the Financing Assumptions—Primary box. The total of $40,000 for improvements has been entered into the Estimate for Improvements section and is captured in Financing Assumptions—Secondary. In this case, since the Primary and Secondary financing will be combined into one note, the same interest rate and term is used. To calculate the total payment, simply add the two numbers. The information in the Comp Averages section suggests a weighted average Price per Square Foot of $81.92. When multiplied by 2,400 square feet, the resulting value is $196,609, which is well above the required value of $188,000 necessary to make the deal work. After factoring in transactions costs, the Profit Margin in the Most Likely scenario reflects a small gain of $712. Now let's take a few minutes to study Exhibit 6.13. Although this model is similar to the Value Play Rehab Analyzer, it is really quite different.

Exhibit 6.12
Property Analysis Worksheet: The Value Play Rehab Analyzer

Purchase Assumptions

Project Name:	Residential to Commercial
Address:	123 South State St.
City, State, Zip:	Anywhere, TX 77520
Contact:	Mr. Please Buy My House
Telephone:	(800) 555-1234

Land	33,000
Building/House	115,000
Closing Costs	3,650
Other Related Costs	350
Total Purchase Price	152,000

Financing Assumptions - Primary

Primary Mortgage or Loan:

Total Purchase	100.00%	152,000
Down Payment	10.00%	15,200
Balance to Finance	90.00%	136,800

	Annual	Monthly
Interest Rate	6.500%	0.542%
Amort Period	30	360
Payment	10,376	865
Interest Only	8,892	741

Financing Assumptions - Secondary

Secondary Financing/Line of Credit:

Total Imprvmnts	100.00%	40,000
Down Payment	10.00%	4,000
Balance to Finc	90.00%	36,000

	Annual	Monthly
Interest Rate	6.500%	0.542%
Amort Period	30	360
Payment	2,731	228
Interest Only	2,340	195

Estimate for Improvements

Appliances		Flooring		Lighting	750
Dishwasher	0	Carpet	2,000	Masonry	0
Disposal	0	Ceramic Tile	0	Parking Lot & Drive	8,400
Microwave	0	Hardwood	0	Other	0
Range	0	Vinyl	1,500	Other	0
Refrigerator	0	Subtotal	3,500	Painting: Exterior	1,200
Subtotal	0			Painting: Interior	2,100
		Foundation	0	Permits	250
Architectural Drawings	0	Framing	0	Subtotal	12,700
Cabinets	0	Garage	500		
Caulking	450	Gas & Electric Hookup	0	Plumbing	
Subtotal	450	Glass: Mirrors, showers	0	Commodes	0
		Gutters	0	Drain Lines	0
Cement Work		Subtotal	500	Faucets	250
Basement Floor	0			Fixtures	250
Driveway	0	HVAC		Hot Water Heater	0
Garage Floor	0	Air Conditioner	1,800	Showers	0
Porches	0	Duct Work	0	Tubs	0
Sidewalks	1,200	Filters	25	Water Lines	0
Subtotal	1,200	Furnace	225	Subtotal	500
		Subtotal	2,050		
Cleaning	1,000			Roofing	7,800
Counter Tops	0	Insulation	0	Siding	0
Decorating	1,500	Insurance Premiums	525	Site Planning & Engineering	2,200
Doors	500	Subtotal	525	Steel	0
Drywall	250			Trim	0
Electrical	500	Landscaping		Utility: Gas & Electric	250
Engineering	0	Irrigation System	0	Utility: Water & Sewer	125
Equipment Rental	0	Lot Clearing	0	Warranty	0
Excavation Work	0	Mowing Services	50	Windows	500
Fences	2,500	Sod	0	Subtotal	10,875
Fireplace	0	Trees, Plants, & Shrubs	1,400		
Subtotal	6,250	Subtotal	1,450	Total Cost of Improvements	40,000

Comp #1

Address:	
Sales Price	179,900.00
Adjustments to Price	1,200.00
Adjusted Price	181,100.00
Square Feet	2,200.00
Price Per Square Foot	82.32

Comp #2

Address:	
Sales Price	186,500.00
Adjustments to Price	1,800.00
Adjusted Price	188,300.00
Square Footage	2,320.00
Price Per Square Foot	81.16

Comp #3

Address:	
Sales Price	189,450.00
Adjustments to Price	(2,200.00)
Adjusted Price	187,250.00
Square Feet	2,275.00
Price Per Square Foot	82.31

Comp Averages

Sales Price	185,283.33
Adjustments to Price	266.67
Adjusted Price	185,550.00
Square Feet	2,265.00
Price Per Square Foot	81.92
Turn Comps Off/On	ON
Est Price/Sq Ft If Turned OFF	80.00

Subject Property — 123 South State St.

Square Feet	2,400.00	
Price/Sq Ft	63.33	
Imprvmnts/Sq Ft	16.67	
Total Price/Sq Ft	80.00	
Estimated Time To		
Complete Project	2.00	

Adjustment to Comps   5.00

Description	Best Case	Most Likely	Worst Case
Est Sales Price	208,609	196,609	184,609
Purchase Price	152,000	152,000	152,000
Improvements	40,000	40,000	40,000
Interest Charges	1,872	1,872	1,872
Taxes	450	450	450
Closing Costs	1,575	1,575	1,575
Total Costs	195,897	195,897	195,897
Profit Margin	12,712	712	(11,288)
Return On Inv	66.21%	3.71%	-58.79%

This model is the Value Play Income Analyzer and is used to measure the value of an income-producing property, such as an apartment building or our soon-to-be-converted office building.

In Exhibit 6.13, notice that we have the same sales price of $148,000 plus $40,000 in improvements, plus $4,000 in closing costs and other costs for a total of $192,000, just as we did in Exhibit 6.12. Notice also that the information in the Financing Assumptions is exactly the same, except that it is consolidated into one section instead of two. The Key Ratios section in Exhibit 6.13 captures important data relative to income-producing property. The most important number to focus on for this example is the capitalization rate. The capitalization rate, or cap rate as it is referred to, is the ratio between Net Operating Income and Sales Price.

$$\frac{\text{Net Operating Income}}{\text{Sales Price}} = \text{Capitalization Rate}$$

Or

$$\frac{\text{Net Operating Income}}{\text{Cap Rate}} = \text{Sales Price}$$

As you can see, this ratio is really a very simple calculation used to measure the relationship between the income generated by the property and the price it is being sold for. This ratio measures the same relationship as that of the certificate of deposit we discussed in Chapter 5. The *price* we are willing to pay for the CD is a function of its *yield*, or rather, the *income* the instrument generates. This is precisely consistent with the relationship between the *price* of an income-producing property, the *yield* an investor expects to receive on her investment, and the property's ability to generate *income*.

The capitalization rate, or yield on an income-producing property, will vary within a given range, generally 8 to 12 percent, depending on a variety of market conditions, including supply and demand for real estate, the current interest rate environment, the type and condition of the property, its location, and tax implications imposed by local, state, and federal authorities. Under the Key Ratios section in Exhibit 6.13, notice the cap rate of 14.25 percent. This number represents the yield of the property as a whole, since it is based on the sales price, and not the equity. Remember that Return on Investment, or ROI, measures that relationship. A yield of 14.25 percent would be exceptional on a

Exhibit 6.13
Property Analysis Worksheet: The Value Play Income Analyzer

Cost and Revenue Assumptions		Financing Assumptions			Key Ratios	
Land	33,000	Total Purchase	100.00%	192,000	Total Square Feet	2,400.00
Building	115,000	Owner's Equity	10.00%	19,200	Avg Sq Ft/Unit	2,400.00
Improvements	40,000	Balance to Finance	90.00%	172,800	Avg Rent/Sq Ft	1.00
Closing Costs	4,000				Avg Cost/Sq Ft	80.00
Total	192,000				Avg Unit Cost	192,000.00
			Annual	Monthly	Capitalization Rate	14.25%
Number of Units	1	Interest Rate	6.500%	0.542%	Gross Rent Multiplier	6.67
Average Monthly Rent	2,400	Amort Period	30	360	Expense/Unit	0.00
Gross Monthly Revenues	2,400	Payment	13,107	1,092	Expense/Foot	0.00

Rental Increase Projections	0.00%	4.00%	4.00%	4.00%	4.00%
Average Monthly Rent	2,400	2,496	2,596	2,700	2,808
Operating Expense Projections	0.00%	0.00%	0.00%	0.00%	0.00%

		Actual			Projected		
Operating Revenues		Monthly	Year 1	Year 2	Year 3	Year 4	Year 5
Gross Scheduled Income		2,400	28,800	29,952	31,150	32,396	33,692
Vacancy Rate	5.0%	120	1,440	1,498	1,558	1,620	1,685
Net Rental Income		2,280	27,360	28,454	29,593	30,776	32,007
Other Income		0	0	0	0	0	0
Gross Income	100.0%	2,280	27,360	28,454	29,593	30,776	32,007
Operating Expenses							
Repairs and Maintenance	0.0%	0	0	0	0	0	0
Property Management Fees	0.0%	0	0	0	0	0	0
Taxes	0.0%	0	0	0	0	0	0
Insurance	0.0%	0	0	0	0	0	0
Salaries and Wages	0.0%	0	0	0	0	0	0
Utilities	0.0%	0	0	0	0	0	0
Trash Removal	0.0%	0	0	0	0	0	0
Professional Fees	0.0%	0	0	0	0	0	0
Advertising	0.0%	0	0	0	0	0	0
Other	0.0%	0	0	0	0	0	0
Total Op. Exp.	0.0%	0	0	0	0	0	0
Net Operating Income	100.0%	2,280	27,360	28,454	29,593	30,776	32,007
Interest on Loan	41.1%	936	11,175	11,046	10,908	10,761	10,603
Dep. Exp. - Building		348	4,182	4,182	4,182	4,182	4,182
Dep. Exp. - Equip.		0	0	0	0	0	0
Net Income Before Taxes		996	12,003	13,227	14,503	15,834	17,222
Income Tax Rate	0.0%	0	0	0	0	0	0
Net Income After Taxes		996	12,003	13,227	14,503	15,834	17,222
Cash Flow From Operations							
Net Income After Taxes		996	12,003	13,227	14,503	15,834	17,222
Dep. Exp.		348	4,182	4,182	4,182	4,182	4,182
Total CF From Ops.		1,344	16,185	17,409	18,685	20,016	21,404
Interest on Loan		936	11,175	11,046	10,908	10,761	10,603
Total Cash Available for Loan Servicing		2,280	27,360	28,454	29,593	30,776	32,007
Debt Service		1,092	13,107	13,107	13,107	13,107	13,107
Remaining After Tax CF From Ops		1,188	14,253	15,348	16,486	17,670	18,901
Plus Principal Reduction		161	1,931	2,061	2,199	2,346	2,503
Total Return		1,349	16,185	17,409	18,685	20,016	21,404
CF/Debt Servicing Ratio		208.75%	208.75%	217.10%	225.78%	234.82%	244.21%
Net Income ROI			62.52%	68.89%	75.54%	82.47%	89.70%
Cash ROI			74.24%	79.94%	85.86%	92.03%	98.44%
Total ROI			84.30%	90.67%	97.32%	104.25%	111.48%
Net CFs From Investment - 1 Yr Exit		(19,200)	135,385				
Net CFs From Investment - 3 Yr Exit		(19,200)	14,253	15,348	161,877		
Net CFs From Investment - 5 Yr Exit		(19,200)	14,253	15,348	16,486	17,670	199,141

	Exit Price	Gain on Sale	Cap Rate		IRR
Estimated Exit Price/Gain On Sale - 1 Yr	292,000	100,000	9.37%	Annualized IRR - 1 Yr	605.13%
Estimated Exit Price/Gain On Sale - 3 Yr	312,000	120,000	9.48%	Annualized IRR - 3 Yr	146.02%
Estimated Exit Price/Gain On Sale - 5 Yr	342,000	150,000	9.36%	Annualized IRR - 5 Yr	104.29%

WWW.THEVALUEPLAY.COM - COPYRIGHT PROTECTED 1998

certificate of deposit. It is also considered high in real estate. This indicates the property's sales price is low relative to its ability to generate income. Translated, it means we are buying the property at a bargain price and that there is plenty of upside in the deal.

The Average Monthly Rent is based on a rate of $1 per square foot per month, or $12 per square foot annually, multiplied by the square feet of the house, which gives us $2,400 of rental income per month. In the market the building is located in, that rate is a conservative number. A vacancy rate of 5 percent is applied for lender purposes. Since the lease will be a net lease, there are no expenses, because they will all be paid by the tenant. Now take a look at the bottom of Exhibit 6.13 at the three different Estimated Exit Prices. Based on the information we know to be true about market rates and capitalization rates, we can sell the property at the end of year 1 at an exit price of $292,000 at a very conservative Cap Rate of 9.37 percent, which will produce a very nice Gain On Sale of $100,000, excluding transaction costs. The internal rate of return, or IRR, is derived by measuring the rate of return over time given a series of cash flows (taken from Net CFs from Investment—1 Yr Exit). In this example, the IRR is an astounding 605 percent in year 1! For those of you who think this kind of return is wishful thinking, may I remind you that these numbers are actually quite conservative and are on the low end of the market, based on the rate of $12 per square foot. Now take a moment to study Exhibit 6.14, the Refinance Analyzer.

The Refinance Analyzer provides you with an alternative to selling your income-producing property. Given a certain set of assumptions, it calculates the maximum loan amount that an investor could borrow, based on the income the property produces. In Exhibit 6.14, the maximum loan amount, based on an 80 percent LTV ratio, is $228,540. It also tells us that we have to be able to get an appraisal in the amount of $285,675, which shouldn't be too difficult, based on the Cap Rate of 9.577 percent indicated in the Key Ratios section. Since the new loan would be a commercial loan, not a residential mortgage, I applied a higher interest rate of 7.5 percent and a shorter amortization period of 25 years. Okay, so you can refinance the property. Big deal, right? Let's see just what the *effect of our handiwork* is.

New Loan Amount:	$228,540
Pay Off Existing Loan:	$172,800
Cash Back to Investor:	$55,740

Exhibit 6.14
Refinance Analyzer

Maximum Refinance - Cash Out		
Max Refinance	80.00%	228,540
Owner's Equity @	20.00%	57,135
Required Appraisal	100.00%	285,675
	Annual	**Monthly**
Interest Rate	7.500%	0.625%
Amortization Period	25	300
Payment	20,267	1,689

Key Ratios	
Total Square Feet	2,400.000
Avg Sq Ft/Unit	2,400.000
Avg Rent/Sq Ft	1.000
Avg Cost/Sq Ft	119.031
Avg Unit Cost	285,674.738
Capitalization Rate	9.577%
Gross Rent Multiplier	9.919
Expense/Unit	0.000
Expense/Foot	0.000

Operating Revenues		Year 1
Gross Scheduled Income		28,800
Vacancy Rate		1,440
Net Rental Income		27,360
Other Income		0
Gross Revenues	100.0%	27,360

Operating Expenses		
Repairs and Maintenance	0.0%	0
Property Management Fees	0.0%	0
Taxes	0.0%	0
Insurance	0.0%	0
Salaries and Wages	0.0%	0
Utilities	0.0%	0
Trash Removal	0.0%	0
Professional Fees	0.0%	0
Advertising	0.0%	0
Other	0.0%	0
Total Op. Exp.	0.0%	0

Net Operating Income	100.0%	27,360
Dep. Exp. - Building		4,182
Dep. Exp. - Equip.		0
Net Income Before Taxes		23,178
Income Tax Rate	0.0%	0
Net Income After Taxes		23,178

Cash Flow From Operations		
Net Income After Taxes		23,178
Dep. Exp.		4,182
Total Cash Available for Loan Servicing		27,360
Debt Service		20,267
Remaining After Tax CF From Ops		7,093
Plus Principal Reduction		3,236
Total Return		10,329

CF/Debt Servicing Ratio	135.0%

Refinance Matrix	
Max Refinance	**CF/DS**
308,529	100.0%
302,479	102.0%
296,662	104.0%
291,065	106.0%
285,675	108.0%
280,481	110.0%
275,472	112.0%
270,639	114.0%
265,973	116.0%
261,465	118.0%
257,107	120.0%
252,892	122.0%
248,813	124.0%
244,864	126.0%
241,038	128.0%
237,330	130.0%
233,734	132.0%
230,245	134.0%
226,859	136.0%
223,572	138.0%
220,378	140.0%
217,274	142.0%
214,256	144.0%
211,321	146.0%
208,465	148.0%
205,686	150.0%
202,979	152.0%
200,343	154.0%
197,775	156.0%
195,271	158.0%
192,830	160.0%
190,450	162.0%
188,127	164.0%
185,861	166.0%
183,648	168.0%
181,487	170.0%
179,377	172.0%

Refinancing the property on the basis of the income approach has allowed us to justify a much higher value than the one based on the comparable sales approach. In this example, refinancing would put $55,740 cash back in your pocket I'm sure you would agree with me that you can find something to do with that much money!

Let's look at one more example. We'll make a quick change in the Income Analyzer by adjusting the rental income from $12 per square foot up to $16 per square foot, which is at the upper end of market rates, and see how that affects the property's value. All other assumptions remain the same. Take a minute to review Exhibit 6.15.

As you can see, by increasing the rents, we are significantly increasing the value of the property. This is similar to increasing the income generated by a certificate of deposit. Since the yield is held constant, it is the value of the certificate that must be increased. With the cap rate held constant in the Income Analyzer of about 9.5 percent, the Estimated Exit Price increases from $292,000 in Exhibit 6.13 to $385,000 in Exhibit 6.15. If the property was sold at the end of year 1, the estimated Gain on Sale is $193,000, which represents an increase of $93,000 more than the Estimated Gain on Sale in Exhibit 6.13. We now have two different versions, or scenarios, of this property—one at the lower end of the income per square foot range and one at the higher end of the income per square foot range. This provides us with a broad spectrum of values ranging $292,000 to $385,000. These values are a direct function of the income produced by the property, so the more rental income that can be justified by local market rates, the more valuable the property becomes. Now let's examine the effect of these changes in our Refinance Analyzer in Exhibit 6.16.

The same assumptions we used in the previous example in Exhibit 6.14 have been applied to the model in Exhibit 6.16. The maximum loan amount, based on an 80 percent LTV ratio, is $304,720. The output also tells us that we have to be able to get an appraisal in the amount of $380,900, based on holding the Cap Rate constant at 9.577 percent as indicated in the Key Ratios box. Here's how it looks.

New Loan Amount: $304,720

Pay Off Existing Loan: $172,800

Cash Back to Investor: $131,920

Exhibit 6.15
Property Analysis Worksheet: The Value Play Income Analyzer

Cost and Revenue Assumptions		Financing Assumptions			Key Ratios	
Land	33,000	Total Purchase	100.00%	192,000	Total Square Feet	2,400.00
Building	115,000	Owner's Equity	10.00%	19,200	Avg Sq Ft/Unit	2,400.00
Improvements	40,000	Balance to Finance	90.00%	172,800	Avg Rent/Sq Ft	1.33
Closing Costs	4,000				Avg Cost/Sq Ft	80.00
Total	192,000				Avg Unit Cost	192,000.00
			Annual	Monthly	Capitalization Rate	19.00%
Number of Units	1	Interest Rate	6.500%	0.542%	Gross Rent Multiplier	5.00
Average Monthly Rent	3,200	Amort Period	30	360	Expense/Unit	0.00
Gross Monthly Revenues	3,200	Payment	13,107	1,092	Expense/Foot	0.00

Rental Increase Projections			0.00%	4.00%	4.00%	4.00%	4.00%
Average Monthly Rent			3,200	3,328	3,461	3,600	3,744
Operating Expense Projections			0.00%	0.00%	0.00%	0.00%	0.00%

		Actual Monthly	Projected Year 1	Year 2	Year 3	Year 4	Year 5
Operating Revenues							
Gross Scheduled Income		3,200	38,400	39,936	41,533	43,195	44,923
Vacancy Rate	5.0%	160	1,920	1,997	2,077	2,160	2,246
Net Rental Income		3,040	36,480	37,939	39,457	41,035	42,676
Other Income		0	0	0	0	0	0
Gross Income	100.0%	3,040	36,480	37,939	39,457	41,035	42,676
Operating Expenses							
Repairs and Maintenance	0.0%	0	0	0	0	0	0
Property Management Fees	0.0%	0	0	0	0	0	0
Taxes	0.0%	0	0	0	0	0	0
Insurance	0.0%	0	0	0	0	0	0
Salaries and Wages	0.0%	0	0	0	0	0	0
Utilities	0.0%	0	0	0	0	0	0
Trash Removal	0.0%	0	0	0	0	0	0
Professional Fees	0.0%	0	0	0	0	0	0
Advertising	0.0%	0	0	0	0	0	0
Other	0.0%	0	0	0	0	0	0
Total Op. Exp.	0.0%	0	0	0	0	0	0
Net Operating Income	100.0%	3,040	36,480	37,939	39,457	41,035	42,676
Interest on Loan	30.8%	936	11,175	11,046	10,908	10,761	10,603
Dep. Exp. — Building		348	4,182	4,182	4,182	4,182	4,182
Dep. Exp. — Equip.		0	0	0	0	0	0
Net Income Before Taxes		1,756	21,123	22,712	24,367	26,093	27,891
Income Tax Rate	0.0%	0	0	0	0	0	0
Net Income After Taxes		1,756	21,123	22,712	24,367	26,093	27,891
Cash Flow From Operations							
Net Income After Taxes		1,756	21,123	22,712	24,367	26,093	27,891
Dep. Exp.		348	4,182	4,182	4,182	4,182	4,182
Total CF From Ops.		2,104	25,305	26,893	28,549	30,275	32,073
Interest on Loan		936	11,175	11,046	10,908	10,761	10,603
Total Cash Available for Loan Servicing		3,040	36,480	37,939	39,457	41,035	42,676
Debt Service		1,092	13,107	13,107	13,107	13,107	13,107
Remaining After Tax CF From Ops		1,948	23,373	24,833	26,350	27,928	29,570
Plus Principal Reduction		161	1,931	2,061	2,199	2,346	2,503
Total Return		2,109	25,305	26,893	28,549	30,275	32,073
CF/Debt Servicing Ratio		278.33%	278.33%	289.47%	301.05%	313.09%	325.61%
Net Income ROI			110.02%	118.29%	126.91%	135.90%	145.27%
Cash ROI			121.74%	129.34%	137.24%	145.46%	154.01%
Total ROI			131.80%	140.07%	148.69%	157.68%	167.05%
Net CFs From Investment — 1 Yr Exit		(19,200)	237,505				
Net CFs From Investment — 3 Yr Exit		(19,200)	23,373	24,833	274,741		
Net CFs From Investment — 5 Yr Exit		(19,200)	23,373	24,833	26,350	27,928	317,810

	Exit Price	Gain on Sale	Cap Rate		IRR
Estimated Exit Price/Gain On Sale — 1 Yr	385,000	193,000	9.48%	Annualized IRR - 1 Yr	1137.00%
Estimated Exit Price/Gain On Sale — 3 Yr	415,000	223,000	9.51%	Annualized IRR - 3 Yr	211.13%
Estimated Exit Price/Gain On Sale — 5 Yr	450,000	258,000	9.48%	Annualized IRR - 5 Yr	148.68%

Exhibit 6.16
Refinance Analyzer

Maximum Refinance — Cash Out		
Max Refinance	80.00%	304,720
Owner's Equity @	20.00%	76,180
Required Appraisal	100.00%	380,900
	Annual	Monthly
Interest Rate	7.500%	0.625%
Amortization Period	25	300
Payment	27,022	2,252

Key Ratios	
Total Square Feet	2,400.000
Avg Sq Ft/Unit	2,400.000
Avg Rent/Sq Ft	1.333
Avg Cost/Sq Ft	158.708
Avg Unit Cost	380,899.651
Capitalization Rate	9.577%
Gross Rent Multiplier	9.919
Expense/Unit	0.000
Expense/Foot	0.000

Operating Revenues		Year 1
Gross Scheduled Income		38,400
Vacancy Rate		1,920
Net Rental Income		36,480
Other Income		0
Gross Revenues	100.0%	36,480
Operating Expenses		
Repairs and Maintenance	0.0%	0
Property Management Fees	0.0%	0
Taxes	0.0%	0
Insurance	0.0%	0
Salaries and Wages	0.0%	0
Utilities	0.0%	0
Trash Removal	0.0%	0
Professional Fees	0.0%	0
Advertising	0.0%	0
Other	0.0%	0
Total Op. Exp.	0.0%	0
Net Operating Income	100.0%	36,480
Dep. Exp. — Building		4,182
Dep. Exp. — Equip.		0
Net Income Before Taxes		32,298
Income Tax Rate	0.0%	0
Net Income After Taxes		32,298
Cash Flow From Operations		
Net Income After Taxes		32,298
Dep. Exp.		4,182
Total Cash Available for Loan Servicing		36,480
Debt Service		27,022
Remaining After Tax CF From Ops		9,458
Plus Principal Reduction		4,315
Total Return		13,772
CF/Debt Servicing Ratio		135.0%

Refinance Matrix	
Max Refinance	CF/DS
411,372	100.0%
403,306	102.0%
395,550	104.0%
388,086	106.0%
380,900	108.0%
373,974	110.0%
367,296	112.0%
360,852	114.0%
354,631	116.0%
348,620	118.0%
342,810	120.0%
337,190	122.0%
331,751	124.0%
326,485	126.0%
321,384	128.0%
316,440	130.0%
311,645	132.0%
306,994	134.0%
302,479	136.0%
298,095	138.0%
293,837	140.0%
289,698	142.0%
285,675	144.0%
281,761	146.0%
277,954	148.0%
274,248	150.0%
270,639	152.0%
267,124	154.0%
263,700	156.0%
260,362	158.0%
257,107	160.0%
253,933	162.0%
250,836	164.0%
247,814	166.0%
244,864	168.0%
241,983	170.0%
239,170	172.0%

In this instance, we are able to obtain a new loan in the amount of $304,720, pay off the old loan of $172,800, and pocket the difference of $131,920. This is another powerful example of how effective the value play strategy can be. We have taken an existing property and created substantial value in it by changing its use from residential to commercial. The ROI on our original investment, if sold using the assumptions in Exhibit 6.14, is a phenomenal 1,005 percent.

$$\textbf{Return on Investment}$$

$$\frac{\text{Profit Margin}}{\text{Primary Down Payment} + \text{Secondary Down Payment}} = \text{ROI}$$

$$\frac{\$193,000}{\$19,200} = 1,005.21\%$$

By now you should have a good understanding of the different valuation approaches and their proper application. We analyzed in depth three real-life examples of how these approaches can be applied. We examined a residential property using the comparable sales approach, 22 duplex units that were sold on the basis of the comparable sales approach rather than the income approach, and finally, a residential property that was converted to an income property and valued using the income approach. A comprehensive understanding of these valuation methodologies is vitally important to your success in this business.

> **Firmness of purpose is one of the most necessary sinews of character, and one of the best instruments of success. Without it, genius wastes its efforts in a maze of inconsistencies.**
>
> *—Lord Chesterfield*

Chapter 7

Seven Steps of Successful Negotiations

In Chapter 5, we examined the three most commonly used approaches for appraising real estate and determined that the comparable sales method was the most appropriate approach to use for single family houses. In the previous chapter, we studied three examples of how those approaches can be applied to real world transactions. In this chapter, we shall examine seven techniques that will enable you to negotiate the best possible price and terms for the purchase of a property. As you will discover over time, many of the buyers and sellers you negotiate with are amateurs, meaning that they do not buy or sell real estate with any degree of frequency. They participate in the market out of necessity. Professional real estate investors, on the other hand, have mastered the seven steps of successful negotiations and use them to their advantage at every opportunity. (See Exhibit 7.1.)

THE PSYCHOLOGY OF NEGOTIATING

One of the most important things to remember when negotiating with others is that you are dealing with people, many of whom develop an emotional attachment somewhere in the process. Most of the buyers and sellers you deal with are not professionals and often find it difficult to separate their emotions from the rational aspects required to conduct business. After a certain point in the process, people become emotionally engaged, which causes them to act in a manner they otherwise wouldn't. This is especially true for sellers.

For example, an individual who has had his property listed for sale for several months begins to worry whether his house will ever sell. Then one day, a buyer comes along who

---

Exhibit 7.1
Seven Steps to Successful Negotiations

1. The Psychology of Negotiating

2. Comprehensive Knowledge of Market

3. Degree of Seller's Motivation

4. Back Door Exits

5. Concessions—When to Make Them and What to Expect In Return

6. The Red Herring Technique

7. The Money Talks Approach

---

expresses a sincere interest in the house. Mr. Seller begins to think there is hope after all. His real estate agents suggest that an offer might be forthcoming. Mr. Seller becomes eager with anticipation at the thought that he can sell his house and move on with his plans. He thinks about all the things he can do with the money he will make from the sale—the new car, paying off some old debts, and buying a nice gift for his wife. Just as Mr. Buyer is getting ready to make an offer, he discovers another house that he likes better and buys it instead. Feelings of despair immediately set in with Mr. Seller. There go all of his hopes and dreams, for it seems as if he will never sell his house now.

I recall one time when I was negotiating for a tract of land in a prime location. The sellers were two older gentlemen who had owned the land for a number of years. They were asking $400,000 for the land. I had expressed a strong interest in the property and had preliminary discussions with the sellers indirectly through a broker. The time came for all of us to sit down at the table to work out the details. I thought the property was priced too high relative to other tracts of land in the area and felt a more reasonable price was closer to $350,000. The two gentlemen happened to be brothers and were well into their retirement years. It was apparent to me that one of the brothers was very eager to sell and was willing to consider the lower price. By sitting across the table from them, it was easy to read their facial expressions. The brother willing to consider the lower price was practically salivating with anticipation at the thought of cashing out. My guess is that in his mind, he perhaps had visions of being out on the water in his new boat down off the coast of Florida. If I were negotiating with him only, the $350,000 price would have been easily achieved. Unfortunately, his brother was not as eager to sell and held out for close to full asking price. I decided that the deal was overpriced and indicated my unwillingness to proceed. The look on the brother's face who already had visions of retirement suddenly changed to one of great disappointment as I announced my decision to terminate the negotiations.

Remember that at some point in the process of negotiating, the party with whom you are dealing will most likely become emotionally engaged. Once she does, it is difficult for her to turn back. In her mind, the property is sold and she is already spending the money. As a professional, you should closely watch the signals sent by the other party's facial expressions and body language. Use these sometimes very subtle, yet very real, signals to negotiate the best price and terms possible.

COMPREHENSIVE KNOWLEDGE OF MARKET

To be successful in this business, you must have a comprehensive knowledge of the market you are dealing in. It is impossible to negotiate for the best price without it. You must understand property values in your respective market as well as, or better than, the parties you are conducting business with. You can use your knowledge to make sound arguments to the parties you are dealing with to support the price and terms you are negotiating for. By showing them what similar properties are selling for, you present reasonable and logical data that will help convince them of your position.

I am very familiar with both housing prices and land prices in my particular market and therefore am better prepared to negotiate for the best possible price. One example that comes to mind centers around several vacant lots in a new residential community that a developer had available for sale. His initial asking price was $46,000 per lot. My research indicated that while there were a number of lots for sale at $46,000 and even more, the lots this seller had were considerably smaller. The lots selling for $46,000 in that area typically ranged in size from a third of an acre to half an acre and may have even offered other features like trees or a walkout basement site. The lots I was considering were much smaller in size, probably no more than a fifth of an acre and had no trees. Since I had done my homework and was familiar with the market, I knew there were comparable lots in another new community within a mile of this one selling for $35,000 to $37,500. I presented this information, complete with the community plot plans, lot sizes, and prices, to the seller to make a valid argument for a lower price. We eventually settled on a price of $36,000 per lot, $10,000 less than his initial asking price.

As a residential builder for Symphony Homes in a very competitive marketplace, it is imperative to control costs through each and every step of the building process, beginning with the acquisition of land. If I had agreed to pay the extra $10,000 per lot the seller was asking, I would have been at an immediate disadvantage to other sellers in the area. To compensate for the difference in price, I would have had to do one of two things—raise the price of the house by $10,000, or absorb the cost within the company. Raising the price would have meant my turnover time for each house sold would increase significantly, which adds directly to the carrying costs such as interest, taxes, and insurance. Absorbing a cost of $10,000 per house was not feasible, either, as it would quickly put me out of business. Although I really liked the lots the seller was offering for sale, had he not conceded, we would not have had a deal. I have enough experience to know that there is always another opportunity just around the corner. To overpay for a particular deal just because I had fallen in love with it, or had become emotionally engaged with, would border on suicide for my company.

Whether you are buying vacant lots, single family houses, or apartment buildings, you cannot afford to overpay for a piece of property. As a professional real estate investor, you must be intimately familiar with the market you are dealing in and possess a comprehensive knowledge of it in order to be truly successful. Without this key information, you will soon discover that you cannot survive in the business of buying and selling real estate.

DEGREE OF SELLER'S MOTIVATION

As a professional real estate investor, it is important for you to know why the seller is selling her property. Knowing the underlying reasons for the sale can potentially give you an advantage during the negotiation process. For example, you want to know if the seller just lost her job and can no longer afford the payments, or if she is perhaps attempting to test the market to see how much her property is worth. In other words, you want to know if your seller is a motivated seller, and if so, to what degree. The more motivated the seller is, the more likely he is to be flexible on both price and terms. While there are many reasons for selling, they typically fall into one or more of seven categories. (See Exhibit 7.2.)

One primary reason sellers sell their properties falls into what is commonly referred to as life-changing events. Life-changing events include events like marriage, the birth of a new baby, a new job too far to commute to, divorce, illness in the family, an accident, or the death of a loved one. These types of events are what I refer to as *high degree motivators*, meaning that one or more family members are often highly motivated to sell the house. They need and want to do so quickly and are unlikely to hold out for top

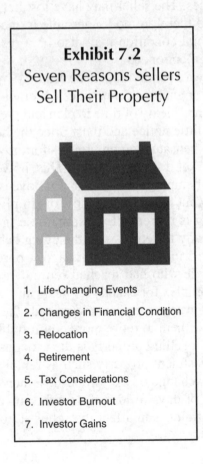

Exhibit 7.2
Seven Reasons Sellers
Sell Their Property

1. Life-Changing Events

2. Changes in Financial Condition

3. Relocation

4. Retirement

5. Tax Considerations

6. Investor Burnout

7. Investor Gains

dollar. The sellers who are affected by these circumstances often have a very real and immediate need to sell and are therefore more likely to be flexible in both price and terms. Life-changing events often create a need to sell that outweighs the need to profit from the transaction.

A couple going through a divorce, for example, will often create a financial hardship for the family, especially if it is a household in which the father is the main or sole provider and the mother is the primary caregiver to the children. In a situation such as that, all members of the family are affected and where one larger house was adequate before, two smaller houses or apartments will be necessary now.

Another reason sellers sell their properties is directly related to changes in their financial condition. These changes may also fall into the high degree motivator category, depending on the degree of financial change. The most likely cause of financial hardship is a change in employment circumstances. The seller may have lost her job. The bottom line is that she is now unemployed and therefore no longer able to meet her financial obligations. Changes in a seller's financial condition may also be a result of one of the other life-changing events previously mentioned.

It is not at all uncommon for an individual to be required by his employer to relocate to another area for one reason or another. Sometimes the employee knows well in advance of the impending move and has plenty of time to plan and prepare. Other times, however, the employee is given very little notice and must price the house for a quick sale. Some employers will actually compensate their employees for moving expenses and also offer to purchase the house at market if it does not sell. This, however, is the exception rather than the rule. The majority of employers give their employees a choice of absorbing these costs on their own (if they want to keep their jobs) or simply leave the company.

Another reason for selling is retirement. At some time in everyone's life, they reach a point at which they are ready to retire. With the aging baby boomers, there are more people than ever who are retiring. Several years ago, I purchased a 25-unit apartment building from an older couple who had reached retirement age. Ironically, the couple had owned the apartment complex for exactly 25 years and had just made their very last mortgage payment. Selling the apartments would provide them with a considerable lump sum of cash that would allow them to retire more comfortably.

Another primary reason for selling property is the tax considerations of the seller. For example, if he is selling investment property such as rental units or commercial space, and is also involved in an exchange of like properties, then the seller is limited by law to a predetermined number of days to identify another investment property and close on it. These strict time constraints can affect the seller at both ends of this transaction, meaning the property he is divesting himself of, and the one he is acquiring. If the seller has not identified a new property to purchase yet, he may not be that motivated and may in fact stall the sale of his property. On the other hand, if the seller has identified another property, which must soon be closed on because of the expiration of that seller's time, then he must be prepared to rapidly strike a deal with a buyer of his property.

Investor burnout is another primary reason people sell their houses. They excitedly purchase their first few rental houses with the notion that at last they have made it. Then reality sets in. The tenants call complaining about the broken air conditioner, or the dishwasher that needs replacing. Then there's Uncle Joe, who just died and they had to help out Aunt Sally with the funeral expenses, so they don't have this month's rent. I've heard enough excuses in my experience to fill a book with. I remember one lady who did everything she could to avoid paying her rent. On one occasion, she stopped by our office to pay her rent. She was in a hurry because she was on her way to work. In the blink of an eye, the lady dropped off a check and was out the door. "Thank you," I called out to her as she whisked away. The amount of rent due from the lady was $575.00. I vividly remember glancing down at the check, and then feeling my blood boil as I realized the amount of the check she wrote was $5.75, not $575.00! Since I knew she worked right down the street, I quickly hopped in my car and confronted her about the error. She acted surprised about the slight oversight, as if she didn't know, but I think she was more surprised by the fact that I caught up with her than anything else. She wrote another check on the spot, and this time it was for the correct amount. In the case of investor burnout, the degree of the seller's motivation will correlate directly with the degree of distress. This is where subtle clues can be detected by direct communication with the seller. If the seller is suffering from burnout related to managing the property, he will most likely be highly motivated, and a highly motivated seller is a flexible seller.

Finally, one of the most compelling reasons for a seller to divest his property is that he is a value player like yourself and is ready to take his gain on sale and move on to the next value play opportunity. The degree of motivation will vary depending on factors such as how much value was created in the deal and timing for entry into the next investment. If, for example, the seller has identified another retail opportunity but needs the cash out of this house, then he may be willing to strike a bargain, knowing that he will make up for it, and then some, on the next transaction. Investors buying and selling in volume are not interested in holding out for top dollar. They prefer to take a little less and keep their turnover high, knowing that the more houses they buy and sell, the more financially rewarding it will be overall.

As you work with and talk to sellers, ask them why they are selling. Listen both to what they do tell you, and to what they don't tell you. Sometimes they will be very direct, as in, "My wife and I just got a divorce." Other times, however, you must watch and listen for subtle clues as to their true reason for selling. They may tell you, for example, that they are retiring, but leave out the part about having already purchased a condo in Florida and are now making two payments, which is really beginning to stretch the budget and "Oh, if we could only sell this house so we could move to Florida." A little probing can often uncover the seller's underlying motives to sell her property.

BACK DOOR EXITS

Back door exits, or escape clauses as they are also referred to, allow you to back out of a purchase agreement at various times throughout the contract period. You should always take care to ensure that several escape clauses are built into the contract, with at least one of these clauses giving you the right to back out right up to the point of closing. The proper application of these techniques can provide the shrewd investor with tremendous bargaining power.

A contingency is a common back door exit used by many investors. The types of contingencies are limited only by your imagination. Some examples include "contingent upon purchaser selling her residence," or "contingent upon seller making repairs prior to closing as indicated on Addendum A." There are also many provisions and conditions that must be satisfied before the purchaser's earnest money "goes hard," or becomes nonrefundable. You can easily protect yourself with a provision such as "subject to satisfactory inspection of the property and acceptance thereof by purchaser." You typically have anywhere from 14 days to 30 days to accept the property, based on its physical condition. The number of days is usually a fill-in-the-blank type of provision, so you can ask for more time if necessary. The seller may not give you more time, but it doesn't hurt to ask. In some instances, there may be approvals required by state and local authorities. For example, if there is a change in the use of the property from residential to commercial, the city board of zoning appeals must review and subsequently approve the change. You certainly want to include language in the agreement that will fully protect you in the event that the approvals are not granted.

One of my favorite techniques is a very simple, yet powerful, back door exit. Right on the first page of most purchase agreements are several paragraphs outlining the financing provisions. The buyer is given the right to obtain suitable financing within a certain number of days of signing the agreement. They usually have anywhere from three to seven days to apply for financing and 7 to 14 days to obtain an approval. Since most sellers assume they are working with a buyer who is fully qualified and will be approved for the required financing, this section of the purchase agreement is often glossed over. Like many places throughout the standardized purchase agreements that are most often used, there is the opportunity to fill in the blank. Under the financing provisions section, there is almost always a blank for the interest rate not to exceed a certain amount and also one for the loan-to-value percentage. Here is where you protect yourself in not one, but two places. If you know that the prevailing market interest rate for loans is 6.5 percent, for example, you fill in the blank with 6.0 percent. Since it is not at all uncommon for buyers to get 95 percent loans, and even 97 percent loans, on houses they purchase, you fill in the blank with 95 percent. You comply with the time requirements as outlined in the financing section, but as a real estate professional buying investment property, you will most likely only be able to get a loan for up to 90 percent of the value. When your approval comes back from the lender offering an interest rate of 6.6 percent and a loan-to-value ratio of 90 percent, the seller believes that you have been approved. While it is true that you have in fact been approved, you have not been approved under the terms and conditions as set forth in the purchase agreement. You can use this very simple, but very powerful, technique as a back door exit on almost any property you enter into a contract on, right up to the very last minute. The seller won't like it one bit, but it is a very real legal out for you.

CONCESSIONS

Concessions can be another very effective method of getting exactly what you want during the negotiation phase. My approach is to always ask for more than I expect to get in the initial offer. For example, I may ask the seller to accept a price substantially below his asking price, to include all of the appliances, to carry back a second mortgage for 15 percent of the deal value, to allow an additional credit at closing for repairs, and to pay for all of the closing costs. I know going in that I will most likely not get all of what I ask for, but then again, you never know. The seller may be just anxious enough to give you everything. On the other hand, he may instead present a counteroffer to partially reduce the price, pay for the closing costs, and give you a credit for repairs, but not carry back a second mortgage or include the appliances. In the seller's counteroffer, he has made several concessions that you must then determine whether you are willing to accept.

Concessions can also be used as a kind of bargaining chip. You tell the seller, "I will agree to X if you will agree to Y." One example of this kind of bargaining is an agreement to pay the seller's full asking price if he in turn agrees to accept only 5 percent down instead of the 20 percent originally desired. Another example is a seller who must have all cash and is pushing for a quick closing. You agree to her request, but only if she concedes to accept $10,000 less than the asking price. Concessions are most effectively used to gain something in your favor related to the transaction in exchange for something else.

THE RED HERRING TECHNIQUE

One of my favorite negotiating methods is one I refer to as the red herring technique. The phrase can be traced back to the practice of escaped convicts who used pickled herrings to throw bloodhounds off their scent. In essence, the red herring technique creates a distraction that is completely irrelevant to the subject it is introduced to. As a professional real estate investor, you can use this technique to throw the party you are negotiating with off the scent, or in other words, to create a distraction. The technique works like this. Let's say the seller is asking $90,000 for his house and wants all cash. You inspect the property and determine that although the asking price appears to be fair, you will make a concerted effort at purchasing it for 10 percent below market value. During the course of your inspection, you notice stored in the garage a pair of prized Yamaha WaveRunners. You decide to write an offer structured as follows:

1. sales price of $81,000
2. seller to carry back a second mortgage for $10,000
3. seller to include two Yamaha WaveRunners
4. seller to pay for all closing costs

Now then, can you guess which provision is the red herring? Of course you can! It's the inclusion of the pair of WaveRunners! Can you imagine how the seller will react when your offer is presented to him? He's likely to breeze right past everything with the exception of the WaveRunners. He'll probably say something like, "What's this? Include my WaveRunners? That buyer must be crazy! There's no way he's getting my WaveRunners!" Meanwhile, he signs off on everything else, but he absolutely refuses to include those WaveRunners. You, of course, didn't care about them to begin with. Your objective was to get your price and terms by creating a distraction that had nothing at all to do with the original transaction.

I recently used this technique to shave $5,000 off an already-below-market asking price. Since the name of our company is Symphony Homes, we obviously have an interest in

■ **Seven Steps of Successful Negotiations** ■

most anything related to music, especially classical music. While inspecting the seller's property, I noticed a very old violin that was carefully mounted on the dining room wall. Proudly displayed, I figured it had probably been in the seller's family for some time. I wrote the offer for $5,000 less than the seller's asking price. To create a distraction, I wrote under the Special Provisions section, "Seller to include violin hanging in dining room." I can only imagine the look of surprise as the seller's agent presented the offer to him. The seller countered the very next day. His agent brought the counteroffer to my office and stated rather emphatically on the seller's behalf that there was no way that I was getting that violin, as it was an old family heirloom. The agent didn't say a word, however, about the lower price. In an effort to mask my true motives, I insisted to the agent that I must have that violin. She reaffirmed the seller's position and again stated that he would not part with it. I finally conceded and signed the counteroffer. The red herring technique is another simple, yet powerfully effective tool in your arsenal of negotiating tactics. Use it wisely to get what you want!

THE MONEY TALKS APPROACH

The *money talks* approach can be an effective negotiation tool that can help you get more of your offers accepted. While the approach is simple in its application, the results can be quite powerful. There is a great deal of truth in the phrase "money talks." It works like this. After you have written your offer to include some of the other negotiation techniques previously described, it is time to present it to the seller. When presenting your offer, attach a large check to it to demonstrate to the seller that you are a serious buyer. As a general rule, the check should be written for between 5 and 10 percent of the deal value. This will depend on the housing prices in your particular market, but generally speaking, a check written for at least $5,000 and up to $25,000 will most certainly get the seller's attention. A large earnest money deposit sends a strong and immediate signal to the seller that he is dealing with a buyer who is both serious and capable of putting a deal together.

Think about it. How many offers have you received where the buyer attached a $500 or $1,000 earnest money check? Probably three out of four of the offers you receive have minimal deposits attached. When I get a buyer interested in one of my houses who shows up with a $1,000 deposit, I usually don't get too excited. On the other hand, if they show up with a check for 5 to 10 percent of the purchase price, they immediately have my attention. I once had a buyer who made an offer for $228,000 on a house valued at $235,000. I watch the profit margins pretty closely, so this is a deal that I would normally pass on. In this particular case, however, the buyer attached an earnest money check in the amount of $12,000. That check immediately got my attention because I knew I was working with a buyer who was both serious and capable of purchasing the house. It took me all of about five minutes to think it over before accepting the offer.

Obtaining the best possible price and terms for the purchase of real estate requires a combination of both art and skill. As a master negotiator, you must take care to exercise each one of the seven steps of successful negotiations discussed in this chapter. To summarize, they are as follows:

1. The Psychology of Negotiating
2. Comprehensive Knowledge of Market
3. Degree of Seller's Motivation
4. Back Door Exits
5. Concessions—When to Make Them and What to Expect in Return
6. The Red Herring Technique
7. The Money Talks Approach

A thorough and comprehensive understanding of each one of these principles can literally save you thousands of dollars on your real estate transactions. The more familiar you become with these principles, the more skilled you will become when negotiating with others.

> **You can have anything you want—if you want it badly enough. You can be anything you want to be, do anything you set out to accomplish, if you hold to that desire with singleness of purpose.**
>
> —*Abraham Lincoln*

PART III

Investing Strategies
for the Smart Investor

Chapter 8

Financing and Closing Considerations

$\mathbb{T}$ he ability to obtain proper financing for the purchase of your investment property is vital to your success. In this chapter, I examine several financing alternatives available to you and discuss the differences of each. (See Exhibit 8.1.) I have also included a sample outline of a business plan that you can use to better prepare yourself when initiating new relationships with lenders or partners. I have also included a section about credit scores and underwriting guidelines. Finally, I provide you with information that will better enable you to understand and prepare for the closing process.

CONVENTIONAL MORTGAGES

Conventional mortgages represent an excellent source for financing your real estate investments. There are a number of loan programs available at any given time that offer a wide range of terms and conditions. Depending on the interest rate environment, conventional mortgage rates can be some of the most competitive of all the types of financing. Unlike bank loans, which are usually linked to the prime lending rate, mortgage loans are typically linked to 10-year T-Bills, or treasury notes, plus some additional spread or margin. The result is that conventional mortgage loans generally carry a more favorable interest rate than do other types of financing instruments.

Conventional mortgages are usually available with 30-year amortization periods as well. The longer amortization period helps you to minimize your monthly cash flow out requirement to the lender by reducing the amount you must pay back each month. By way of comparison, a loan through your local bank may offer only a 15- or 20-year amortization period. This is not always the case, however, because sometimes interest-only

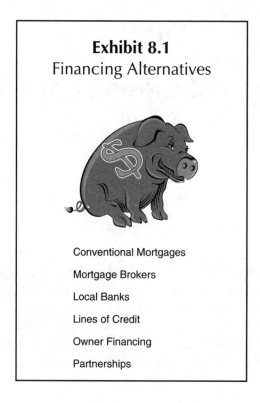

loans are available from a bank. Since no principal payments are being made, the monthly cash flow out can be reduced even further.

Another advantage of using a conventional mortgage company to finance your purchase is that there are a number of companies that will lend up to 90 percent of the purchase price on investment properties. This means you only have to come up with 10 percent for your down payment. For those of you who are accustomed to reading the nothing-down types of books, keep in mind that the selection of available investment opportunities is much narrower. You may spend more time searching for a deal that requires very little down and discover that the upside for creating value and subsequently flipping the property is limited. I prefer to use a little more of my cash and have a much broader selection than to spend time looking for that proverbial needle in a haystack.

While conventional mortgage companies are overall a good source of financing, there are some drawbacks to using them. One such drawback is the documentation required by the lender on each and every transaction. Mortgage companies are notorious for demanding excessive documentation. For example, if a large deposit has recently been made into your bank account, the lender will want documentation to determine its source. Other disadvantages to using a conventional mortgage company are the fees charged for the loan. Depending on the lender, these may or may not include a loan application fee, an underwriting fee, a loan origination fee, and whatever other creative fees the lender can come up with.

MORTGAGE BROKERS

Just as real estate brokers play an important role in matching up buyers and sellers, so do mortgage brokers play an important role in matching up buyers and lenders. Mortgage brokers usually have many contacts in the industry, they know which lender is best suited for the type of financing you are seeking, and they know who's offering the best deal. Experienced brokers have well-established relationships directly with the lenders and usually have two or three that they do a large volume of business with. While you can generally expect to pay 1 percent to the broker for his or her services, the fee can be well worth it if you are working with a professional broker who has solid relationships with several lenders.

The broker's service can sometimes make the difference between having the financing for your deal be accepted or not. Furthermore, brokers know how to qualify your particular property before ever sending it to a lender because they know what each lender will accept and what they will not accept. A good mortgage broker can usually tell you if he can place your loan after spending just 10 to 15 minutes with you on the phone. He knows what questions to ask to qualify your property and which lender is likely to be the most interested in financing it.

LOCAL BANKS

Conventional bank financing is commonly available through a smaller local bank. These types of banks may operate with just a single branch and $15 million in deposits, or they may be somewhat larger with as many as 5 to 10 branches and $150 million in deposits. One advantage of using a local bank is they can often offer borrowers a greater degree of flexibility than other lenders, such as mortgage companies. For example, they may provide the money for your rehab improvements, or a percentage thereof, in addition to the financing for the property itself.

Smaller banks are also likely to be much more familiar with the local area and would therefore have a greater degree of confidence in the specific market than a larger regional or national lender would. Personal relationships with your local banker are more easily established than with other types of lenders like conventional mortgage companies. You can go into the bank, introduce yourself, and sit down and talk directly with the lender. This gives you the opportunity to sell yourself and your project. Once a relationship has been established and the banker gets to know you and is comfortable with you, future loan requests will be much easier and likely require less documentation, possibly as little as updating your personal financial statement.

Local banks are good sources for rehab loans because the lender knows the loans are short-term in nature. The banks are also able to generate more fees because of the shorter duration of these types of loans. A local bank may not give you the best terms initially, but the more business you do with them and the more comfortable they become with you, the more leverage you will develop in negotiating more favorable terms with them.

As your relationship with a lender matures, you should seek to establish a predetermined line of credit. This will enable you to borrow money up to your credit limit. For example, with a $1 million line of credit, you will have the ability to purchase several properties at one time. With an average selling price of $100,000, you could effectively purchase up to 10 houses. This depends, of course, on the specific terms the lender has set with respect to the loan-to-value ratio and the collateral required, if any, on each house. Since the lender knows you are in the rehab business, money from your line of credit can usually be used for the repairs, too. Again, the lender may limit the percentage of borrowed funds by a predetermined loan-to-value ratio.

LINES OF CREDIT

There are several types of credit lines available to almost anyone. Some of the more common ones are home equity lines of credit, national credit cards like MasterCard and Visa, and individual store credit cards. The terms and conditions vary widely with these types of credit. The most favorable interest rates and the longest terms are typically found with home equity lines of credit, while national credit cards and store credit cards tend to offer higher rates and shorter repayment terms.

Many of you already own your own home. For those of you who do, you are most likely to be already familiar with home equity lines of credit, or HELOC loans. These are merely second mortgages secured by your principal place of residence that allow you to borrow against the equity in your home, oftentimes up to 100 percent of the value of your home, and sometimes even more. Since this type of loan is secured by your residence, the interest rates are usually lower than with other types of credit. HELOC loans provide you the flexibility of borrowing against your home at will by simply writing a check. These funds can be used for just about anything you want and represent a good source of funds to be used as a down payment, as well as for rehab money.

For those of you who insist on that nothing-down deal, you can easily borrow money against your home equity line of credit and use it for the down payment on an investment property. Since those funds are borrowed funds, they do not represent your cash equity. If, for example, you purchase a house for $85,000 and then borrow $70,000 from your local bank and the remaining $15,000 from your home equity line of credit, you have in essence a true nothing-down transaction because 100 percent of the funds used to purchase the house are borrowed funds. You should be aware, however, that this is easier to do with a local bank than with a conventional mortgage lender. Mortgage companies tend to require more documentation and often want to know where the money for your down payment is coming from. You can easily overcome this requirement, however, by depositing the funds at least two months in advance into your bank account. Lenders usually do not require more than the last two most current bank statements, so as long as the money is in your account before those two periods, the lender will not see the deposit and will therefore not question it. This practice is in no way dishonest. You are simply borrowing money against an approved line of credit and placing the funds into your bank account. The borrowed funds will, however, show up on your credit report and will therefore increase your overall debt-to-income ratio, so if you are already maxed out on credit cards, this may not be the way to go.

National credit cards like MasterCard and Visa also represent a good source of funds. Credit cards are available to almost anyone and can be used for just about anything. Most credit cards offer you the capability of getting a cash advance against your credit limit. You can also write checks that can be used for almost anything, including your investment property. National credit cards tend to carry higher interest rates than do other forms of borrowing, so you should use this source of funds prudently.

Individual store credit cards can provide you with even more buying power. National hardware stores like Home Depot offer credit cards to their customers, enabling them to purchase materials from their store. If you are in the rehab business, this can be an excellent source of short-term credit that can be used to finance up to 100 percent of the required repairs on your rehab project.

While lines of credit can be a great source of borrowing power, I caution you to use them wisely. Remember that you are using these funds for investment purposes, so be sensible and responsible in the way you use them. Don't go max out all of your cards thinking you can conquer the world. Remember that the money has to be repaid at some point. Your objective is to earn a predetermined rate of return on all funds borrowed for investment purposes, including the many types of credit lines available to you.

OWNER FINANCING

In an owner-financing arrangement, the seller does exactly as the name implies. She provides the buyer with some form of financing. It may be that she carries the entire note, or only a portion thereof. If the seller owns the property free and clear, for example, then she may be willing to provide you with 100 percent financing. What is more likely, though, is that the seller will want a minimal down payment, even if it is only $1,000. If the seller still has a large underlying mortgage on the property, then she may be agreeable to carrying back a second mortgage for a smaller amount like 10 percent of the purchase price, for example. You will still have to obtain a mortgage for the property from a more traditional source such as a mortgage company, but having the seller carry back a second allows you to get into the deal with less money down. One caveat you should be aware of, though, is that not all lenders will allow a second mortgage of any kind to be attached. Before you proceed with this option, make sure the mortgage company does not have a provision in place that would prevent you from attaching a second mortgage to the deal.

There are several advantages of an owner-financed arrangement. One benefit is that the seller is not required to conform to all of the underwriting guidelines that banks and mortgage companies are. The seller is likely to require very little in the way of documentation. Unlike conventional mortgage companies, the seller providing owner financing doesn't care where the money for the down payment comes from just so long as it comes from somewhere. On the other hand, traditional lenders like banks and mortgage companies can be very particular where your down payment comes from. In many cases, the money cannot come from a family member or friend. Moreover, you must be able to prove that the money is your own and did not come from a relative. Another advantage of using owner financing is that it enables you to save a considerable sum by avoiding the fees and transaction costs commonly assessed on new loans. There are no loan application fees, no underwriting fees, and no loan origination fees. Finally, the time needed to close a deal involving owner financing is much less than for traditional financing arrangements since there is virtually no loan approval process required.

Another form of owner financing is known as a wraparound mortgage. Under this arrangement, the seller retains title and continues to make his mortgage payments to the lender while the new owner makes his mortgage payments directly to the seller. Be careful of any due-on-sale clauses in the deed of trust that may expressly prohibit this type of financing arrangement. Lenders normally are not very fond of the transfer of ownership interests without their knowing about it.

Although second lien positions are the most common form of owner financing arrangements, owners or sellers are not limited to just debt financing. They may be open to an equity agreement wherein they retain a small portion of ownership interest. Instead of being required to make monthly payments to the seller, the buyer and seller agree to share in the profits of the newly formed entity. Depending on the specifics of the agreement, the original seller may also be entitled to a share of any capital gains when the property is later sold again.

PARTNERSHIPS

Using the resources of a partner can be an excellent form of secondary financing. The type of partner I am referring to in this section is a friend, family member, or business acquaintance. Partnerships can be structured in any number of ways. For instance, capital injections by partners can take the form of debt or equity, partners can play an active or passive role, and terms for the repayment provisions can be defined in various creative ways.

If your partner agrees to invest in your project using equity, then he or she will share the risk with you. If you lose, your partner loses, but if you win, your partner also wins and shares in the profits. On the other hand, if you don't want to give up any of the profits, then you would have your partner participate on the debt side by making a loan to you. In this case, the loan can be secured by the property or any other collateral you may have, or it may be an unsecured loan as well. You may decide to have your partner actively participate by using whatever skills he may have. If your partner is mechanically inclined, for example, you may consider having him perform some of the maintenance. Conversely, you may choose to have your partner play a passive role, wherein his only function is to provide capital. Repayment provisions can be made in any number of ways. For example, debt payments can be made periodically such as monthly, quarterly, or annually. You might also agree to repay the debt with all interest due when the property is sold. If, on the other hand, you are flipping several properties a year, it may not make sense to repay the debt when the first property is sold. You will likely want to have your partner agree to an ongoing arrangement that provides you the flexibility to buy and sell at will with a predetermined repayment date both parties agree on. In summary, allowing a partner to participate can benefit you by providing additional capital for a project that may otherwise be out of reach, and by contributing services of specific skills that you may be lacking.

YOUR BUSINESS PLAN

Preparing a professional-looking, comprehensive business plan and presenting it to potential lenders and partners is certain to set you apart from all of the dozens of applicants they meet day in and day out. Preparing a business plan will also compel you to clearly define your real estate investment objectives. Physically going through the motions of formalizing your business plan forces you to think through each and every step of the process and subsequently assess the soundness of your plan. Your vision of where and how you want to grow your company begins in your mind with your thought processes. Recording your thoughts in a formalized manner allows you to crystallize them. You can refer back to your business plan as often as needed to make sure you are on track to reach your objectives, and also to adjust your course as necessary.

Furthermore, presenting your business plan directly to a potential lender or partner will demonstrate to her that you are a serious investor who is looking to establish a long-term relationship. By following the step-by-step process you have outlined in your business plan, the lender will also be able to judge for herself the soundness of your plan. In short, it will enable her to establish a level of comfort with you and your transaction that may not otherwise be possible. You must remember that prospective lenders and partners are human beings who will judge you not only by what they see on your loan application, but also by what they see in the way you present yourself to them. You must be prepared to sell yourself and your abilities to them. Their assessment of you is based on both objective evidence and subjective qualities they observe about you. The objective evidence is drawn from the items that are in black and white before them, such as your loan application and credit scores. The subjective qualities you will be judged on are more subtle in nature and include things like the way you present yourself, your level of professionalism, and whether or not they perceive you to be credible.

The use of a sound business plan is most effective when dealing with local banks or partners. These are the people you are most likely to get to know on a more personal level. A business plan is of little or no value to mortgage brokers since they are more interested in packaging your loan request and shipping it off to any one of many underwriting departments. Although formalizing your business plan will require a good deal of time and effort on your part, a comprehensive and professional-looking plan can pay big dividends by providing you with the much-needed capital to fund your purchases.

Exhibit 8.2 provides a sample outline for some of the more essential items you will want to include in your business plan. These items can be organized in a very professional manner in a notebook that contains tabs and dividers.

WHAT EVERY BORROWER SHOULD KNOW ABOUT CREDIT SCORES

Most lenders today use what is known as FICO scores to determine your ability to borrow money and repay a loan. FICO is an acronym for Fair, Isaac, and Company, which uses an elaborate model to calculate data collected over a period of time about specific individuals. This historical data is then used to assign a credit score to that individual. The scoring system uses factors like payment history, number of creditors, debt-to-income ratios, outstanding balances relative to credit limits, length of credit history, types of credit, and reported income. Before the final score is calculated, previously established weights are assigned to each variable according to the criteria set forth in the model. When lenders order your credit history, they typically get it from all three of the credit-reporting agencies—Equifax, Experian, and TransUnion. All three services may not have exactly the same information, so the credit scores may vary among them. Lenders will often use either an average of the three scores or the median score.

The credit score range is from 300 to 850, with 300 being extremely poor and 850 being a perfect score. It is highly recommended that you do everything in your power to maintain as high a score as possible. If your score is 700+, you are considered to be an "A" borrower and will have no problem qualifying for a loan, provided you meet whatever other criteria the lender has set forth.

Credit scores are used much like SAT (scholastic aptitude test) or GMAT (graduate management admission test) scores. The first thing university administrators want to know when students apply for entrance is how well they did on the required standardized tests. The tests are used to measure students' knowledge and aptitudes in various subjects and the results are quantitatively summarized in the form of a numerical score. Just as admissions administrators use these scores to set minimum standards for matriculation into their schools, so do lenders use credit scores to set minimum standards for lending money to prospective borrowers. Credit scores serve as a valuable tool to lenders because they are purely objective in measuring the ability of a borrower to repay a loan and the probability that he or she will default. They remove all elements of subjective judgments that could be considered discriminatory, such as race or religious preferences.

Some lenders will make loans to just about anyone. They don't care what your score is as long as the property is generating adequate income to service the debt. These

---

Exhibit 8.2
Components of an Effective Business Plan

- Executive Summary—A one- or two-page summary of your plan.

- Company Profile—Background information about yourself, including experience and education, and information about your company.

- Financial Statements—Personal and company financials.

- Primary Market—Define your intended market area.

- Business Strategy—Provide in detail your specific short-term and long-term objectives for your company.

- Marketing Strategy—Define your target market and include specifics of how you intend to market your services and/or properties.

- Capital Requirements—List short-term and long-term anticipated capital requirements.

- Financial Analysis—Provide supporting financial tables.

- Summary—Summarize your proposal and close with sound reasons as to why the lender or partner should work with you.

- Exhibits—May include photographs, surveys, tax returns, purchase agreements, addendums, and so on.

Table 8.1 Interest Rate Matrix

Property Rating	Borrower Rating			
	A	B	C	D
A	6.00%	6.50%	7.00%	7.50%
B	6.50%	7.00%	7.50%	8.00%
C	7.00%	7.50%	8.00%	8.50%
D	7.50%	8.00%	8.50%	9.00%

lenders will, however, adjust their interest rates accordingly by applying a matrix grid that matches your ability to repay with the condition of the property. You can see by looking at Table 8.1—Interest Rate Matrix, that borrowers who fail to maintain good credit are usually penalized as a result. The logic is quite simple. Lenders charge a higher rate of interest to offset the higher risk represented by borrowers with poor credit. The bottom line to you as an investor is to work hard to maintain the best credit rating possible. Doing so will enable you to borrow money more easily than those who have poor credit, and also at much more favorable terms and conditions.

UNDERWRITING GUIDELINES

All lenders have established criteria for making loan decisions. These criteria are referred to as the lender's underwriting guidelines. These guidelines form the basis for all decisions made to either approve or decline a loan applicant's request. They represent the lender's policies and procedures that all new loans under review must conform to before being granted final approval. A lender's underwriting guidelines may include elements such as the loan-to-value (LTV) ratio, the debt service coverage ratio (DSCR), a borrower's debt-to-income ratio, the size and term of the loan, and information about the subject property.

To ensure that the lender's underwriting guidelines are conformed to, the lender will require specific information about the property and the borrower in order to do a full and proper analysis of a loan request. This information includes items such as the purchase agreement for the property, credit reports from all three independent agencies, verification of employment and income, bank statements, and tax returns. See Exhibit 8.3 for a more complete list. Giving the lender a complete documentation package will enable him to expedite the processing of your loan in a timely and efficient manner.

Exhibit 8.3
Required Loan Documentation

Formal loan application

Purchase agreement and all related addenda

Personal financial statement

Income tax returns for a minimum of two years

Credit reports from three reporting agencies

Bank statements for a minimum of two months

Verification of employment, wages, and earnings

Verification of property taxes

Property insurance binder

Third-party reports, including survey and appraisal

Once the lender has all the necessary documentation, you can usually have an approval within two or three days. This is, however, a general time frame and may vary according to the volume of loans being processed at any given time. The underwriter will often come back and ask for more information to clarify something you have already submitted. For example, if your bank statement shows an unusually large deposit being made into your account, the underwriter is likely to require supporting documentation as to the source of those funds.

You should be aware that smaller local banks are usually not as nitpicky about requiring you to document the source of funds. Banks customarily require only the first page of your account statement to document the amount of funds you have and not necessarily their source. You can use this to your advantage if you wish to make a deposit from a borrowed source of funds, such as a line of credit from a home equity loan or a credit card. Making a deposit of this sort does not mean you are being dishonest or breaking any laws. Unless the bank asks you specifically where the deposit came from, you are not required to disclose it to them. Even if they do ask, local banks tend to not be as particular about you borrowing money, for example, from a home equity line of credit as a conventional mortgage company may be.

After securing financing for your property, the next step is to begin preparing to finalize and close the transaction. Depending on the size of your acquisition, the closing process can be fairly simple and straightforward, or it can be quite involved with extensive documentation required. It is also time to begin planning and defining what your role as a strategic manager will be. This, too, will depend on the size of the transaction, as well as your level of experience.

THE CLOSING PROCESS

The closing process is the time when everything comes together to finalize your transaction. You have studied the market and analyzed numerous investment opportunities, you have successfully negotiated terms and conditions acceptable to both you and the seller, and you have sought out the best financing alternative for your property. It is now time to bring all the parties together to close the sale. Before you commit yourself by signing on the dotted line, however, you will want to take time to thoroughly review all of the related closing documents, and in particular, the title report, closing statement, deed of trust, and promissory note.

The title report, also known as the abstract of title, provides information about the property's chain of title. In other words, it gives a history of ownership, judgments, liens, and anything else that may have been recorded against the property over time. The title insurance company issues an insurance policy to the buyer and a separate policy to the lender that guarantees the title is clean and that there are no encumbrances that may adversely affect the new owner.

Closing statements, also known as settlement statements, are commonly prepared by the title company handling the closing. They detail by line item all of the associated debits and credits assessed to both buyer and seller. These include items such as the sale price, amount of earnest money deposit, principal amount of the new loan, any existing loans or debts that must be satisfied, prorated adjustments for taxes and interest, and various fees charged by the title company. Exhibits 8.1, 8.2, and 8.3, and Table 8.1 collectively provide you with some of the detail from a commonly used closing settlement statement form.

You should take the requisite time to review each and every charge on the settlement statement to verify its accuracy. Errors are often inadvertently made for one reason or another. The title company may, for example, have the incorrect payoff amount of the seller's loan, or they may calculate the prorations incorrectly, or they may not be aware of a credit you are entitled to because of a specific clause in your purchase agreement negotiated by you and the seller. Don't assume that because the closing officer works at the title company and acts as the facilitator in numerous closings that "she must be right because she is the closer and she should know." Precisely the opposite is true. Because the closer does act as the facilitator in numerous closings each and every day is all the more reason she must rely on you to provide accurate information for the settlement statement.

The inherent risk to you by neglecting to review the closing statement can be substantial and potentially cost you hundreds or even thousands of dollars. Here in Michigan, for example, the state and county assess what is referred to as a transfer tax. The transfer tax is calculated as a percentage of the sales price and is collected at closing on all real estate sold. It is just like paying tax on a new car, new furniture, school supplies for the kids, or just about anything else Uncle Sam can get his hands on. The tax rate applied is usually about one percent or just a little less, so for every $100,000 in property value sold, approximately $1,000 in taxes is assessed. Unless otherwise stated, the seller is responsible for paying this tax. In my purchase agreements, however, I require the buyer to pay the tax. Unless the title company has been made aware of this, the transfer taxes will be placed on my side of the settlement statement, which is the incorrect side. This error, which has been made many times, could easily cost me two to three thousand dollars. Although I thoroughly review all of the charges on the statement, this is one in particular that I am very careful to check for accuracy.

The lender is responsible for preparing the deed of trust and the promissory note. These documents outline the terms and conditions under which the lender has agreed to lend you money. Repayment terms are specified, including the amount of the loan, the interest rate and amortization period, and any prepayment penalties that may be imposed. Other lender requirements that may also be included are escrow conditions for taxes and insurance, minimum insurance amounts, standard of care for property condition, and default provisions.

By taking the time to more fully understand all of the requisite closing documents, you will be better prepared to ensure that the closing for the investment property you are purchasing will go smoothly. For the most part, you can have confidence in the expertise of those individuals who are preparing all of the related forms, but you must also keep in mind that these individuals are human and prone to make mistakes just like anyone else. Protect your interests by carefully reviewing all of the closing documents. Doing so may potentially save you thousands of dollars.

> Set a goal to become a millionaire for what it makes of you to achieve it. Do it for the skills you have to learn and the person you have to become. Do it for what you'll end up knowing about the marketplace, what you'll learn about the management of time and working with people. Do it for the ability of discovering how to keep your ego in check. For what you have to learn about being benevolent. Being kind as well as being strong. What you have to learn about society and business and government and taxes and becoming an accomplished person to reach the status of millionaire is what's valuable. Not the million dollars.
>
> —*Earl Shoaf*

Chapter 9

Assemble a Winning Team of Professionals

To truly be successful as a real estate investor, you need to assemble a winning team of professionals. If you are only buying and selling one or two properties a year, like most investors, you will be involved in much of the work yourself. As you begin to participate in more and more transactions, however, you will soon discover that you can no longer do everything by yourself. In fact, you will find that the best use of your time will be spent coordinating the efforts of others. By delegating some of the responsibilities to your team, you are able to achieve much more than if you tried to do everything yourself. For example, an ox by itself could pull only a single covered wagon, but when you have two oxen yoked together, they can pull several wagons. This well-established concept can be summarized as the "sum of the parts is greater than the whole." It is a phenomenon known as *synergy*. Synergistic effects are created when individuals who might otherwise work independently instead work together. The individuals are able to achieve much more working together in a collective effort than they can on their own. (See Exhibit 9.1.)

SCOUTS AND DEALERS

Perhaps the most important element of your winning team of professionals is to have dedicated scouts and dealers working on your behalf. As you recall from Chapter 2, both scouts and dealers can provide you with a steady source of property leads. Leads from these sources, as well as others, are the lifeblood of your business. Without them,

Exhibit 9.1
Your Winning Team
of Professionals

Scouts and Dealers

Office Manager

Property Rehab Manager

Local Lender or Mortgage Broker

Real Estate Attorney

Title Company

Real Estate Agents

it will be very difficult to be successful in the business of flipping properties. You should work to build relationships with several different scouts and dealers. You also need to take time to establish investment criteria that best suit your objectives so that the individuals you are working with know what types of opportunities to present to you. You don't want them spending needless time on deals that you have no interest in. Furthermore, you don't want to waste your time either by looking at deals that don't meet your needs.

The relationship between you and other scouts and dealers is mutually beneficial. The more opportunities they bring you, the more you will buy from them or their recommendations, and the more you buy from them, the more money they will make. It is a win-win relationship. You may also decide to hire a full-time scout of your own. In addition to paying them a small base wage, I recommend implementing an incentive system in which they are rewarded for every deal they bring to you that you end up buying. They will quickly learn exactly what kind of opportunities you are most interested in and bring you only the cream of the crop.

OFFICE MANAGER

An effective office manager is another key individual on your winning team of professionals. Before you can have a good office manager though, you first have to have an office. Most people who invest in real estate start out buying and selling a little at a time. As their capital base grows, so does their ability to increase the volume of transactions. At some point in the process, it will become necessary to discontinue your part-time operation out of your home office and begin a full-time operation out of an office building. When you reach that point in your business, I recommend that one of the first people you hire is an office manager. You can delegate many of the lesser responsibilities to that person, which in turn enables you to focus on growing your business. Office managers can handle many of the more repetitive day-to-day tasks that can take up so much of your time. They can furthermore be trained over time to take on greater responsibilities such as some of the accounting and marketing functions.

A good office manager can also be trained to perform functions like scheduling and coordinating all of the necessary parties involved in a closing, as well as attending the closings for you. You may initially be uncomfortable turning that responsibility over to another person, but after about your fiftieth closing or so, chances are you'll be more receptive to the idea of having someone attend them for you. I find that while most closings go smoothly, they typically require a minimum of no less than two hours of my time. By the time I drive to the title company, wait for the closing officer to finish preparing the documents, sign off on everything, and drive back to my office, I have at least two hours invested in the process, and sometimes more. While selling and closing the deal excites me, I find sitting in title companies to be quite boring. Hire a good office manager and use your time where it counts the most, buying and selling properties.

PROPERTY REHAB MANAGER

I cannot stress enough the importance of hiring a rehab manager. This person will take the "rehab" out of rehabbing for you. The property rehab manager's primary role is to coordinate and schedule the subcontractors for all of the required renovations. A handyman is often the most well-qualified person for this type of job. You want somebody managing the crews who can determine what exactly needs to be done, and then to make sure that the repairs are done correctly. A handyman can also save you money by doing a lot of the smaller repairs himself; however, this depends on the number of houses you have undergoing repairs at any given time. If you have several houses being worked on simultaneously, one rehab manager may not have time to do any of the repairs. On the other hand, if you only have two or three in progress at any given time, then your rehab manager will most likely be able to make some of the repairs while at the same time scheduling the other contractors. Remember that the most effective use of your time is not to fix the houses yourself, but rather to oversee the efforts of those who do. By hiring a property rehab manager, you are, in effect, delegating that responsibility to someone else. This allows you to focus on building your business.

LOCAL LENDER OR MORTGAGE BROKER

Another very important component of your real estate business is financing. For this reason, it is essential for you to have one or more lenders or mortgage brokers as members of your winning team of professionals. You must have access to capital, and preferably to large sources of it. It usually becomes necessary to establish relationships with several lenders or mortgage brokers to meet your growing needs for financing. In the initial stages of your relationship, you will most likely secure financing on a case-by-case basis. As the lender becomes more comfortable with you, however, the process of obtaining financing becomes much easier.

Unless you already have a strong personal balance sheet yourself, these types of relationships are not formed overnight. They can sometimes take years to form. I am very fortunate in that I currently have the ability to pick up the phone and secure financing within about five minutes for many of the projects I am involved in. Access to capital is vital to your success in this business. Work hard to establish sound relationships with lenders in your area who can provide you with the financing needed to enable you to be successful.

REAL ESTATE ATTORNEY

Another member of your winning team of professionals that you will want to consider is a real estate attorney. The yellow pages are full of attorneys and most of them advertise the area of law they specialize in. Look for one that specifically advertises real estate services. A few minutes on the phone with them will give you an idea of their level of expertise. Don't be intimidated by them just because they carry the title of attorney. It is quite likely that you know just as much about real estate in general as they do. You hope, of course, that they are more knowledgeable about real estate law. I prefer to work with attorneys who own investment property themselves. This gives them an added level of experience that real estate attorneys who only practice law do not have. Adding this individual to your team of professionals will provide you with the legal expertise needed from time to time during the course of your business.

TITLE COMPANY

A competent title company is another essential member of your winning team of professionals. While most title companies offer similar services such as providing title insurance and closing services, they vary greatly on the degree to which they can provide those services. Over the years, I have worked with many different title companies. Each one seems to have its own unique set of nuances.

Without mentioning any names, until recently, I had a relationship with a national title company that had a deplorable operations department. The firm's outside salesman contacted me and wooed me over to their company. The salesman, Derek, was himself a shining example of what it means to be customer focused. He was extremely attentive to me individually and was proficient at addressing all of my needs and concerns. "This is great," I thought. "Here's a guy who really cares about his customers and is always willing to go the extra mile for them." What I didn't know, however, was that while Derek was about as good an outside salesman you could hope for, the company's operations department was just the opposite. I sent them seven or eight deals right off the bat and ended up having problems with almost every one of them. I had problems with scheduled closings that had been confirmed for a certain date and then mysteriously disappeared from their book. I had problems with their people in operations who were supposed to be capable of preparing all of the title work, but just couldn't seem to get it right. And finally, I had problems with their closing officers who proved themselves to be incapable. Derek was great. The rest of the company was a mess.

Now that I've lamented over my poor experience with them, let me conclude on a more positive note. The title company that I have since switched to is quite the opposite from the one I recently left. For the most part, I can send them a deal, schedule it, and show up at the closing with everything properly prepared and in order. Although I pay a little more for the title services at this company, it's worth it to me. I don't have near the headaches and frustrations working with them as I did with the previous company. Find a competent title company in your area and include them on your winning team of professionals.

REAL ESTATE AGENTS

Top producing real estate agents are vital elements of your winning team of professionals. You should plan on including as many of them as possible on your team. If an agent knows you are a serious buyer, she will work to bring you the types of deals you are most interested in. As with scouts and dealers, you must establish predetermined criteria that meet your investment objectives for the sales agent. The better they understand exactly what you are looking for, the better they will be able to meet your investment needs.

If you limit yourself to just one agent, then you have only one set of eyes and ears on the lookout for good deals to bring to you. On the other hand, if you enlist the aid of several real estate agents, you will increase the number of potential investment opportunities for you to take advantage of. Each agent has her own sphere of influence, or circle of friends and associates with whom she interacts on a daily basis. You never know when one of them will come across that gem of a deal just waiting to be discovered.

When it becomes time for you to sell your property, you will likely want to have more than one agent working on your behalf then as well. Those of you who are licensed agents are likely to disagree with me on this point, but please allow me to explain. The reason I prefer to use more than one agent is because I know that agents tend to specialize in certain areas by farming specific communities. Yes, I know, you can list the property for sale in the MLS just like any other agent and gain access to a broad spectrum of buyers, which is certainly very important, but unless you are familiar with the area you have the listing in and physically work that area, you are doing your seller a disservice.

I have seen, for example, agents take listings clear across the county and even into the neighboring counties before. These areas may be as far as fifty miles from where they live and work. No matter how hard you try, you can't convince me that you can effectively sell a house for me in an area that you know little or nothing about. Your marketing efforts will be limited to a few newspaper ads and to the MLS. An agent selling in another market that far away is likely to have no personal contacts or relationships in that area. They know absolutely nothing about the town or city except the name of it. They know nothing about the school district, which is vital information to anyone with children. Chances are, they haven't even been to the community except to write the listing agreement. Yet I see this all the time—a real estate sign in a homeowner's yard that I know good and well is not from that area. To be successful in the business of buying and selling investment properties, it is essential for you to include several real estate agents who can create a pipeline of inventory for you, as well as represent you effectively when it becomes time to sell.

In summary, we have examined the merits of building a first-class team of people who can help mobilize you to effectively reach your investment objectives. Each member of the team is vital for your success in the real estate business. You may initially go through a trial and error period in which some members of the team have to be replaced for one reason or another. In time, however, you will eventually assemble a winning team of professionals who, when working together, can help you achieve much more than you could ever hope to on your own.

> **Few people are capable of expressing with equanimity opinions which differ from the prejudices of their social environment. Most people are even incapable of forming such opinions.**
>
> *—Albert Einstein*

Chapter 10

Three Keys to Maximizing Your Potential

There are three important keys that when properly applied will empower you to maximize your potential as it relates to buying and selling houses. In this chapter, I examine several post-entry strategies you should give serious consideration to long before you close on the property. I also analyze the advantages and disadvantages of doing the required repairs yourself, versus hiring the work out. Finally, I review several methods to increase the marketability of your property. The proper and systematic application of the three precepts outlined in this chapter enable you to maximize your potential in the real estate arena. (See Exhibit 10.1.)

POST-ENTRY PLANNING

Your post-entry strategy is the specific plan of action you will take immediately upon the closing of your property. I want to emphasize the word *immediately*. Remember that time is of the essence and every day that passes by without being fully utilized costs you money. This is why you must plan well in advance of the closing date for the work required to prepare the property for its eventual resale. Minimizing the turnaround time on each deal is crucial to helping you maximize your profits.

One of the best ways to begin preparing is by scheduling the contractors who will be making the repairs (assuming you are not doing the work yourself) two to three weeks before the scheduled closing date if possible. Don't make the mistake of waiting until after you close to begin thinking about scheduling. You will lose valuable time by doing so, and remember, time is money because you are paying interest on the borrowed funds. The best time to tentatively begin the scheduling process is when the contractors first

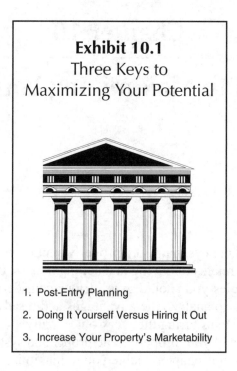

Exhibit 10.1
Three Keys to
Maximizing Your Potential

1. Post-Entry Planning

2. Doing It Yourself Versus Hiring It Out

3. Increase Your Property's Marketability

come out to the property to provide you with bids for the work that must be performed. This information, as you recall, is used in your assessment of the viability of the project. After factoring in all the costs and expenses related to the project, as well as market comparables, then and only then are you able to accurately measure the expected return in profits this particular project will generate.

When you meet with the contractors, you can provide them at that time with a general idea of when you expect to close. Be sure to express to the contractors how important it is to you for them to be available when you need them. Explain to them that you don't like to lose even a single day if possible. Once you have established a firm closing date with the seller and the title company, you can then notify the contractor so as to schedule a specific date and time for him to make the repairs. The key is to establish your post-entry plan well in advance and to be prepared to execute it as soon after the closing as possible.

DOING IT YOURSELF VERSUS HIRING IT OUT

Is it better to do the work yourself and try to save money, or to hire as much of the work out as possible and try to save time? This is a question that many real estate investors struggle with, especially those who are just starting out. While there is no one right answer, it's important to understand the advantages and disadvantages of both methods.

For those of you who may be more mechanically inclined, it is natural for you to feel and believe that you should do as much of the work yourself in an effort to save money. Allow me to share a personal example with you of the differences between two individuals who have different skill sets. The first individual is my brother, Tim, who has very strong mechanical skills and can fix almost anything. In fact, one of my earliest memories of him fixing something occurred when I was about three years old. Tim was around five at the time. I remember coming outside to play one day only to discover that he had taken all of the wheels off of my shiny, red tricycle. Another time, he completely disassembled our swing set. While Tim was exceptionally good at taking things apart, he had not yet learned how to put them back together, thereby rendering my tricycle and the swing set useless. Tim has come a long way since then. Not only has he become an expert at taking things apart, he is now extremely proficient at putting them back together.

The second individual in this example is none other than yours truly. While I lack the natural mechanical skills that Tim has, I do have very good organizational and management skills. I recall in my teenage years that I was always very particular about keeping my bedroom as neat and orderly as possible. I was probably the only child in the family who made his bed without having to be asked to do so. My personality demanded structure and order. Later, my service in the United States Air Force reinforced these concepts, especially the training I received at boot camp (also known as basic training) at Lackland Air Force Base in San Antonio, Texas. Our beds had to be made perfectly with blankets folded taut enough to literally bounce a quarter off it. Everything in our footlockers had to be placed in exact and precise order according to our training manuals. If it wasn't, believe me, you would hear about it from the drill sergeant.

I never will forget one experience in my early days at basic training. I had only been there a few days and had just received my Air Force fatigues, which were all green. Since they were brand new, none of the insignia had been sewn on yet. With our heads freshly shaven and new uniforms adorned with no insignia, we were referred to as *pickles* because that is exactly what we looked like, a bunch of green dill pickles running around. Anyway, being brand new in the service, I was not fully aware of all the rules. My drill sergeant's name was of all names, Sergeant Carter, and believe it or not, he bore a strong resemblance in both manner and appearance to the Sergeant Carter in the old Gomer Pyle TV sitcom. One afternoon while wearing my fatigues, I put a pencil in my shirt pocket. After all, that's what pockets are for, right? Wrong! Little did I know that I was grossly out of uniform. That's right, that little pencil sticking out of my pocket was not supposed to be there, and boy, did Sergeant Carter let me know about it. He literally stood nose to nose with me and bellowed out something like, "Airman, what's wrong with you!?! Don't you know you're out of uniform! You better get that #*!#*!#*! pencil out of your #*!#*!#* pocket and don't ever let me see it in there again!?! Do you understand me!?!" "Yes sir!" came my immediate reply, and believe you me, he never did see that pencil in my pocket again because I wasn't about to put it in there and run the risk of another verbal thrashing. In fact, to this very day, I sometimes have second thoughts about putting a pencil in my shirt pocket.

With Tim's strong mechanical skills, he has quite naturally developed a mindset to fix or repair things himself, including his rental properties. After all, why pay somebody to come in and rehab a house when you can do it yourself and save money? I must say that I have to give him credit for taking on some tough jobs. Over the years, I've observed Tim take on bathroom and kitchen remodeling, replace badly worn flooring, do tile work, along with painting, roofing, plumbing, and air conditioning work. I'm sure I've left some things out of that list, but you can name just about anything having to do with repairing a house and Tim has done it.

While I, on the other hand, have done a few things like painting and mowing the lawn, I don't hesitate to call in the pros to take on the other work. First of all, I don't have the skills necessary to perform some of the more involved repairs, and secondly, I don't have the desire to do them anyway. This is not to say that I couldn't learn how to make some of the more complex repairs, but I have no desire to. As one who is naturally well organized and possesses good management skills, I much prefer to call in the proper tradespeople and pay them to do the work. I consider this to be a much better use of my time than trying to do the work myself. I naturally enjoy planning and preparing for upcoming events, so long before I close on a property, I take time to ensure that my tradespeople, who are all more skilled than I am when it comes to fixing houses, are ready to perform the work as soon as I need them. For me, this is a much more efficient process than trying to do everything myself.

I recall one time in particular when Tim had just purchased a single family house that he was going to renovate and subsequently flip. About the same time, I had just purchased an apartment building that was also in need of some extensive rehab work. Tim, Mr. Do-It-Yourself, was committed to doing most of the rehab work by himself.

Although he did have a little bit of help, Tim did most of the work on his own. I, on the other hand, Mr. Hire-Everything-Out, was committed to doing none of the work myself and hiring all of it out. Since Tim had a full time job, he was only able to work on the house after work and on weekends. As I recall, he spent every bit of three to four months of giving up nights and weekends to make the necessary renovations before finally completing all of the work and getting the house ready for resale. Meanwhile, since I already had all of the bids in for the required repairs on my apartment building before I had even closed, I was ready to go the day after closing. Within about thirty to forty-five days, the trades were completely finished with the repair work and my property was ready for resale. In addition, since the building was fully occupied by tenants, I began initiating increases in the rents, which were justified by the recently completed improvements.

This example is meant to be an observation of fact only and is certainly not intended as a criticism of my brother, Tim, whom I love dearly. It is instead intended to illustrate the differences in the way the same tasks can be accomplished. Tim has his way of doing things, and I have my way of doing things. While Tim is saving money, I am saving time. Since to me, time is money, I am really saving both time and money. To flip properties on a large scale, you cannot possibly do all of the required repairs yourself. You must decide if you are in the business of fixing houses, or if you are in the business of buying and selling houses. If it is the latter, then you cannot afford to spend your time doing the repairs. The only exception to this may be when you are first getting started and are doing only one or two houses a year. At that level, you can probably justify taking the time to do some of the work on your own, but once you start ramping up your operation, you must begin scaling back your hands-on involvement and take care to make the best and most valuable use of your time, which is to organize and manage. Once you have your tradespeople in place and have fine-tuned your system, you then have the ability to do 10, 20, 50, or even 100 houses per year.

Although it may initially appear that an investor would be giving up some of the profits by hiring out the rehab work, this is not necessarily the case. The key is to purchase the property at the right price to begin with. In Chapter 6, I described and provided several examples of appropriate analysis methods to be used when selecting an investment property. I recommend that you factor into your analysis of potential investment opportunities the cost of having contractors do the required repairs. If your analysis does not provide an acceptable rate of return on your invested capital, then you simply pass on it and move on to the next deal. Do *not* fall into the trap of rationalizing your analysis by saying that since you really like this deal, you will go ahead and do all of the painting, for example, just to make the numbers work out. You are much better off passing on it and waiting for another opportunity, for it will surely come.

INCREASE YOUR PROPERTY'S MARKETABILITY

Congratulations! You've worked hard over the last few weeks or months renovating your investment property. You have increased the house's value by a significant amount, and it is now time to sell it and capture the profit margin in it that you have created! There are several things you can do to enhance the marketability of your property and to increase the exposure it receives. They include preplanning, heightened visibility through the MLS, offering a marketable product, pricing your property competitively, and offering incentives. (See Exhibit 10.2.)

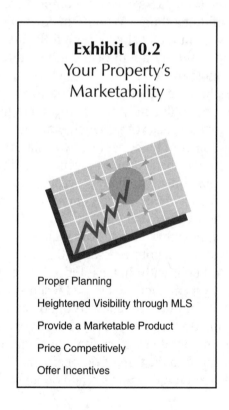

Exhibit 10.2
Your Property's
Marketability

Proper Planning

Heightened Visibility through MLS

Provide a Marketable Product

Price Competitively

Offer Incentives

1. Preplanning—Proper planning from start to finish is essential for you to be successful in this business. This includes planning for the sale of your property. After all, you are not rewarded for your efforts until the sale has been completed. Only then do you profit from your labors. You may be thinking that of course you are going to plan to sell your house, but you'd be surprised at how many investors wait until they get to that phase of the process before they even begin to consider how they will sell their property. In the Post-Entry section of this chapter, I discussed the necessity of scheduling your subcontractors long before the actual closing occurred so that you would be ready to go with your improvements immediately following the consummation of the sale. The proper planning of your exit strategy is equally important, if not more so, than the post-entry strategy. Ideally, you should begin thinking about how you are going to sell your house even before you purchase it. You should have already taken the steps to establish a well-defined sales plan so that you are ready to implement it immediately at the appropriate time.

2. Heightened visibility through the Multiple Listing Service (MLS)—The Multiple Listing Service, or MLS, is a requisite tool to provide your property with maximum exposure. This means, of course, that you will have to list your property for sale with a licensed real estate agent, unless you happen to be a licensed agent yourself. When your house is placed in the MLS, you gain immediate access to hundreds and even thousands of sales agents who have a potential interest in your property. Any one of them may have a prospective buyer with whom they are working who may be interested in exactly what you are selling. You cannot afford not to have your house listed for sale in the MLS. Remember that you are in the business of buying houses, refurbishing them, and selling them as quickly as possible. Your role in this business should be that of a manager. You are there to facilitate the process and to ensure that things happen when they are supposed to happen. You can certainly make the argument that you can save money by not having to pay the sales agent's commission, but that would be a weak argument at best. Using that logic, you are reverting to the "I can do it myself and save money" mode. Trying to sell the house yourself and save money is no different from trying to do all of the repairs yourself and save money. That rationale is shortsighted and will prevent you from maximizing your potential in this business. If you are not a licensed real estate agent already, I recommend you find a top-producing agent who has a proven track record of being a mover and shaker. In other words, look for a competent agent who is serious about helping you sell your properties as quickly as possible. In Chapter 2, I described the role of the dealer as it relates

to flipping properties. I mentioned that while dealers can be a good source for bringing you investment opportunities, they can also be a good source for selling those properties for you once the necessary improvements have been made. Dealers are particularly fond of this type of relationship because it enables them to double dip, meaning that not only do they earn a commission when they sell the property *to* you, they also earn a commission when they sell the property *for* you. If you have a good relationship with a sales agent or dealer and are listing several properties with her on a continuing basis, chances are she will be willing to negotiate her fee structure with you. The most important thing for you here, though, is to maximize the visibility of the property you are selling so that you can gain ready access to as large of a pool of buyers as possible.

3. Offering a marketable product—To further enhance the marketability of your house, you must offer a product that people want. As simple as this may sound, this is an important point that shouldn't be taken lightly. Recall from Chapter 3 that as an investor who is in the business of flipping properties, you are not interested in carrying your inventory any longer than necessary. That means you should carefully study the area you are considering investing in to determine which vicinities are selling with the shortest average number of days on the market. The type of location best suited for selling your properties in a timely manner is a neighborhood that is typically between 10 and 30 years old. These neighborhoods represent where the average middle class citizen lives. The ideal location is one in which the majority of homes are well maintained and in an area that is not suffering from functional obsolescence. The area should be well established, have good schools nearby, and continue to have homes that sell in a shorter-than-average number of days compared to surrounding communities. Characteristics of this kind of neighborhood often include mature landscaping, pristine lawns, and homes that are well cared for. Be sure that the house you purchase fits in with the rest of the houses in this kind of neighborhood. I have seen, for example, an ultra contemporary house in a mostly traditional neighborhood sit on the market for much longer than other houses in the same neighborhood. You can't wait, of course, to make these kinds of decisions when it's time to sell. They must be made long before you even buy. In addition, your investment property should be presented to prospective buyers in its most favorable condition. Common sense necessitates that after all of the subcontractors have finished their work, you must be willing to spend a little extra on a good cleaning service to put the finishing touches on your house to make it really look like new. House cleaning services typically do not cost much and will be money well spent.

4. Competitive pricing—If you did your homework before purchasing your investment property, you should already be intimately familiar with pricing in your market. I recommend making your house available for sale at a price just below market. As an investor who is in the business of flipping properties, you do not have time to sit on your house for an indefinite period in an attempt to hold out for top dollar. Remember that you have carrying costs including interest, taxes, and insurance, so the quicker you sell, the quicker you can relieve yourself of those obligations. In addition, you have a lost opportunity cost, meaning that as long as your investment capital is tied up in one property, you are limited in your ability to take advantage of other opportunities. You have become capitally constrained. Time is money in this business, so the quicker you can sell your property, the more money you will be capable of making.

5. Offering incentives—If you are like most people, chances are, you are motivated by money. Your prospective buyers will be motivated by money, too. You can use many different types of incentives that have some monetary value to encourage prospective buyers to purchase your house instead of the one down the street. For example, you can offer a credit at closing for landscaping, which will enable the buyer to help beautify the exterior of their new home shortly after they move in. For many buyers, especially those who are first-time home buyers, it takes everything they have financially just to move in, so they will greatly appreciate having a little extra at closing. Whether the money is used for landscaping or any other purpose is really irrelevant. Your objective is to give them a reason to buy your house now rather than to continue to shop around. Other incentives include agreeing to pay the buyer's closing costs (or a portion of them), offering to throw in a free appliance package, or giving them a gift certificate from a local moving company to help offset their moving expenses.

In summary, we have discussed the three most important keys that when properly applied will enable you to maximize your potential in the real estate business. We examined a variety of post-entry strategies, analyzed the advantages and disadvantages of doing the necessary repairs yourself versus hiring the work out and finally, reviewed several methods to increase the marketability of your property. The three principles outlined in this chapter will enable you to maximize your potential in the real estate arena when regularly and consistently applied. Each of these essential elements takes time to master. You must be willing to not only apply yourself, but to be patient as you do so. Life is full of adversities and challenges that can test the measure of who we are. We must be willing to meet these challenges with courage and determination. We must be prepared to respond, not to react, to adverse circumstances. When we rise up to meet whatever challenges life presents us with, then and only then do we become victorious. Then and only then are our characters and our moral fiber strengthened. Then and only then can we become the kind of person that we truly wish to be.

> I hope that I shall always possess firmness and virtue enough to maintain what I consider the most enviable of all titles, the character of an honest man.
>
> —*George Washington*

PART IV

It's a New Day in Real Estate

In Chapters 11 through 14, I have included a special section taken from our weekly radio program, "It's a New Day in Real Estate." The radio show is a half-hour program produced by the Symphony Homes Family of Companies, in which I am one of the co-hosts. The program is prerecorded once each week, and runs four times on the weekend on two different stations. The radio program provides our company with a forum to share ideas covering a variety of real estate–related topics with tens of thousands of listeners each and every week. It has turned out to be one of the most effective marketing tools we use because we are able to share information about the real estate market, housing, buying and selling, investing, home improvement tips, financing suggestions, and a number of other real estate topics in a manner that is presented as informational. Rather than push our products and services in the traditional commercialized environment (which we also do in other media outlets), we share information and ideas while very subtly suggesting that, as the local experts, our company is available to help with any needs our listeners may have.

The following chapters are from a special eight-week investor series. The series was designed for the beginning investor and covers a wide variety of topics. The chapters feature me, an office manager from Real Estate One Symphony Homes, Carol Eberhardt, and John Sticker, the previous owner of Preferred Mortgage, Home of Loan John. John's background lends itself to the financial structure of almost any transaction, which as many of you know, is essential to being able to successfully put deals together.

The information shared in the following chapters is provided in a dialogue format as taken from the radio program. I hope you enjoy reading and learning from these chapters as much as we enjoyed recording them!

Chapter 11

Radio Program: Weeks 1 and 2

INVESTMENT WEEK #1

STEVE: Our focus for this radio program is going to be on investing in real estate, and particularly here in the Genesee County market. As you indicated, this is such a great time to begin taking a serious look at investing. We know that the market is a little bit soft right now; however, we are very optimistic about the 2007 and 2008 outlook. We expect to see price appreciation and improvement in prices just because of some of the things that we see going on in housing—the demand is somewhat stable and the inventory of available housing stock is beginning to come down, thereby decreasing the difference in the supply and demand ratio. So right now, although prices are a little bit soft, it's a great time to be able to get into the market and to be able to make investments.

Today we want to talk about price appreciation over time. I've got a chart here in front of me that shows the historical new home sales average price over a 40-year period. The average sales price in percentage growth indicated in the chart is from 1963 to the year 2002, so it covers about a 40-year period. What this chart shows us is that the average sales price back in 1963 of a new home was $19,300. So, Carol, how would you like to go out and buy a new home today for $19,300!

CAROL: Actually, I bought my first house for right around that price.

STEVE: Probably not going to happen today, though.

CAROL: No, Steve, you're right. Not for that price!

JOHN: It's only 40 years ago! That's what's so amazing to me.

STEVE: That's 40 years ago, well, in the year 2002, the average sales price for a new home had risen from the $19,300 to $228,300. That's a total increase, according to the chart here, a total increase in value of almost 1,100 percent over that 40-year period. And if you take that out and divide that number and annualize it, then you come out with an annualized growth rate of about 6.37 percent. So that really is not that bad, compared to the stock market, to other investment vehicles, and other investment opportunities that you might have.

CAROL: Well, I think it's fabulous, because history tells us this. I think it's really important for anyone who's thinking about investing, even quite frankly in the stock market to the housing market, is history. We don't change the numbers. It is what it is, and we know that *historically* things rally, things come back, things continue to grow, and that's the important thing to remember. Get out of your head what the media is telling you today and be smart enough to analyze what history is saying you should do.

STEVE: You know, Carol, that's a great point. If you were around 40 years ago and happened to be in a position to buy five new homes for an average sales price of $19,300, their value today would be worth a little over $1.1 million. So just by buying five new homes back in 1963, today you could own them free and clear, and you'd have your retirement portfolio right there with just five rental houses.

JOHN: Steve, I think it is so important that as we go through this and we're going to explain all the different ways in how being involved in real estate helps with your finances. But here we do have a 40-year investment with the good, the bad, and the ugly, and the average is still over 6 percent, almost 6 percent that the house is going to appreciate each year, and of course we're going to get into the tax incentives that are out there. So it's actually much larger than the 6 and a half percent that you're seeing in the annualized growth rate of that home. But you know, the government gives us a lot of extra reasons to be involved in real estate, and we're going to talk about those in just a bit.

STEVE: That's right, John. Let's move on now to the second benefit that we've identified here to owning real estate and investment property. The second one is that as you purchase a home, most homes are set up on 30-year fixed notes. Not all of them are, of course, as some might be 20 years, some might be some of the newer mortgage products, like the 40-year, but as you're paying that monthly payment, each month a little bit of the principal portion is paid down. Initially in the first few years, most of the payment goes to interest, but by about the tenth or twelfth year, you begin paying a little bit more toward the principal balance, and toward the end of the 30-year period, most of the payment is being applied directly toward the principal. So by the end of that 30-year period, you have completely paid for the house. So that's the second benefit. The first benefit, once again, is that we get the natural price appreciation that occurs over time in the value of real estate and then secondly, as we have a tenant in there, it is the tenant who is actually paying for this house and they're reducing the debt, or the loan amount, that is owed on it, so at the end of the 30-year period or 20-year, depending on how you make your payments, you can actually own that real estate free and clear.

JOHN: And that's what's so beautiful about being involved in real estate! You are leveraging an asset, the house, to get the capital to purchase it so that you can have a tenant make the payment for you to create a retirement or investment portfolio—an asset that is, in fact, paid off in 30 years if you did a traditional 30-year mortgage. You're actually leveraging an asset using somebody else's money and then you're going to have a tenant make that payment for you to pay it off. And that's what makes real estate such a viable option for building wealth.

STEVE: You're exactly right, John. Let's move on now to the third benefit that we've identified here. And this has to do with what you alluded to earlier, which is the reduction in tax liability. The IRS code actually requires this. Folks, it's not even an option! We're actually required to depreciate assets such as real estate investments, and in particular rental houses. The average depreciation schedule now, as I recall, is over a 27-and-a-half-year period, so you're going to depreciate the value of your rental property over a 27-year period, approximately. And without getting into the mechanics of how that actually works, let me just say that what this does for you is that by owning rental property, it actually sets up a built-in tax shelter. You're able to depreciate these assets, which lowers the amount of taxes that you will owe. So that truly is a very real benefit, especially to some of you who may be in a 30 or 35 percent tax bracket. You want to do everything you can to reduce your overall tax liability and your exposure to Uncle Sam. Carol, I don't know about our listeners here, but I know I don't get overly excited about writing those tax checks each year!

CAROL: And I'll tell you I have a conversation with my tax person every year about what I can do to get this liability down, so this is a perfect time to pick up the phone, talk to your tax person, and educate yourself on how this is going to benefit you personally. I think you might be surprised at how much money you're going to save and how seriously you really do need to think about investing in real estate at this particular time. Remember the time is right now and we've all been in that place where we've second-guessed or we've been a Monday morning quarterback and we said if we would have only bought that McDonald's stock when French fries were thirteen cents. We'd be millionaires today, but you can't do it unless you take that first step.

STEVE: That's right, folks. You've got to be willing to take that first step and have the courage to get out there. And you know, if you're still a little apprehensive and you just want to talk to somebody about it, any one of us here on the panel on our program today would be more than happy to talk to you. We've got all the tools, all the resources, in place. We can help you with the financing, we can help you find rental properties, we have quite a few in inventory ourselves, most of which are already leased out. You actually even have the opportunity to buy rental houses with tenants already in them! I know that's a concern for some people, because they have these preconceived fears of, "Wow, if I'm going to buy this rental house, what happens if I can't rent it out?" Well, don't worry about that. We've got tenants in place in most of our houses and we can easily fill the rest. We even have a property management service in place. We can provide you with a turnkey service and all you're doing is buying these rental houses and you really don't even have to hardly give them a second thought. Once again, we can provide the tenants because we already have the property management service in place. All the things that make investing in real estate very easy for you.

Now let's move on to the fourth benefit of investing in real estate that we've identified, and that is the fact that because you're charging rent each month, you want to buy your properties right so that you have what we refer to as a positive cash flow. That means that the difference between what the tenant is paying, and let's just pick a number and say $700 of monthly rent that your tenant is paying, is greater than your monthly expenses. So your mortgage payment, let's just say, for example, might be $500 a month, and you might have additional $50–$100 a month on average in maintenance and repairs and things like that. So in this example you'd have a total liability of $600 a month. But you would have $700 of income, rental income, coming in to offset that. And so although $100 a month isn't a whole lot, you have at least created a positive cash flow situation. And now, let's just think, that's with one house. If you multiply that times 10 houses or 20 houses, that $100 grows significantly. So now you've got possibly $1,000 a month or $2,000 or $3,000 a month in net positive cash flow, and so you know, once again, this is another great reason to own real estate.

JOHN: Folks, I can't encourage you enough. Now is the time! Usually, one of two things are happening. If rates are really good, the prices of houses are usually being driven upward because of the fact that rates are really good, so you're usually paying a premium for the house. In reverse order what tends to happen is if the housing market is getting a little soft, then the economy usually is soft at that time and interest rates are starting to rise, so then you're paying a little bit more for the mortgage if you're getting a good deal on the house. But right now, folks, you're getting rates near historic lows *and* you're getting a huge opportunity because the inventory out there is large. You're getting a great deal on the house, you're getting great pricing on your mortgage. And you know, Steve, as we go through these four benefits, that's what I love about this! Now let me get this straight. We get to buy a house, and, of course, that house historically goes up in value over 6 percent a year. We then go ahead with a mortgage payment that's being made on the house by our tenants, so we're reducing the principal on the loan balance. Then we have the tax shelter of being able to write off all the expenses and reduce our tax liability on our own income and the property to almost zero. And then this investment is going to further increase from the positive cash flow on a monthly basis. Can it get any better than that?!

STEVE: You are exactly right, John. That's four great reasons to get into the rental market right now, folks.

INVESTMENT WEEK #2

CAROL: I'm Carol Eberhart, and I'm with Real Estate One Symphony Homes. I'm here with Steve Berges from Symphony Homes and John Stricker, Loan John from Preferred Mortgage, and we're here today for part two of our series in understanding and investing in real estate. And one of the reasons we decided to do that is because right now is the absolute prime time to get yourself educated and to stick your toe in the water. Isn't that right, Steve?

STEVE: You better know it, Carol. Today we want to talk with the folks about what we refer to as the OPM principle, and we're going to define that here in just a few minutes. But what I want to share with our listening audience, first of all, is how I initially got my start in real estate. A number of years ago, when I was in the Air Force, I came across a book at the bookstore. Some of you may remember this, or may have read it, but at the time it was a pretty popular book. It was written by a man named Mark O. Haroldsen, and the name of the book is *How to Wake Up the Financial Genius Inside You.* Well, I'll tell you what. I picked that book up and just couldn't put it down. There was a lot of great material in there. The book was about a young real estate investor who by the age of 31 had acquired enough real estate to declare himself a millionaire. He had been very successful in it and then as many real estate investors do, they go on to write books and teach other people the secrets of their success. Kind of like what we're doing here with our listening audience today. But you know, I want to share something that really was the key to my success in real estate. And it's all about a chapter in Mark O. Haroldsen's book called "The Lever and the Fulcrum." In chapter six of his book, and this was published back in about 1976 or thereabouts, so it's been a few years, but Mr. Haroldsen writes, "Archimedes, the Greek mathematician and physicist, calculated the law of the lever. He is reported to have said that if he had a lever long enough and a place to stand, he alone could lift the world." In real estate, the same principle applies. If you have a long enough lever, you can lift or buy properties that are so large that you heretofore have not even dreamed of such purchases. The OPM formula, other people's money, is the formula for using leverage.

CAROL: So when you hear the term *leverage,* people leveraging their money, this is what they're talking about.

STEVE: That's right, Carol. He goes on to explain in the chapter about the differences of what a fulcrum is and what a lever is. Mr. Haroldsen describes a fulcrum as being the support, or the base on which the lever turns, or is supported. And so the fulcrum is what supports the lever. And in the case of real estate, the fulcrum is the use of other people's money. So, on one end of the lever is your initial investment, however small that may be. It might be $1,000, it might be $500, or it might be more than that. On the other end of the lever is the real estate, and so in the center you have the fulcrum, which supports that and allows you to lift, or leverage, that real estate. There are a couple of different approaches that you can use for leverage and they generally take the form of either debt or equity. Let me just give you a couple of examples. Debt is usually the most common type of financing, and it's provided in some form of a loan or investment financing, which our friend John here can tell us all about. But there are lots of ways to acquire debt to be used to purchase real estate. Some of these include using the traditional financing sources you might have depending on what kind of line of credit you have, maybe credit cards or home equity loans, family members, or friends who may be willing to loan you some money. And then you're financing with that debt. One of the key differences between debt and equity is that debt typically requires some kind of a monthly payment. Not always, but it oftentimes does. There's a fixed rate of interest that's typically applied to the mortgage instrument. In some cases, it may actually be if it's an adjustable rate investment instrument, that the rate would adjust periodically up or down. John, I think you can tell us about these option ARMs, which are sometimes available. They give investors the benefit of having a greater cash flow in the initial stages because the interest rate is lower.

JOHN: Absolutely Steve. You know, we use a lot of these different types of programs because unfortunately, a lot of times when you're just starting out you have the least amount of cash to work with. It's almost like a graduated lease that goes up over time when people are starting out in a retail space. So what we've done and made available for investors is debt financing with lower interest rates and lower payments. And a lot of times we'll lock these in for five years and the payment will gradually get bigger each year, but what it allows you to do is step into an investment with very little money down and a low monthly payment. As the years go by, the payments and the interest rates get higher, but it allows you to step into an investment vehicle such as a rental house with little or no money down. The monthly payments are low at first, so as you're getting started in the real estate business, you aren't massively undercapitalized. This enables you to survive and get the project rolling, and then, of course, turn and acquire more properties over time.

STEVE: Right, so even though the monthly payment may be going up in subsequent years, let's say years three, four, and five, to offset that, you also have your rental income that's going up as well. So if you started out leasing a rental house that's $700 a month, the next year you may bump the rent to $720 or $725, and the next year it may go to $740 or $750, just depending on what the market will bear. That will help you keep up with those payments as the interest rate increases, but it's a great opportunity as John said to get started with a lower rate and to be able to establish a positive cash flow. Now one of the disadvantages is that debt must be serviced and so as we've already indicated, oftentimes you are required to make monthly payments on that debt. If you compare that to an equity investment, equity usually takes the form of somebody such as a friend or partner or family member who has cash that they can put up. But generally, when you are investing in real estate with equity, you are not having to make monthly payments, so that gives you the benefit of immediate cash flow. But one of the primary disadvantages of equity is that shareholders generally want a larger return of the profits.

JOHN: Yes, and of course, there's less risk when using equity financing, but then there's also less upside when there's less risk for you. That means when you're doing equity financing, you're sharing that equity over time, whether it's quarterly, semiannually, or annually, where you'll be taking a portion of the profits and the equity of properties being gained and you'll have to share that with your stockholders and maybe other people, which, of course, does reduce the amount that you'll generally keep.

STEVE: That's an excellent point, John. Let's move back to investing with debt and talk about that for just a minute. If we compared an investment in real estate to an investment in, let's say, the stock market. Let's just assume we've got $100,000 to work with and we're going to buy some shares of stock ABC. Well, generally John, as you know, when you're investing in the stock market you can't obtain the kind of leverage that you can investing in real estate.

JOHN: No you can't. That means if you want to buy $100,000 worth of stock, guess what? You've got to have $100,000! And in real estate, this is the best part about this and why I got into this market. I absolutely love and have a passion for this. If you want to buy a $100,000 house, hey, you know what? I can do it with either zero money down or 10 or 20 percent, but the maximum people generally come up with is 20 percent. So you want to buy a $100,000 investment, for example, and assume the buyer puts down 10 percent, that's only $10,000 compared to the stock market. Now, Steve, you and I both know you can't go to your stock broker and say you want to buy a $100,000 worth of stock and by the way, I have only $10,000.

STEVE: Yes, now you do have that opportunity through the use of highly leveraged instruments like options and things like that. But those are really for the skilled and more astute investors who really understand the risk and nature of options. And I'm sure some of our listeners are quite skilled at doing those things. I know that I personally haven't been that successful investing in stocks and more times than not, I've lost money. My success has been in the real estate market. But to carry your example a little bit further, let's say we had this $100,000 asset that we're buying and we have a choice of purchasing stock for $100,000, which requires 100 percent of our investment, or we have the opportunity to purchase a rental house for $100,000 and we're going make the assumption here that we only have to put down 10 percent. So here we have an investment that's only required $10,000 of our money versus one that has required $100,000. Let's just look at a typical example here using 5 percent. If our investment of $10,000 grew at an annual rate of 5 percent, now that 5 percent is on the overall purchase price, so that's 5 percent on the growth of the asset. The asset at the end of one year is now worth $105,000, and if you look at just that $5,000, that represents your gain on the $10,000 investment that you put in. So it's really simple math here. Five thousand over 10,000 is a 50 percent return on the investment. Now, John, let's compare that to the same investment that we made in the stock market, and our investment grows from $100,000 to $105,000 and now our gain is represented by taking 5,000 over 100,000, because that's what we had to come up with, and that gives us a simple rate of return of only 5 percent. That's about what you would get in an average CD or money market account. So given a choice, John, would you rather have a 50 percent return on your investment or a 5 percent return?

JOHN: You know, Steve, I'm going to have to go with the 50 percent return on invest-ment. What is so dynamic and so incredible about this annual appreciation rate is that using the laws of leverage, we're able to buy an asset that's worth $100,000 using $10,000 and as we talked last week, the housing market has grown on average 6.5 percent annually over the last 40 years. So even the 5 percent is actually smaller than the historic 40-year average. Basically if history tells us the future, you have a guaranteed return on your investment of 50 percent, as indicated in this example.

STEVE: And that's only for the very first year. If you carry that a little bit further, and let's look at our table here. When we compare this in year 25, the investment has now grown in value by using simply 5 percent, from $105,000 or actually $100,000 in year zero, all the way up to $338,000, representing a total return of 2,386% over a 25-year period. You cannot get that in the stock market.

JOHN: And Steve, this is exactly why in the "Forbes Top 100 Wealthiest People of the World" over half of those people are real estate moguls. And you know what? You start out one house at a time. That's what I tell my investors all the time, "You know, we're going do it real slow, one house at a time, and we're just going to keep on moving forward."

CAROL: And that's the point, John. The first jump off the curb is the hardest, but once you do it one time and understand the economics of it, and quite frankly, being hooked up with a company like Real Estate One–Symphony Homes, where you're able to get the jump on the housing market, gives you all the more advantage. Investors get the inside track on what's going on in the market, and this allows them to make intelligent decisions rather easily with some good solid counseling on our part, which helps them all the more.

STEVE: You're exactly right, Carol. Now, Carol and John, I've got a question here for you, and I'm going to give you each a choice. Here's your choice: If I give you the opportunity to work for me for $1,000 a day for 35 days, now that's sounds pretty good, $1,000 per day. Not too many people make that kind of money. Okay, that's choice number one, I'm going to pay you $1,000 a day for 35 days. Now here's choice number two: I'm going to pay you one penny on day one, and each day for 35 days I'm going to double your wage. That means on day two I'm going to pay you two cents, on day three I'm going to pay you four cents, and so on until day 35. Now which choice sounds better? You know with the $1,000 per day, you've got $35,000 at the end of the period. Which one of those sounds like the better choice?

JOHN: Over 35 days, I would have to believe the $1,000.

STEVE: That $1,000 sounds pretty good, doesn't it?

CAROL: That sounds right to me!

STEVE: $35,000! Sign me up!

JOHN: Let's do it!

STEVE: Well, let's take a look at the math here. We actually have some tables to compare these two choices. At the end of day eight, we've got $8,000 on choice one, and on choice number two, with doubling our one penny, we're up to $2.55. Okay, choice number one's looking pretty good. Let's look at day 16. We're up to $16,000 on choice number one, and we're up to $652 on choice number two. That $16,000 is looking pretty good to me!

JOHN: Yes, it's looking pretty strong.

STEVE: Now let's move down to day 24. We're at $24,000 on choice number one, but look what has happened to choice number two, where our investment by the magic of compound interest has now grown from the one penny a day to $167,000.

CAROL: Oh, you're making that up, Steve!

STEVE: No, Carol. Do the math. It works out! And let's move on to day number 35. We know, of course, we've got $35,000 on choice number one but look at choice number two at $342,255,000! So, I'll tell you what! Although the choice wasn't clear before, it sure is now. The rate of $1,000 a day sounded pretty good at first, but that really pales in comparison to choice number two, which started out at a meager one penny a day. That penny a day compounded at a rate of 100 percent grew to more than an incredible $342 million.

JOHN: That's absolutely incredible! And folks, that's why it's so important. If you want to make the leap and get into the real estate market, give us a call right now at 1-866-LOANJOHN. That's 1-866-LOANJOHN. We can show you how to take advantage of the principle of leveraging money to use to buy an asset that is going to have gains so that you can create millions of dollars in wealth for yourself. As a matter of fact, we have a segment next week that's called "How to Build a 10-Million Dollar Retirement Portfolio," so be sure to tune in next week! You're listening to "It's a New Day in Real Estate" and we'll be back in just a moment.

Chapter 12

Radio Program: Weeks 3 and 4

INVESTMENT WEEK #3

CAROL: It *is* a new day in real estate, and we're back again talking about investing in the real estate market and what it takes to do that. And we're lucky to have Steve Berges, who is the broker of Real Estate One Symphony Homes, with us. As always, and fortunately for us, Steve is the expert in the investing market. He's written lots of books on the subject.

STEVE: And while we're on the topic of building wealth, today we're going to talk about how to build a $10 million retirement portfolio.

JOHN: Steve, I was looking at this and looking at your table and chart. Now folks, you want to be sure and listen up, get your pen, get your paper, really make sure you make it to this investment seminar because this is the yellow brick road. All you have to do is follow it and Steve is going to make you a multimillionaire if you do this. And it's a fact proven by history, and of course, history tells us a lot about the future, so listen up to what he has to tell you. It's how to build a $10 million retirement portfolio by simply investing in real estate. Steve, what's the first step in this exciting process of building a retirement portfolio of this magnitude?

STEVE: Well, the first thing we need to understand here is that building a $10 million portfolio does not happen overnight. We're not here to sell any kind of get-rich-quick schemes or anything like that. We want our folks to understand that just like anything else, if you want to get good at it, you have to apply yourself and it takes time.

CAROL: Well, you have to educate yourself.

STEVE: Yes, you have to be educated and informed. If you want to be the star basketball player on a team, it's not going to happen overnight. You have to work hard, you have to practice every day, you have to get out there and shoot the hoop and do everything that it takes to be a star. And it's no different from applying yourself in building a retirement portfolio, especially one of this magnitude. So let's just take a minute to review a table I have here that we can step through and help our listeners understand how this exciting process works. To begin with, we have some assumptions that we've made. We're going to assume that our investor, Mr. Investor, is going to purchase one rental house for $200,000 a year for 10 years. So, one house a year for 10 years at $200,000 per house. Remember now that a rental house in your area could be more or less than that. In Oakland County, that would probably be about right. In California, that's probably going to be low. But, that's the assumption that we've made. We're going to invest in one rental house per year for 10 years. Then we're going to quit buying rental houses so that we'll have a total of only 10 houses all together.

JOHN: Steve, now you've really piqued my curiosity. I'm going to buy one house a year as the proposed investor at $200,000 per year. I'm going to buy houses—one a year for 10 years, and you're telling me that at some point in time in my life, I have the potential to have a $10 million retirement portfolio?

STEVE: You better believe it, John!

JOHN: All right, you have to walk me through this and tell me how this works. I can't believe that by investing in only 10 houses, a person can amass a fortune that size!

STEVE: These are not overly aggressive assumptions that I'm making here. These are, in fact, fairly conservative assumptions. Okay, let's just walk through this with our listeners. We're going to buy one house a year for 10 years and then we're going to quit buying houses and the estimated average value is $200,000. Now we talked—I think it was last week or the week before—about some of the benefits of buying and investing in real estate and one of those was just through simple price appreciation. We've established that over the last 40 years the average historical percentage gain in value is about 6.37 percent. So I've used a value and annual growth rate of only 6.37 percent. I think you would agree with me, John, that's not an overly aggressive number.

JOHN: No, it's not. It's actually just as you said, quite conservative.

STEVE: For some markets, that's low, very low, and in some markets that's about the average. But over a 40-year period, 6.37 percent is the average. So, if we buy one house a year for 10 years, each house will grow in value. For example, house number one purchased in year one at the end of that year, using the factor of 6.37 percent, has grown a little over $12,000 in value. And now house number two is going to do the same thing. So at the end of year number three when you've got three houses that you've purchased, you now have $39,000 in value simply from price appreciation. If you then just walk up the scale, by the end of year 10, your value, again just through simple price appreciation—this does not include, John, all the other benefits that we talked about in buying and owning real estate. So at the end of year 10 . . .

CAROL: And you're not even talking about tax benefits or anything like that?

STEVE: No, it's just simple math and growing and increasing in value through price appreciation. We're now up to $682,000 at the end of year 10. By year 12, here's the number that everybody seems to shoot for. They say "Wow, I want to be a millionaire." Hey, we want you to be millionaires! At the end of year 12, if you follow this simple formula, this very simple strategy, the value that these houses have appreciated or grown in value is $1,035,000. And now let's look at . . . we'll step this up a little bit, by year 17, you hit the $2 million mark. By year 21, you hit $3.2 million, and it just goes right on up the ladder from there, four million, five million, six million. So the $10 million retirement portfolio that we're referring to is actually in year 35. Now you say, "Hold on a minute, I don't know if I have 35 years to wait around for a $10 million portfolio." Well, folks, if you take the steps now, you don't have to wait for 35 years. Let's pose the question another way. If you don't take action now, what are you going to have in 35 years? The answer is—nothing. So ask yourself the question: Would you rather have $10 million at the end of 35 years, or would you rather have nothing?

JOHN: Well, it sounds to me like they can't afford *not* to do something, Steve.

CAROL: Well, I think the great thing about this, and Steve and I were talking about this the other day in the office, is understanding that as you start buying houses and you think "How am I ever going to be able to afford to buy 10 houses? It's just not going to happen." Well, the reality of it is that you're building equity in the first houses that you buy, so can't you use the leverage of the equity in those houses, Steve, to help you purchase the next one?

STEVE: Well, that's actually a very good question for John because John, the master of finance, can teach us all about refinancing and pulling cash out of these deals as the assets grow in value. And so John, I know you've got some help for our listeners.

JOHN: Absolutely, Steve! Our listening audience absolutely can use this. As we look at this, if it's just a simple 30-year loan, at year 35 you're going to have 5 of those houses completely paid for. The other thing that this table is not taking into account are the tax depreciation benefits and the write-offs that you get, as well as the gains that you're going to be making by paying down the principal over the next 35 years. Also, the fact that we will be pulling that equity out because it does you no good to let it just sit there, and putting that equity to work. We talked a week ago about compound interest. Folks, it works the same way when you flip it the other way. Compound income and having that equity go to work for you to generate a compound interest rate in the positive direction adds up as quickly as it does when you're paying that interest. When you take all of these benefits into consideration, Carol, this is an extremely conservative table. And Steve, I know that our listeners could actually do very much better than this, but you want to be very realistic about getting people excited about investing in the real estate market.

STEVE: John, remember that this is if the investor does nothing more than just buy 10 houses and stop right there. Think about how this $10 million can really grow and these gains can rapidly accelerate if two houses a year were purchased, or even three or four houses a year. You know, it just boggles the mind the potential that this very simple formula has, this very simple strategy, that anybody can take advantage of. You don't have to have a degree from Harvard or anything like that to be able to take advantage of this simple, yet very powerful strategy. Just look at some of the wealthiest people in the world, like the Donald Trumps, who made their money in real estate.

JOHN: And Steve, we're looking at very general assumptions here, and let's face it, if you do your homework and you educate yourself and go out there and work hard and get good at this, you're going to get even better returns than those outlined in this strategy. You're going to be able to buy right because you're going to have your fingers on the pulse of the real estate market. This is just the basics, folks. This is just the average over the next 35 years and what it's going to produce for you. This is the good and the bad. And I know that if you're educated and you do the work you can assume far better results than these.

STEVE: That's the key right there, John. You have to be willing to take action. You cannot sit back in a passive role on the couch and channel surf and be thinking about these things. You have to get up off the couch, put the bag of chips away, and begin looking seriously at real estate and get in the game. If you want to play the game, you have to get into the game. It's just like being the star basketball player. If you want to be good at it, you've got to practice, and yes, it's going to take some effort. As I said before, this isn't any kind of a get-rich-quick scheme that we're promoting. It does take work. You have to take action, but that's where the fruit lies, in your efforts.

INVESTMENT WEEK #4

CAROL: Hi! I'm Carol Eberhardt, and it *is* a new day in real estate! We're here again this week with Steve Berges and John Stricker and we're talking about investing in real estate and understanding how to do that. I'll tell you, I find that as a Realtor, as soon as someone finds out I'm in real estate, it's kind of like going to the doctor. Instead of talking to me about the ache they have in their elbow, however, people invariably say to me, "You know, I was thinking about buying some real estate." Almost 100 percent of the time when I meet a stranger and we start talking about what we do for a living, the first thing they want to know is, "Okay, give me a 10-minute crash course on how the heck I know what to buy." In other words, people want to know how to tell the difference between a good deal and a bad deal. I know that's a hard thing for people to learn right off the bat, because let's face it, right now in Genesee County, there are more listings than there have ever been. It's kind of like having too many wallpaper books to choose from. How do you know which one to choose, because there are just too many choices!? Investors today are in the wonderful position of having many options to choose from. There are more options today for you as an investor than there has ever been before. So the question becomes: How do you know which house to buy and how do you go about finding it?

STEVE: Well, Carol, you're absolutely right in that there are a lot of choices. For those of us who are schooled in the process of understanding because we're in the real estate market every single day, we know what these choices are and how to go about finding them. We buy and sell real estate for ourselves, and we help our clients do the same thing. But for those people who are just getting started in investing, you're absolutely right, Carol. There are lots of choices. Those people who are just getting started, however, are not necessarily aware of these choices and how to go about making them, and that's what we want to talk about today.

CAROL: Well, Steve, they really don't understand what a good deal is and what might not be such a good deal. This really is the dividing line between making a good investment decision and making one that might be just a little marginal.

JOHN: Carol, you're absolutely right. And I think it's so important that as we go through this, we need to help our listeners gain a better understanding of exactly how to go about buying that first property. When you make the decision to become an investor, you are committing yourself to a business. Just like with any business, when you commit yourself to your craft, the first thing you want to do is surround yourself with quality people who know what's going on so you can learn from them. You want to know that you are dealing with a real estate professional who's in the market every day. This helps you to really understand the dynamics of the market. So you have to really do your homework to make sure that when you sign your name on the dotted line and you hand the check over to buy a property, that you've done the proper research and you're buying right. Understanding these basic principles can make you or break you as an investor.

STEVE: John, that is so true. You can't just throw money at a property and expect to get back more than you put into it. One of the things I also teach the clients we work with is that there's an easy way to go about finding property and there's a hard way. And the hard way is to try and do it all yourself. The easy way is what we refer to as "finding undervalued properties the autopilot way." There is a mechanism, a network of people, that you can build and surround yourself with that will actually help bring deals to you to make it very easy to buy and sell. One of the most important factors for investors to understand, however, is that the people, the network, or the team that you surround yourself with needs to know and understand that you truly are committed, that you're not just out kicking the tires and that you are in fact a serious investor. And believe me, when they know and understand that, the deals will come to you. You will have more choices than you could ever imagine.

The very first thing that we have on our list here of how to find undervalued properties the autopilot way is to establish relationships with professional real estate agents. Agents know and understand property values and we can look at a house, do the proper analysis, and tell you what's a good deal and what isn't a good deal. They also have access to properties such as foreclosures, HUD properties that have been insured by the Department of Housing and Urban Development and later taken back. And they have a process in place whereby you are allowed to bid on those houses. Many of these foreclosures are readily available. There are some pitfalls, however, to be aware of. Understand also that while foreclosures and HUD houses do in fact represent a viable investment opportunity, it is a competitive niche in the market. There are a lot of people who are going after those, so sometimes the price gets bid up and there's not always a lot of value left in them for investors.

JOHN: That's right, Steve. I've seen it happen several times where people get emotionally involved in these HUD houses, and through the bidding process they end up paying more than retail.

STEVE: John, those are what we refer to as "distressed sellers" and they come in all shapes and sizes. There are many reasons homeowners are in financial distress. In fact, I've written at least an entire chapter or two that we'll get into that discusses distressed sellers, and how to go about identifying opportunities to help them. We don't have time for that today, unfortunately, but certainly some very good material and very worthwhile in helping our listeners to understand that with the real estate process. As we've said before, we're in the market every day, and because we're active investors, we are actually purchasing some of these houses at significant discounts. We know how to buy, and we buy smart. We purchase these houses ourselves at well below retail or market value, so we're buying these houses at wholesale prices. And because we are involved in the market, we have our companies in place to help us manage the entire process, everything from buying and selling, to financing, and even managing them.

That's right. We have a property management company in place that we turn the houses over to once we purchase them, who in turn rents them out for us. They take care of the property management, the leasing, the renting, the qualifying, the filling out of the application, making sure that we're not getting a deadbeat tenant in there who can't pay their rent on time. They're responsible for all of the collections and the maintenance as well, so it's really a turnkey process. And because we have so much inventory right now ourselves, you know we're in the market to buy and sell, we're not necessarily here to buy and hold. We buy and sell, buy and sell, buy and sell over and over and over. We have many houses ourselves in inventory, so Real Estate One–Symphony Homes is actually a good resource for our listeners because we can take these houses, package them, and offer them in a bulk sale. We can sell two houses or four houses or eight houses in bulk at discounted prices. And in most cases, as I said earlier, these houses are already leased out. It's a turnkey service. Our management company rents them out and takes care of them so that you don't have to worry about knocking on a door and collecting rent and those kind of things. Of course, if you want to do that, you're certainly free to do that and certainly welcome to manage them yourself. Our tenants are not deadbeat tenants. We have good, qualified solid tenants in our properties.

JOHN: You know, Steve, I listen to you say how you're offering all of this. You're offering a service where you'll find the properties, buy them at wholesale, a lot of times have tenants in them, and then offer these properties for sale to our listeners. Gosh, when I first got into the real estate market, if somebody would have done that for me, I can't think of the tens of thousands of dollars I would have saved through mistakes and just going through the learning curve that we're offering to people out there who are looking to get involved in this.

CAROL: Steve, I want to talk a minute about what it means when you connect yourself with a real estate professional. A lot of people don't realize that we're in a loop.

Just like any other profession, we network with one another and at any real estate gathering that I've ever been to, and to tell you the truth, even when I bump into a real estate friend at the grocery store, rarely is the first question, "How's your kids?" It's usually, "What do you have listed that I might be interested in?" or, "I've got a really hot listing coming up if you've got a client who's interested in it." So we have this kind of underground network that is always going on. And you, as an investor, need to take advantage of someone who is on that inside track, because we have the ability to ferret out things even before they hit the multilist. This is particularly true in our office. When someone in the office is going to list something, you better believe that the other agents in the office know it before it hits the multilist. We also have what's referred to as *hot sheets* for those of us who are working actively in the business every day. These hot sheets tell us what was listed the day before. So we don't even have to look for it, it's just delivered to us in our e-mail box every day. If we have a relationship with someone who we know is looking for something specific, we're right there and believe me, you are right on the edge with us and we're going to pick up the phone and we're going to get you in to the inside track. No time lapse, no waiting for it to hit the newspaper, you're going to get it before anybody else does.

JOHN: That's right Carol, and you know, I love this, Steve. You have written here about advancing your team of scouts. You know it's a very cost-effective way to find properties. Why don't you explain a little bit about that.

STEVE: Sure John, when I refer to a team of scouts, a scout is nothing more, if you think about the old days when you had the cowboys and Indians, the cowboys or the militia . . .

CAROL: The posse, are you talking about the posse?

STEVE: Well, no, not exactly, more like an advance party. A scout is someone who's going to go out and going to look through their binoculars or telescope and look for the enemy on the other side of the hill or the mountain. So, when we say advance your team of scouts, a scout is really nothing more than somebody that you have a relationship with. It might be another student at college, it might be a co-worker, a friend, an associate, or anyone like that who is constantly on the lookout to help you identify opportunities. They may have heard of a neighbor who's selling because of a divorce, or perhaps a death in the family. The more of these type of people you have, the more contacts they will have, and the greater your opportunity will be to have them bringing deals to you. Of course, in most cases, they're not going to be willing to do that for free. I would encourage them by offering a little incentive, like a referral fee. If they bring you a deal that makes sense and that you end up buying, you could say, "I'm going to pay you $300 for every deal you tell me about that I end up buying."

JOHN: You know, Steve, it's so true. Just being Loan John in the business, everybody that I come in contact with knows I'm in real estate, so they often bring those leads in. It's a great way to get a hold of wholesale properties. You have another method listed here called "Build a Solid Wholesale Network." How exactly do we go about doing that?

STEVE: Wholesalers play an important role in bringing opportunities to investors by acting as a wholesaler for those investors who can in turn sell at the retail level. For example, wholesalers, who're often licensed real estate agents, make their money off the commissions and sometimes a slight markup. I've got a couple of contacts in the industry here that I know that these guys deal primarily in foreclosed properties, who have the contacts and the relationships with lenders who need to dispose of foreclosed properties. They're bringing opportunities to an individual who wants to buy at wholesale and then take that property and maybe spend a little bit of money on repairs, or whatever the case may be, and get it leased out and possibly sell it at resale. So they may want to flip the house, as the term is referred to, or they may just want to buy and hold that property. But the wholesaler is not trying to maximize his or her gain on the sale of that house. They really are looking for a slight gain of 2 or 3 percent typically paid in the form of a commission.

JOHN: They like to do a lot of volume at that level.

STEVE: That's right. Wholesalers are looking to do volume, so they mark up the price of the house minimally for a quick resale. They usually have a network of buyers they work with whom they can notify as deals become available. Carol referred to this network of buyers as having a hot sheet of 10 or 20 or 50 people who are on the list. The information is faxed to the investors listed on the hotsheet and whoever wants it, whoever steps up to the plate first, is going to get it.

Chapter 13

Radio Program: Weeks 5 and 6

INVESTMENT WEEK #5

CAROL: It *is* a new day in real estate, and we're here again today to talk with you about real estate investments, and one of the reasons we're doing this is because we've had an absolutely overwhelming response from a number of people who are definitely interested in jumping into the real estate market right now. This is the best time to start thinking about investing! If you've ever had an inkling of a thought of getting into the market, now is the time to do it. Today we're going to be talking about five conventional techniques to financing, so take out your pen and paper and get ready to take some notes!

STEVE: Well, Carol, there are so many different ways to finance investment property that the opportunities are almost limitless. One of the things we're going to talk about today, as you've all ready mentioned, are five conventional techniques that we referred to earlier. These are the more traditional sources of financing, but what I really like about these traditional sources is the fact that we can mix and match these in a myriad of combinations.

CAROL: Steve, are you saying that people don't have to be gazillionaires to get themselves into the investment market?

STEVE: Well, I'll tell you, Carol, when I first started investing in real estate, I certainly was not a gazillionaire. In fact, I barely had anything at all to work with. And this first one here, the very first technique we referred to, is just a simple line of credit, which is one that I used quite often during that period of time, and believe it or not, I still use this today. When we refer to lines of credit, it's important to understand that there are all different types of lines available. Some of the most common are available through credit cards like MasterCard and Visa. You can easily get a $5,000 cash advance, depending on what your credit limit is, or even a $10,000 or $20,000 cash advance, again depending on what your credit limit is.

Another technique that I really like and that I've used many times is the home equity line of credit, also known as a HELOC loan. If you have a house that's worth $100,000, and let's say, for example, that you owe $70,000 on your first mortgage, you can very easily get a HELOC loan, or home equity line of credit. This type of loan is readily available and so very easy to get. I know that my friend John here, with Preferred Mortgage, can help our listeners get a home equity line of credit.

JOHN: You know, Steve, I help people all the time get the home equity credit lines that we put in place for folks on their primary residence. This gives them the availability to write a check right out of that account to spend any way they like, such as investing in real estate. A lot of times you can use these home equity credit lines, these other lines of credit as your down payment, so investors can use a combination of the two to truly maximize their leverage and walk into these investments with zero out of pocket.

STEVE: That's the beauty of real estate investing. You can mix and match using these various financing combinations. And just as you said, John, you can get a 90 percent investor loan and then use your Visa or MasterCard for the other 10 percent, which gives them a true nothing-down deal. I love that concept! Investors have the ability to purchase a house with no money out of their pocket. Now, of course, that money has to be repaid. Anything you buy that you get a loan for has to be repaid. The key point is the fact that you didn't have to go to the bank and withdraw $10,000 or $20,000. You instead had a line of credit that was available to you to borrow from. You're able to use that line of credit to purchase an asset that's going to generate a higher yield than the debt that's required to repay it. As you recall, John, we talked previously in our investors' series about the four benefits investors can enjoy from owning investment real estate. The growth, the appreciation, the depreciation, the cash flow—all those different things that we talked about previously. Another technique that we have is referred to as *private money* or *hard money loans*. These sources are readily available and they're generally easy to get for investment-type properties. One of the specialized areas that these private money loans are available for are investors who are interested in flipping properties. Private money loans are generally intended for short-term use and one of the primary reasons for that is because the interest rates do tend to be higher. You might pay anywhere from 12 to 18 percent, which is comparable to a credit card, but the idea here is if you can buy a house for $50,000 and put $20,000 into it in rehab money and turn around and sell it for $90,000 or $100,000 and do that within a 90-to-120 day period, then the return is certainly worth it. So if you have to pay a little bit higher interest rate on that loan, it's going to be worth it to you, because of the return it can produce.

JOHN: And again, you know anytime that we have layers of risks, the cost of the money is a little bit higher. When you're purchasing these investment houses and you don't have anybody in it right away and you need to rehab it, it might seem like a higher interest rate relative to other mortgage products, but really it's a great deal. It's an opportunity, it's an avenue that you're able to use to leverage to get an asset into play without tying up your own money. So you can sell it, and of course, create a return.

CAROL: Well, isn't the reality of that, John, that it's a get-in-and-get-out kind of thing? And when you look at it, really it's only the short term that you're borrowing that money. So you're not looking at a high interest rate over an extended period such as 10 or 15 years.

JOHN: You're so right, Carol. Because you're in and out so quick, the cost of borrowing that money because of the rate of return that you're looking to get really isn't much of a concern at all. Now, if you were to hang on to that and pay it for 12 or 18 months, then of course, it's going to eat away at your profit. But as quickly as so many people do the rehabs, it really doesn't affect their bottom line on the project too much.

STEVE: Okay, guys. We've talked about lines of credit, we've talked about private money, and hard money loans. The third technique we want to talk about are bringing in debt and equity partners. I've used these sources a number of times myself and continue to do so. A partner, of course, is somebody that you're going to bring in to help you achieve your investment goals. When we refer to a debt partner, that is somebody who is willing to loan money to you. It may be just enough money for a down payment, or it may be more. For example, if you don't have a MasterCard that has a $10,000 or $20,000 line on it that's available to you for a cash advance or something like that, then you might consider approaching your mom or dad, uncle, brother, sister, or anybody that you know who might be willing to loan you the $10,000 or $20,000. And remember, that's the portion that can be combined with these other investor loans that we've talked about. So once again, you're able to raise money to put together a nothing-down deal. And yes, you have to pay the loan back, but that's just part of the process.

An equity partner, on the other hand, is someone who is willing to contribute funds, again $10,000 or $20,000, $50,000, or whatever it happens to be, but the way you're going to repay that individual is that they become an actual partner with you. They have ownership in the property. Typically you're going to pay a higher rate of return using equity than you would using debt. You're going to give a percentage of the profits away with an equity partner as opposed to a debt partner, who's just loaning you money. When debt is used, a fixed rate of return is usually agreed upon and the loan is guaranteed. When equity is used, however, the partner shares the risk with you and the return is not guaranteed unless the project is successful.

CAROL: The reality of that is, so what? If you give away part of your equity, but you actually make money and you don't have to spend any of your own to do it, then you're that much further ahead than you otherwise would have been.

JOHN: Well, it is a way, that, and I would say that as an investor, it's probably one of the ways that I would hold out to do the least amount of the time, because you do give away a greater share of the profits. You're always better off if you can borrow from a line of credit or from a family member and pay a fixed rate of interest. You're better off paying the interest rate than paying a percentage of the yield. So it is a way that you can get in, once again, with zero money and it's another very creative way. But it is more costly, isn't it, Steve?

STEVE: Well, John, I always say half a pie is better than no pie at all! Using an equity partner does give you the opportunity to buy property if you have somebody that wants to form a partnership with you. It might even be that you find a property and your partner is the one who is responsible for doing the maintenance on it. I've been in relationships like that, where I'm the one who's out making the deals while my partner was more of a hands-on maintenance type of guy. In fact, my brother and I bought some property together—some duplexes. He was the guy on the rehab side, so it actually worked out quite well.

CAROL: If you need to do your first deal or so like this in order to give you the capital to begin to restructure other deals, it's at least an option for you to get yourself into the market.

JOHN: Good point, Carol.

STEVE: All right, gang! That brings us to our fourth technique, which is just using a standard conventional mortgage. Now then, you might say, "Well that doesn't really sound like much of a technique" but believe it or not, it is, because . . .

JOHN: That I can help people with.

STEVE: Let me give you an example of how conventional financing can help. I've done this myself, and in fact with one, the apartment building that I owned, I actually used this technique to pull about $300,000 in cash out of the deal. Here's the way it works, folks. Let's just say, for example, that you purchase a property that's in foreclosure for $45,000, then you put $25,000 into it for repairs, so you now have a total of $70,000 invested in it. The next step is to go to the bank to get a conventional loan. The lender will order an appraisal, and let's assume in this example, that the property appraises for $100,000. If you get an 80 percent loan, you're able to pay off the $70,000 in debt and now you've got $10,000 to put in your pocket to go out and buy another house. If you get a 90 percent investor loan, now you've got $20,000 to put in your pocket. So in a period of just three to four months, you bought a house for $45,000, put $25,000 into it for repairs, and then turn around in three or four months and pull $20,000 out of the deal!

Now then, guys. I don't know about you, but most folks don't make $20,000 in a month or two! If you apply the law of leverage that we've talked about before, you can take that $20,000 and go out and buy two more properties or three more or five more or 10 more properties and repeat the cycle over and over. Imagine if you pulled out $20,000 on every deal and you did 10 deals a year—that's $200,000! I don't know about the rest of you, but for me, that isn't chump change.

JOHN: That's a wonderful thing. You still have 10 to 20 percent equity in the properties and the possibility of a positive cash flow on a monthly basis.

STEVE: Okay, let's move on to our fifth and final technique for today. This technique has to do with our broker and investor programs, and this is where my buddy John comes in. Working with a mortgage broker offers some very definite advantages. Let me just also point out that the conventional loan technique that we talked about a few minutes ago requires the borrower to approach the lender directly. If you have financial relationships with these individual lenders, for example, you can talk to them yourself and try to shop your deal among them. By using this fifth and final technique, you actually have someone else do the shopping for you. That someone is a mortgage broker.

JOHN: Absolutely, Steve. As a mortgage broker, this is where I come in. To get in touch with us, you can give us a call at 1-866-LOANJOHN, or you can log on to our web site at loanjohn.com. We have over 108 different investors and we have our fingers on the pulse of the finance world. We know where to go, based on your credit score, based on the type of collateral, and based on the LTV, to get you the best financing possible. Whether it's to pull cash out to refurbish a house, or pull cash out so you can buy more houses, we can help you. As the broker, we can help you with any one of these financing needs because we have access to not just one bank or one mortgage company, but to well over 100 different lenders and investors. Of course, because we're in the finance market every day, we're able to stay up with the ever-changing guidelines, which lately have been changing on almost a daily basis. We know where to go to get the best rates and the best programs based on your credit and the type of collateral being offered. Using a mortgage broker who's in tune with the finance market can make all the difference in the world for investors.

STEVE: Well, and let's face it John, if you're not in the mortgage business, if you're not in the industry shopping every day, then you have no idea where to go. I know for myself that in the past, when shopping for lines of credit for Symphony Homes to use for construction purposes, it usually has been me one on one with the lenders establishing and building relationships with them. What a terrific advantage you offer, John, as a mortgage broker, because now our investors only have to come to one person. They just call you and you already know where the money is. You know which lenders and which investors are doing what kinds of deals. And that makes it very easy for you to match up the needs of the investor with those of the lender.

JOHN: That's right, Steve. The best part is, folks, that I have banks that come to me because rumor has it if they don't lend any money, they don't make any money! I have banks that are just as eager to lend you the money as you are to borrow it. So if you want to find out more about this type of financing or any one of the ways that we talked about today, you can always contact our office at 1-866-LOANJOHN, or you can log on to our web site at loanjohn.com, where you can actually do a mortgage calculation and look up all the different types of mortgage products that we have available. And there's some quick calculations that you can do in there as well.

STEVE: Okay, folks. We've covered quite a bit of information here in the short time we've had. We've talked about lines of credit, private money and hard money loans, debt and equity partners, conventional mortgage financing, and last but not least, broker and investor programs that my friend John offers.

INVESTMENT WEEK #6

CAROL: It *is* a new day in real estate, and we're here again this week talking about investments and investment property, investment financing, and everything you need to know to get yourself into the real estate market. And right now, all we hear are negative things about the market—the press has not been good to us. The reality of the situation is, if you're smart, if you understand what your potential is, then this is the absolute best time to get yourself into this market and to start making money.

So today, we're going to be talking about high leverage techniques for financing your investment properties. So Steve, talk to me today about leverage and leveraging money.

STEVE: Well Carol, last week we spoke about the five conventional techniques to finance your investment properties. When we say conventional, we are referring to the more traditional methods of financing, and this week we want to talk about four more sophisticated methods, what I refer to as high leverage techniques. The first one of these methods that we're going to talk about is the short-sale strategy. Many of our listeners are probably not familiar with the term of short sale and how exactly that works. Well, let me just take a minute to explain the process and what we mean by short sale. One of the biggest challenges that investors of foreclosed properties find is that when they take on a foreclosure, oftentimes there's not any money left in the deal, so it doesn't make any sense to buy it. The property's been foreclosed on, the bank wants to recoup the amount of money they've loaned on it, which is sometimes as much as 90 to 100 percent of its value.

If you have a house that's in foreclosure, for example, and the homeowner owes $100,000 and that's all the property's worth, then you are faced with the challenge of saying "There's no money left in this deal." The approach to overcoming this shortfall is what we refer to as a *short sale strategy*. In essence, the way this process works is that you're going to get on the phone and negotiate with the lender who holds the note on the property and talk to their loss mitigation department. You will ask them if they will consider working out a short-sale solution, and taking 70 cents on the dollar or 60 cents on the dollar or 50 cents on the dollar in the first mortgage position. Sometimes that's a little bit difficult to do, but let's get back to our example here that's valued at $100,000, and let's assume that we have a $60,000 first mortgage and a $40,000 second mortgage on the property. What will happen is that when the house goes into foreclosure, the lender who is in the first lien position is the one who will be in control. The lender in the second lien or third lien position most likely will get very little or next to nothing on their loan. So in a short-sale strategy what you actually want to do is talk to the lender who holds that $40,000 note.

CAROL: Steve, I think the one thing that listeners need to understand is that the banks don't want to take the house back. The reality of it is, and we all hear this on the news every day, is that there are more properties on the market today that have been foreclosed on than ever before. The bank has been forced to be in a position of managing all of these properties, trying to get them sold and having to list them with Realtors. To tell you the truth, they'd rather talk and get rid of the house and take a little loss then have to add it to their inventory. The cost of carrying these houses can be enormous when interest charges, taxes, insurance, utilities, maintenance, and vandalism are all factored in. It only makes sense for lenders to negotiate with investors and try to come to a mutually beneficial agreement. The investor gets a break on the price of the house and the lender gets a nonperforming asset off the books and frees up capital to loan out again.

JOHN: You're absolutely right, Carol. There's just a lot of cost associated with these houses. First of all, when a house goes into foreclosure, a lot of times the bank has to worry about its condition as it sits there vacant. Secondly, as the house is retained in the lender's portfolio, it can really eat up a lot of the bank's profits. As you've already stated, the lender has to pay property taxes, utility, maintenance, and all of the related upkeep. So you're absolutely right, when you do a short sale it can be a very useful tool to pick up properties on the cheap.

STEVE: You're exactly right, John. As I mentioned in the example here in the $40,000 second mortgage that I referred to earlier, the lender who holds that second note in the amount of $40,000, they know the way the game's played, and they know that if a deal goes into foreclosure, they'll be lucky to get anything at all. So if you offer them, let's say, 25 cents on the dollar, which is $10,000, you might say, "Wow, who in their right mind is going to take $10,000 on a $40,000 note?" Well, the way the lender's viewing this, is he knows that there's a very high likelihood, or probability, that the deal's going to go to foreclosure. Being in a second lien position, if it does, in fact, go to foreclosure, the lender will most likely end up with nothing.

I know for myself, and this is very common . . . you've heard about selling notes and discount on notes and things like that. This really is the same process or strategy. I've got an example here to share with our listeners. I actually held a note on a mobile home that I owned a number of years ago that I sold to a couple for $17,500. They gave me a $2,500 down payment, which left a loan balance of $15,000. They agreed to an interest rate of 12 percent, so by the end of the first year after paying on the note, they owed a little over $14,000. I had an investor who offered me a little over $11,000 for that $14,000 note, which represented a difference of almost $3,000. You might think, on the one hand, that I'm losing $3,000, but the way I viewed it was that a bird in the hand is worth two in the bush. I took the investor's offer of $11,000 and never looked back. In addition to buying the note at a discount, the investor continued to collect a very generous interest rate on it. So, that was what the investor wanted and at the time the cash worked well for me, too, so it was a win-win situation for both of us.

JOHN: I think that's a very useful way in getting cash to use as working capital. I think you also have an example in here, Steve, about how companies actually sell their receivables to raise cash to use as working capital. And a lot of times, that's exactly what you are helping the bank do, is raise cash that is sitting there so you can get those bad loans off the books and get some of the capital back in play to reinvest into assets that are going to perform.

STEVE: John, that's a process known as *factoring*. Just, for example, you hear of furniture stores or any number of retailers who sell their receivables. They advertise no payments for three years and that kind of thing. Well, guess what? There might not be any payments and they might say zero percent interest, but oftentimes what they're doing is selling those notes or receivables for cash and they're getting their money up front. A lot of times these businesses have to, because they have to be able to replenish their inventory; that is, go out and buy more inventory to sell all over again.

Okay, guys, moving on to the second technique that we want to talk about today is what is referred to as a *subject to* technique. A subject to financing technique is similar to something you've likely heard of before, but probably not too much in recent years. It's similar to assuming a loan from the seller. The subject to method is similar to the loan assumption method except that you're not actually assuming the loan. What you are doing instead is taking over the property *subject to* the existing terms and conditions that the lender already has in place. And so it's kind of like taking control of the property without actually taking the legal liability for the note.

Let's look at an example. If you're working with a seller who is in distress—they need to get out of their property or they want somebody to make the payments for them—then you can structure an agreement with them such that they're going to vacate the property. You might give them $2,500 for moving expenses, but then they're going to move out. You then take control of the property subject to the existing terms and conditions of the note using a very simple quitclaim deed. This means that you're now going to be responsible for making the payments. Your goal is to get somebody in there and either rent the property out or turn around and get it sold for profit. So you are actually not assuming legal liability for the note, but you're just agreeing with the individual who's selling it to you that you're going to be responsible for making the payments. And once again, this is referred to as a *subject to* strategy.

JOHN: Steve, it's a very useful and a very good way rather than actually assuming the property. You're assuming the equity position in the property by assuming responsibility for the note and the payment. It's just a fantastic way if you can negotiate that to enjoy the benefits of the property without having the legal liability.

STEVE: Right! And as I just mentioned, the title can actually be transferred using a quitclaim deed. While that might seem a bit scary for some people, it really is a simple instrument that's used to transfer title and can be done very easily. With a quitclaim deed, there is no warranty or guarantees with the title. It's different from a warranty deed, but that's the way this process works, and it's very easy to do. The beauty of this technique is that you're not legally liable to the lender, because it is the seller's name that is on the mortgage, not yours. If things don't work out, the lender will come after the person whose name is on the note.

CAROL: Steve, our next topic is referred to as a *purchase option* technique. To tell you the truth, I'm not sure I get that one. What's that all about?

STEVE: Well, Carol, a purchase option technique actually happens to be one of my favorites, because that's the method that I can use to leverage a large piece of land or investment property with very little money down. We recently used this technique to acquire or take control of approximately 80 lots, which is about $3 million worth of land. We put up an option in the amount of $10,000. I haven't done the math, but I know that's less than 1 percent.

JOHN: Yes it is, and I think it's a beautiful thing.

STEVE: So, in this very recent transaction, I was able to take control of almost $3 million worth of property using a purchase option for only $10,000.

CAROL: So, let me see if I understand this concept. What you're telling me is that you actually didn't give the seller any money, but instead just *promised* to pay him?

STEVE: Well, that's not exactly right. The seller did get some money. He got $10,000.

CAROL: Well, I know, but on a very valuable piece of property. So he's willing to take that little bit of money on a property that's worth that much money?

STEVE: That's right, Carol. Yes, he is. There are certain constraints that we have to follow, certain things that we are required to do during this option period, but that's the way it works. A purchase option gives us the right to buy the land at a predetermined price. It gives us legal control of the property. Now I have a couple of things that I can do with that option. I can either buy the 80 lots myself one at a time, or 10 or 20 or 40 at a time, and cash the seller out. Or, because I hold a legal interest in the property, I have legal control of it. I can actually take my interest and sell it to another individual such as another builder or investor. Let's say I pay my option price to purchase these 80 lots at $3 million and then find somebody who comes along and wants to buy it from me for, let's say, $4 million. Wow! Hey, that's pretty cool, isn't it, John?

JOHN: Yes, Steve, it sure is!

STEVE: I just made $1 million on my 80 lots and I only had to put up $10,000 to do it. Let's bring this back to our investors now. The way this technique would work for them using an option to purchase rental property is very similar. The same thing is being done, but on a much smaller scale.

CAROL: I need to just clarify something, Steve. So once you do that, the person that sold you that option can't sell the property out from under you now?

STEVE: No ma'am, they absolutely cannot.

CAROL: You really have the control?

STEVE: That's exactly right. We have a contractual agreement between us that gives me full control. I have what is referred to as an *equitable interest* in the property. Although title has not been transferred, I control the property. It's important that title is not transferred because that affects the assessed value of the property. Once title transfers, then I become responsible for the taxes and liability; all the issues that go with that. So, once again, I have what's referred to as an equitable interest in the property.

JOHN: Now Steve, I've heard of people using this type of technique to buy houses in a preforeclosure status. This is where buyers go in and make an agreement to option the house with the person who has the house that's going into foreclosure. And this is a way you actually can sell the house and make anything above and beyond what the costs are.

STEVE: That's right, John. If you're working with a family that has experienced a job loss or some other financial hardship and they're about to lose their house to the foreclosure process, you might agree to give them $2,500, for example, over and above what is owed on the house. So let's just say the seller owes $60,000, but the house will appraise for $90,000. But meanwhile, you've given the current owner $2,500 to help them out with some of their more immediate needs. You may even agree to make their monthly payments for a period of time. Let's say you do a six-month option with the homeowner. That gives you six months to go out and find another buyer for that property to turn around and sell it for $90,000. The beauty of this plan is that you are not really assuming the risk. Yes, you're going to be out a little bit of money, your option premium, but you have the opportunity to possibly enjoy a $30,000 gain on that property.

JOHN: Yes, and I think that's another very useful way, folks, that we're going to teach you when you come to this investment seminar on how you can exercise options with very little money out of pocket using the tools of leverage and the tools of options to create. We have another method that we're going to show you and talk to you about, but these are all going to be covered in our seminar. And it's so exciting—I get really excited about this Steve—showing people how they can create wealth no matter what market conditions they're faced with.

STEVE: Well, if you're just getting started, one of the ways that can be used to buy property is the *lease option* method. It's similar to a purchase option in that it grants the right for investors to purchase property at a predetermined price with any given period of time. But lease options are a little bit different in that they combine the basic lease or rental agreement with an option-to-purchase contract. So I might use, for example, a lease option technique with somebody that I've already purchased property from and now I'm going to lease it to a tenant and give them an option to purchase that property. So while I am giving them the right to buy, that gives me a viable exit strategy for a house that I bought, let's say, for $50,000. In this situation, I'm going to do a lease option with the buyer, and after 12 to 16 months, they're going to turn around and buy the house from me for, let's say, $80,000. This strategy nets me a cool $30,000 in a very short period of time.

So just a quick recap, folks. We've talked about four high-leverage techniques to finance your investment property. They are the short-sale strategy, the subject-to technique, we've talked about purchase options, and last, but again, not least, is, of course, our lease-option technique.

Chapter 14

Radio Program: Weeks 7 and 8

INVESTMENT WEEK #7

CAROL: It *is* a new day in real estate, and I'm Carol Eberhardt, and I'm here today again with Steve Berges and John Stricker and we're going to continue in our series this month of investing in real estate and understanding exactly how to do that. I'm really excited about this process, guys, because in today's market we are getting just a ton of phone calls from folks who are really interested in stepping off the curb and getting into the investment market but aren't quite sure exactly what to do. Although investing in real estate can seem complex, it's really quite simple once you get the hang of it. There are a lot of things to consider, from the financing, to where and how do I find the house that I want to buy, and who's going to help me, and am I going to spend too much money and not get a decent return. Other things to consider are am I going to rent it, keep it, flip it? Sometimes it's hard to know what to do and what the best choice is.

Now we're going to move today into something that's a really interesting topic, mainly because it not only affects the rental market but if you own property today, this is something that you really need to understand. We're going to talk about the concept of understanding the value. I find that's the one thing that clients have the hardest time understanding. We kind of have a joke around the industry, Steve and John. Every client that comes in the door tells me that their house is probably worth more than it actually is because they've got the heavy duty nails in there along with extra insulation and they know that there must be a lot of value in that. The problem is that most home owners truly don't understand how value is arrived at in today's market.

STEVE: That is so true, Carol. Value is so important, and it's such a fundamental principle that investors absolutely must understand to be successful in the real estate market. Whether you're investing in rental property, or shopping for a new home, or shopping for appliances, you need to understand the concept of value. So we do want to spend a few minutes today talking about value and why it's so important. John, I've got a question for you here. Let's shift our focus from the real estate market to the stock market for just a minute. Who is the individual, the king of investing, that comes to mind to you when it comes to value?

JOHN: When it comes to value investing, it has to be Warren Buffett.

STEVE: Well, you are exactly correct, sir. Warren Buffett, as we know him, is the king of value. He's the guy who's out there buying and scooping up all the assets at prices that are well below market value. Whether it's real estate, precious metals, silver, stock, commodities, insurance companies, you name it, Warren Buffett is out there scooping it up. He is buying when everybody else is saying, "The sky is falling, the sky is falling," and they're all selling. Warren Buffett knows and understands the principle of value. He's looking at the intrinsic value of various commodities or assets and their ability to produce income while others believe their value may be somewhat diminished. He's looking at the income that those assets are yielding relative to the price that's being paid for them. So while everybody else is yelling, "The sky is falling, the real estate market is falling apart, and the bottom's falling out. We're selling, we're selling!" Well, guess who's stepping in and buying? You have the astute people, like Warren Buffett, who understand the relativity of the value. He's buying at prices that are largely depressed because he knows that over time that the market is going to stabilize and it's going to begin to improve and then those assets will eventually come back in favor with investors. So while people are beginning to invest back into those assets, at some point, Warren Buffett, who begins to see a top in those markets, will begin very quietly selling. He's buying at the bottom and selling at the top. He's what we might call a contrarian investor.

JOHN: If you watch what he does, it's exactly that. When he starts seeing people panic and things that just don't seem like they're at the top of their game, you start looking at him and he has this remarkable ability to be able to recognize where there's value, where there's appreciation, where he can get into the market at a reasonable price, and ride it out. And, of course, by the time everybody else catches on, they're starting to buy where he's starting to sell. Buffett almost creates his own buy-low-and-sell-high market. The truth of the matter is that he's done this so many times that he's become such an icon in the investment world. There are, in fact, many people referred to as "Buffett watchers" who watch his every move. They look to Buffett's activities in the marketplace to try to anticipate what's hot and what's not.

STEVE: That's right, John. It's exactly as you've stated. The group of individuals known as "Buffett watchers" are watching to see exactly what he's doing because what he does as far as his investment portfolio goes has to be publicly disclosed. These investors watch to see what Warren Buffett is buying, and then oftentimes they will do likewise. But you know, to become as astute as Warren Buffett, we need to learn to think like him also. It's imperative for us that we have a sound understanding of the principle of value as it applies to real estate. Let's just talk about that here for a minute. When we consider the concept of value, let's take just a minute and talk about the example of shopping for an appliance. To determine what the best value is, we have two components, price and features. Price is not necessarily a function of value when we think about the value a particular item provides us. That really comes down more to comparison shopping. We're comparing that particular appliance to all other appliances that are similar. And then if we're shopping for the best value, it becomes a function of price, so we're really looking at which particular appliance has the most features and offers the most benefits for the best price. Once we're able to identify that, after having shopped at four or five different stores that sell similar appliances, we find the one that we liked that seems to offer the most for the money. Then and only then do we feel like we're getting the best value. When you apply the same kind of logic to real estate, that's really what you're doing. You're comparison shopping. To help determine what that value is, we have a term referred to as . . . Carol?

CAROL: A comparative market analysis?

STEVE: Okay, that's one of them, but there's another word that I'm looking for. . . .

JOHN: An appraisal!

STEVE: Thank you, John! We do what is called an *appraisal* on the property. I have a quote here from William Kinard in which he defines an appraisal. It says, "An appraisal is a professionally derived conclusion about the present worth or value of specified rights or interests in particular parts of real estate, under stipulated market conditions or decision standards; moreover, it is or should be based on [the] professional judgment and skill of a trained practitioner." So we are relying very heavily, Carol, on the professional opinion of other individuals who are schooled and trained, who have a particular set of skills as to help us determine value when it comes to real estate. Now you and I both know that we don't always necessarily agree with the opinions of appraisers.

CAROL: Exactly, and what ends up happening is that an appraiser not only looks at value but also looks at market conditions at the same time. So it becomes a multifaceted concept and therefore becomes difficult sometimes for the average consumer because they don't understand that their competition actually affects their values sometimes. So the appraiser takes a big-picture look at what's going on, not only with your particular property, but within the market and how it compares with the other properties on the market, just exactly the same way as we shop for washing machines or refrigerators. It's the exact same process.

STEVE: Well, let's just take that appraisal process a little bit further. While the appraisal itself is supposed to be an objective opinion using a given set of objective data and facts, you're looking at other houses in this case, or other parcels of land, and if you're valuing land or whatever the case may be, it is somewhat subjective. Although the appraisal profession attempts to make the process as objective as possible, it is still an *opinion* of value. We were discussing off mike earlier that we have a house that's currently under contract, one of our new homes, and the appraiser is giving us somewhat of a difficult time because he's not wanting to attribute value to certain options and upgrades. He is, in fact, challenging our assertion of value, and we on the other hand, as builders in that particular neighborhood and market, have a better feel and understanding for value, and in this case, than the appraiser, because he tends to do appraisals in a number of areas and doesn't know this specific neighborhood as well as we do. So the appraisal process, while somewhat scientific and objective, is also subjective as well. And it depends in part on the individual comps that the appraiser chooses.

JOHN: That's right, Steve. There's no doubt that the appraisal process is subjective. A lot of times in the lending business we have appraisals come in and there are a lot of times I have an issue or concern with the type of appraisal that I'm getting because it is just one person's opinion. Where they can go ahead and subtract and add value based on a lot of things they personally see into it and sometimes we have to speak with the appraisers to make sure that we're getting the best value for our clients.

CAROL: I think one of the things that we need to caution consumers about is when they look at an appraisal, particularly on their own property, is to make sure that the appraisal is done with comparing houses in the same neighborhood, if possible. Oftentimes, appraisers in their zeal to find like houses go way out of the area, when indeed that is not truly a reflection of value, so I know that when I look at them, I always look at what houses the appraiser is comparing them to because obviously something on one end of the county is going to have a different value from one sitting on the other end of the county. So it's important as a consumer that when you're really looking at an honest value that you look at the strength of the comparables that are put in front of you.

STEVE: We're focusing on valuation and thinking about this in investment terms, and although not entirely in investment terms but similar to the stock market if we can just shift our thinking back over to the stock market. If you recall, John, in the late nineties, '98, '99 and the year 2000, we saw the Dow go into new highs, and NASDAQ in particular, and approaching new highs. And at that time, value didn't matter because prices were going up, but as we know, a lot of investors bought in toward the top. We saw the crash and many of those investors lost their life savings or a good portion of it, and so it really is important to understand this concept of value. So proponents of the buy-and-hold strategy would argue that because the holding period extends over many years, price really doesn't matter as long as investors could purchase real estate with favorable enough terms. We've heard some of the late night gurus who suggest you can go in and buy with no money down, and don't worry about the price because price doesn't matter as long as you're getting in with no money down. Well, guess what, folks. Actually, nothing could be further from the truth, because price does matter. It's precisely this kind of misinformation that led thousands, if not millions, of investors over the cliff in the collapse of the stock market over a three-year period, which began in the year 2000. So, this law of relativity that we've been talking about really must be taken very seriously. This law is so important, in fact, that every investor's success or failure depends upon obeying it. And if the relativity of value as it applies to real estate is disregarded, the fate of investors buying it will be no different from the tens of thousands of those who lost their life savings in the stock market. So let's try to get into the habit of thinking like Warren Buffett—remember, he's the value king. You can rest assured that the principle of value is always foremost in his mind, regardless of the type of asset that he may be investing in, so let's try to keep that in mind here as we're thinking about investing in the real estate market here in the Genesee county area.

INVESTMENT WEEK #8

CAROL: It *is* a new day in real estate. I'm Carol Eberhardt, manager of Real Estate One Symphony Homes, and I'm here today with Steve Berges and John Stricker from Preferred Mortgage, and we're here again this week to talk with you about the concept of investing in the real estate market. And one of the reasons that we're doing that is because right now is the prime time, and particularly with the weather breaking and spring coming and the real estate market heating up, to think about investing in real estate. So, if you've ever had an inkling about doing this, you need to listen up, get out your pencil and paper, take lots of notes because the opportunity is right here in Genesee County and you don't want to let that pass you by. So today we're going to talk about another aspect of investing. We're going to move on to understanding value, and Steve, where are we at, today?

STEVE: Carol, last week, as our listeners may recall, we talked about the importance of understanding value and having a first firm grasp on that concept. We talked about the relativity of value and why that was so important. We compared that to the stock market and how it's very important to understand value. You can't just say, "This stock is going up in price and therefore it's a good buy. I'm going to jump on board and hope to make some money," because what inevitably happens is that that price comes down and if you have overpaid, without getting into calculations like price-to-earnings ratios and things like that, if you overpaid for that stock and you have a collapse in the market, then you'll be in trouble like so many tens of thousands and hundreds of thousands of investors who lost quite a bit during the stock market collapse there in the 1999, 2000, '01 time period. That's why it's so important to understand this concept of value. We talked about Warren Buffett and how he's the value king. He's the guy who's in there scooping up the bargains when everybody else is saying "Sell, sell, sell!" He's in there buying and doing the exact opposite. Buffett takes a contrarian approach.

So we've talked already about value and today we want to get into a little bit more of this process of valuing real estate. The three most common methods to do what we refer to as valuing real estate as an appraisal and we touched a little bit on that last week, but we want to talk about the three most common appraisal methods today, and those are the replacement cost approach, the income capitalization approach, and then also the sales comparison approach. Let's just start with the replacement cost approach. That method is used primarily as the name suggests. You're thinking about having something insured, for example, the house that you live in. Let's assume your house is worth about $150,000 and that it was built in 1960. To use the replacement cost approach, that's important in this example because you want to know what it's going to cost if the house burns down in its entirety. Now, we certainly wouldn't wish that upon anybody, but it does happen and that's why we have insurance. That's why insurance companies are in business, so they can offer that protection, but they rely on this method of appraising a house referred to as the replacement cost method so that we have a good understanding of what it's going to take to actually replace your house, to rebuild it, to reconstruct it.

CAROL: And typically what I find, Steve, is that they pretty much attach a price per square foot value. They might determine, for instance, that it's going to cost them $100 per square foot to reproduce your house. So it's important to understand exactly where or what their definition of replacement is when you're looking at value that way.

STEVE: That's so true, Carol, and that value will vary, depending on the neighborhood. If you bought the house in an older neighborhood, for example, houses that were built in the 1940s, well, the replacement cost approach method of valuing the house may in fact be higher than one of the other approaches, for example, the sales comparison method, which we'll talk about in just a minute. That value will most likely be higher because of what it costs in today's dollars versus what it cost in 1930 or 1940 dollars is certainly going to be significantly more.

Now, the second appraisal method that we have is referred to as the income capitalization method. I know that might sound a little bit intimidating to some of our listeners and we won't spend too much time on this approach, but suffice it to say that the income capitalization approach is used for appraising income-producing properties such as retail strip centers, apartment buildings, office buildings, and essentially any kind of real estate that is income producing. It could even be used for rental houses, although usually is not used for an individual rental house. It may be used for them if you have, for example, a package of 20 or 30 houses. You might use the income approach on something like that.

To better understand the income approach, assume you have a $10,000 certificate of deposit in the bank account that is yielding 5 percent. What you are doing with the income capitalization approach is that you're taking the present value of that income stream that the asset or deposit is generating, and you are capitalizing it back to come up with a value, and that's exactly the approach that's used. It doesn't matter if it's cash in a certificate of deposit and the yield is 5 percent, which you might refer to as the cap rate, or if it's a multifamily apartment building yielding approximately 8 or 10 percent. You refer to those as the cap rate and those numbers are used to calculate the value on these types of assets. So again, without spending too much time on that, because that's not really what our program is about, just suffice it to say that we've got the income capitalization approach that is used to value and appraise income-producing properties. Now Carol, what is our third approach that we're going to talk about today?

CAROL: The third method, Steve, is the sales comparison method. Oftentimes, when you're talking to a Realtor and they use the word *CMA,* what they're talking about is a *comparative market analysis.* In a nutshell, that is simply looking at the homes that have sold in your area that are the most like yours. It's just that simple. We try to compare apples to apples. Sometimes it's not that easy to do. The tough ones, quite frankly, are the ones that are way out in the country with not a whole lot of houses around. But the whole concept of it is to compare like properties and to get as close geographically as you can to do that.

STEVE: The sales comparison method is based on the premise of what we refer to as *substitution*. That premise or notion maintains that a buyer would not pay any more for a piece of property than the cost of purchasing an equally desirable substitute in its respective market. So if you have two houses that are identical in square footage, the features and benefits that they offer, and are in the same neighborhood, then relatively speaking, those houses should be fairly close in value. Now you do have certain things that affect that value. If you have a 1,500-square-foot house in one neighborhood but it is a newer community, versus a 1,500-square-foot house in another neighborhood that is maybe declining in value, and you have certain factors, maybe that the crime rate is high there, then it becomes a less desirable area. Those are the kinds of things that will affect the value of a house.

JOHN: That's why we're always using when we're looking at a sales comparison method, houses that are as close to each other as possible. For instance, houses that have the same approximate square footage, the same number of garages, equivalent acreage, and things like that. That way, when we start to compare these properties that are really similar to each other, we get a really good feel for what people are willing to pay. What they were willing to pay for a like kind of property within the last six months or so is likely to be very close to what they are willing to pay now. And that's of course why appraisers do use replacement cost in many of their formulations, but where they put four or five different comparisons down, it is for the sales comparison method. This is based on what people have paid for a similar property in a similar area.

STEVE: John, that's an excellent point, something that you just mentioned there. The appraisals are based on properties that have actually *sold*. So let me just help clarify that. I just want to really emphasize this point. Your neighbor's house three doors down might be for sale for $150,000 and you believe therefore that because your house is similar to theirs that your house must also be worth $150,000. Well, guess what, folks? The appraiser cannot use the neighbor's house that is currently listed for sale at $150,000. Instead, he has to rely on houses that have already sold. Like it or not, that's all the appraiser is allowed to use. Now he certainly can look at other factors such as those that are listed for sale, and can take those into consideration, but when it comes right down to it, the appraisal report, the analysis that they do, has to be based on similar properties that have actually sold. So just because your neighbor has her house listed for sale at $150,000 does not mean that it's worth 150,000.

In fact, we're in the market every day and because we look at these comps, we have a good idea of what's going on with respect to price and value. Sometimes we can pull the history on a given house and can see that it's listed for $150,000, but we can also see that it's been listed for sale for the last 18 months and has had very little activity. What that means is that although buyers are seeing the listing, they are not interested in it because they're comparison shopping. Remember we talked about the relativity of value. Buyers are comparison shopping. They're looking at these houses and saying, "For $150,000, I can get a similar house that's a little bit newer and offers a little more square footage." So it's very important to remember that just because your neighbor's house might be listed for sale at a particular price, what you really want to focus on and rely on is what your neighbor's house sold for, because that's what the appraiser is going to be looking at.

JOHN: That's so true, Steve. As I was pulling some comps for a house yesterday that I was preparing for a client who is listing with us, I pulled everything that has sold in the last six months. Although I also did look at, but put very little weight on, are things that have been listed in the last six months but haven't yet sold. I did, however, use them as a rough guideline, but I really put most of my emphasis on what has actually sold in the last six months. It doesn't mean that we're not going to look at these other listings, but when it really comes down to putting hard numbers on something, it's what somebody is willing to pay, and has paid, that it's worth.

STEVE: Carol, maybe you can share with our listeners some of the other things that appraisers look at when they are appraising a property.

CAROL: Well, of course, condition is a big part of it. Also, what upgrades the house has and how well it's been maintained. It's a very similar process to that of the used car industry. If you look at two cars of the exact same age and one looks like it's been through several wrecks, had a bad patch job, and the tires are bald, and then compare it to the one sitting next to it which is the same age and is looking pretty good with low mileage. Common sense tells us that the value is going to be greater on something that is maintained better and is in better overall condition.

Of course, the age of a house is going to make a huge difference, so if you're in, for instance, a neighborhood that has houses that have been built over the course of a year or many years or a community that has a high diversity of different types of houses, the age is going to make a huge difference.

STEVE: Now Carol, does that mean that I can't compare one of my newly built 2007 models to something that was built back in 1945?

CAROL: That's right, it does mean that you can't.

STEVE: Thank you for clarifying that for us.

CAROL: There's a huge difference. And of course we know if you've shopped at all for houses, then you understand the difference in what people are looking for today and in what they're willing to pay. People are in general going to be willing to pay more for a newly built home that is loaded with all the latest gadgets than they are one that is much older and is bordering on the verge of functional obsolescence.

JOHN: Floor plans.

CAROL: Absolutely, floor plans make a huge difference. So, for instance, gone are the days when people want lots of teeny, tiny little rooms that are chopped up with little teeny, tiny bedrooms. They want a flowing floor plan, something that's open, with cathedral ceilings. You may have the same square footage as your neighbor who lives down the street, but if your floor plan is not as desirable, then the value is not going to be there.

JOHN: That's generally referred to as functional obsolescence, where the floor plan is largely outdated and just isn't what people want anymore. For example, the quad-level and tri-level homes were fairly popular once upon a time, but today you can hardly give them away. You've got to walk up 15 stairs, walk through the front door, and then either go up or downstairs again. People just don't want that. The single story ranch, which has become very popular, has taken its place.

CAROL: And of course the upgrades make a huge difference. Buyers are smart today, John. They do a lot of shopping, because there are a lot of choices out there. Quite frankly, if they walk into your kitchen and you have granite and you have a soap stone sink, and you have hardwood floors that are in pristine condition, because you've updated . . .

JOHN: They understand the value in the home.

CAROL: Absolutely. Walk into the house next door and it's got laminate, you're going to lose from a value standpoint.

JOHN: Well, Carol, I think we're seeing all the time with so many shows on TV, buy this house, flip this house, do this, and do that. People are becoming so educated that it makes it fun to work with when we're showing them these types of things because finally, they're really starting to understand the value in their house. Whether it might be undervalued or the value of another house is worth making the move up to, or having some more upgrades added, all makes a difference in the minds of shoppers.

STEVE: To summarize, we've talked about the three different appraisal methods. We have the replacement cost approach that we've talked about, the income capitalization method, and finally, the sales comparison method. And each one of these methods has an appropriate time and place to use them. For our purposes most people are generally concerned with the sales comparison method because they're wanting to know "What is my house worth today?"

PART V

Case Study Analysis and Epilogue

Chapter 15

Case Study Analysis: How *You* Can Go from Zero to $20k in 90 Days or Less!

The precepts discussed in the previous chapters of this book all come together in this chapter in the form of a case study analysis. Analyzing real estate in this manner provides a greater understanding of the investment process as it applies to flipping properties. This is where sound theory and ideas are converted to practical application in their intended form, where everything we have discussed throughout the book is demonstrated. The case study used in this chapter pertains to a house that had been foreclosed upon and was subsequently bought by my company from the federal Department of Housing and Urban Development. As you read through the analysis, think about the principles discussed in this book and pay particular attention to how the principles we have discussed in this book apply.

CASE STUDY: FROM $0 TO $20K

The example used in this case study is one of a house I found for sale on the HUD web site. This house had previously been under contract by another buyer. The buyer's financing apparently fell through, however, because the house was placed back on the market through the normal HUD process. Sometimes when a house suddenly appears back on the HUD web site it can represent a good opportunity for buyers. You can tell whether the house has been listed on the HUD site before by looking at the listing date. The original date appears indicating that the house has been in the HUD system for a while. Such was the case for this house. The minimum bid on it was $22,000. Before ever taking the time to drive around and look at houses, I want to know what comparable sales in the surrounding neighborhood look like. A quick search in the MLS indicated that other houses in that area were selling between about $60,000 and $75,000. I knew from experience that on a deal like this I might have to invest up to $20,000 in improvements, so just doing some quick mental calculations suggested there was probably enough profit margin in it to warrant a drive to the house.

As I drove through the neighborhood, pride of ownership was evident at almost every yard and every house. The lawns were neatly cared for, there were no junky cars or boats around, and there were very few "For Sale" signs. These were all indications that the neighborhood was fairly stable. An inspection of the house revealed that it would need to be painted both inside and out. It also needed a new roof, new kitchen cabinets, new flooring, new lighting, and several other minor improvements. After driving through the neighborhood and inspecting the house, I used the Value Play Rehab Analyzer to estimate the potential profit in this flipping opportunity. The Analyzer indicated a profit ranging from about $19,000 to $27,000, which falls within an acceptable rate of return on smaller deals such as this one. After determining that the level of profit generated from this transaction would be acceptable, I placed a bid for slightly more than the $22,000 HUD asking price just in case there were any other investors bidding that day. When you see a deal like this, there isn't time to sit around and think about it. Remember that there are other investors looking at these houses, too.

I was notified the following day that HUD had accepted my bid and would be ready to close within the next 30 days. The pictures included here are actual photos of the house taken before the renovation had begun and after it was completed.

THE VALUE PLAY REHAB ANALYZER

Now take a few minutes to review Exhibit 15.1—Property Analysis Worksheet for Wood Lane. The worksheet featured here is a proprietary model I developed that I use to quickly and easily analyze potential value play rehab and flipping opportunities. Once I have gathered all of the necessary data, I can input the information into the model and in just a few minutes, know with a reasonable degree of accuracy whether or not a deal makes sense, based upon my initial assumptions. All I have to do is key in the information and the model automatically makes all of the calculations. This dynamic model has been instrumental in generating lucrative profits for me and thousands of other investors as

Before Interior Kitchen

After Interior Kitchen

Before Exterior Side

After Exterior Side

Before Exterior Front

After Exterior Front

Before Interior Living Room

After Interior Living Room

Exhibit 15.1
The Value Play Rehab Analyzer Property Analysis Worksheet

The Value Play Rehab Analyzer Property Analysis Worksheet
July 1, 2007

Purchase Assumptions

Project Name: Case Study
Address: 123 South State St.
City, State, Zip: Flint, MI
Contact: Symphony Homes
Telephone: (800) 555-1111

Land	0
Building/House	22,200
Closing Costs	750
Other Related Costs	0
Total Purchase Price	22,950

Financing Assumptions - Primary

Primary Mortgage or Loan:

Total Purchase	100.00%	22,950
Down Payment	10.00%	2,295
Balance to Finance	90.00%	20,655

	Annual	Monthly
Interest Rate	7.500%	0.625%
Amort Period	30	360
Payment	1,733	144
Interest Only	1,549	129

Financing Assumptions - Secondary

Secondary Financing/Line of Credit:

Total Improvements	100.00%	14,575
Down Payment	10.00%	1,458
Balance to Finance	90.00%	13,118

	Annual	Monthly
Interest Rate	7.500%	0.625%
Amort Period	15	180
Payment	1,459	122
Interest Only	984	82

Estimate for Improvements

Appliances		Flooring		Lighting	225
Dishwasher	0	Carpet	1,200	Masonry	0
Disposal	0	Ceramic Tile	0	Other	0
Microwave	0	Hardwood	0	Other	0
Range	0	Vinyl	425	Other	0
Refrigerator	0	Subtotal	1,625	Painting: Exterior	800
Subtotal	0			Painting: Interior	1,200
		Foundation	0	Permits	0
Architectural Drawings	0	Framing	0	Subtotal	2,225
Cabinets	1,700	Garage	0		
Caulking	75	Gas & Electric Hookup	0	Plumbing	
Subtotal	1,775	Glass: Mirrors, showers	300	Commodes	100
		Gutters	250	Drain Lines	0
Cement Work		Subtotal	550	Faucets	125
Basement Floor	0			Fixtures	225
Driveway	0	HVAC		Hot Water Heater	0
Garage Floor	0	Air Conditioner	0	Showers	100
Porches	100	Duct Work	0	Tubs	0
Sidewalks	0	Filters	25	Water Lines	0
Subtotal	100	Furnace	250	Subtotal	550
		Subtotal	275		
Cleaning	250			Roofing	3,350
Counter Tops	450	Insulation	0	Siding	0
Decorating	0	Insurance Premiums	325	Site Planning & Engineering	0
Doors	0	Subtotal	325	Steel	0
Drywall	150			Trim	100
Electrical	0	Landscaping		Utility: Gas & Electric	350
Engineering	0	Irrigation System	0	Utility: Water & Sewer	125
Equipment Rental	200	Lot Clearing	200	Warranty	0
Excavation Work	0	Mowing Services	125	Windows	600
Fences	850	Sod	0	Subtotal	4,525
Fireplace	0	Trees, Plants, & Shrubs	400		
Subtotal	1,900	Subtotal	725	Total Cost of Improvements	14,575

Comp #1

Address:
Sales Price	61,500.00
Adjustments to Price	1,500.00
Adjusted Price	63,000.00
Square Feet	735.00
Price Per Square Foot	85.71

Comp #2

Address:
Sales Price	76,250.00
Adjustments to Price	0.00
Adjusted Price	76,250.00
Square Footage	1,125.00
Price Per Square Foot	67.78

Comp #3

Address:
Sales Price	68,700.00
Adjustments to Price	0.00
Adjusted Price	68,700.00
Square Feet	950.00
Price Per Square Foot	72.32

Comp Averages

Sales Price	68,816.67
Adjustments to Price	500.00
Adjusted Price	69,316.67
Square Feet	936.67
Price Per Square Foot	74.00
Turn Comps Off/On	ON
Est Price/Sq Ft If Turned OFF	75.00

WWW.THEVALUEPLAY.COM - COPYRIGHT PROTECTED 1998

Subject Property 123 South State St.

Square Feet	875.00
Price/Sq Ft	26.23
Improvements/Sq Ft	16.66
Total Price/Sq Ft	42.89
Estimated Time To Complete Project	4.00

Description	Best Case	Most Likely	Worst Case
		Adjustment to Comps	5.00
Est Sales Price	69,128	64,753	60,378
Purchase Price	22,950	22,950	22,950
Improvements	14,575	14,575	14,575
Interest Charges	844	844	844
Taxes	500	500	500
Closing Costs	2,765	2,590	2,415
Total Costs	41,634	41,459	41,284
Profit Margin	27,494	23,294	19,094
Return On Inv	732.68%	620.75%	508.83%

well. This particular deal netted a little over $20,000 and was sold almost as soon as it was finished. As the title of this chapter suggests, this flipping opportunity went from $0 to $20K in 90 days or less!

PURCHASE ASSUMPTIONS

Under the Purchase Assumptions section, the basic property information is listed, including a project name, address, and pricing information. The value of the land doesn't really matter as long as the price of the land plus the price of the house is equal to the total purchase price. It is placed there for those investors who may wish to separate the two values for tax purposes. The purchase price of the house in this case study was estimated to be $22,200 with approximately $750 in closing costs, bringing the total acquisition cost to $22,950.

PRIMARY AND SECONDARY FINANCING ASSUMPTIONS

There are two sections for Financing Assumptions—one for primary financing and another one for secondary financing. The primary financing section is used for the main source of lending, which can be in the form of a loan from a mortgage company, bank, hard money lender, or a private individual, as this example illustrates. The line of credit available to me to purchase bank REOs and HUD houses provides 90 percent loan-to-value financing, leaving me to come up with the balance of 10 percent for the down payment. The secondary financing section is used for any additional loans that may be needed for improvements. For lower cost improvements such as the one in this example, you may wish to use all cash. On the other hand, if the cost of the improvements is greater than the amount of capital available to you, then this is the section to use. Rates and terms are typically different for a line of credit, such as a home equity line or a credit card, than they are for a regular mortgage, so having two sections for financing allows investors to more accurately determine the related carrying costs. In this example, I have assumed borrowing at a 90 percent loan-to-value ratio.

ESTIMATE FOR IMPROVEMENTS

Under the Estimate for Improvements section, there is quite a bit of detail that provides investors with the ability to estimate the costs for virtually everything in a house. Estimating these costs accurately is essential for the proper analysis of an investment rehab and flipping opportunity. The more experience you have, the easier estimating costs become. At first, you may need to obtain bids or estimates from contractors to help determine how much the required repairs will cost. As you gain experience, however, you'll be able to estimate many of the costs yourself. The Total Cost of Improvements in this example was estimated to be $14,575.

COMPARABLE HOME SALES

The next section of the model allows investors to enter information for comparable home sales. This information is needed to help make accurate projections of the estimated resale value of an investment property. If you don't already have access to the MLS in your area, any real estate sales agent can provide comparable sales data for the area you are interested in. There is also an area in this section of the model for making adjustments to the sales price of the comps. This provision permits buyers to compare houses on an apples-to-apples basis. If, for example, the home you are buying has a two-car garage and the comparable home sale has a three-car garage, you will need to revise the price downward in the Adjustments to Price section. This is exactly how real estate agents and appraisers derive the market value of a house. They start with an average price per square foot of several similar houses and make compensating adjustments to estimate value. For the subject property, I used three comparable sales that were representative of the one I was thinking about bidding on. I did not make any adjustments to them because I was comfortable with the values as they were. The price per square foot on these comps ranged from a low of $69.09 to a high of $83.67.

COMP AVERAGES

The Comp Averages section simply takes an average of the three comps sales prices to come up with an average sales price to be used for the subject property. This number is then divided by the average price per square foot. The result is a weighted average price per square foot. This section also has a provision that allows the comps section to be turned on or off. As you become familiar with a specific market or neighborhood, you are likely to already know what the average sales price per square foot is, so you don't need to key in sales comp data. Instead, you can turn the comps section off and plug in your own estimate. In this example, the average sales price of the houses is $68,816, the average square feet is 936, and the average price per square foot is $74.

SUBJECT PROPERTY

The average sales price per square foot is then fed into the Subject Property section. All of the information keyed into the rest of the model is summarized in this section. The square footage of the subject property must be known so that an accurate comparison can be made. The purchase price per square foot is automatically calculated, as is the total cost of the improvements per square foot. The two numbers are then added together to calculate the total cost of the project. In this example, the Total Cost of Improvements of $14,575 was added to the Total Purchase Price of $22,950. The resulting sum was then divided by 875 square feet for a Total Price per Square Foot of $42.89. Below that is a provision allowing users of the model to estimate the total time for completion of the renovations and resale time, which is represented in months. In other words, the model calculates the carrying costs for interest based on the amount financed, a factor that many novice investors do not consider. In the example here, the number of months is set to 4.00.

The Adjustment to Comps cell is used to create the Estimated Sales Price for three different sales scenarios—Best Case, Most Likely, and Worst Case. In this example, $5.00 per square foot is used. For the Best Case Sales Price, the model adds $5.00 to the Price Per Square Foot cell in the Comp Averages section, and then multiplies the sum of the two by the square feet of the subject property (there are slight rounding differences in the model). Here's how it works:

Best Case Sales Price

$$(\text{Avg. Price/Sq Ft} + \text{Adj to Comps}) \times \text{Subject Property Sq Ft}$$
$$= \text{Best Case Sales Price}$$
$$(\$74.00 + \$5.00) \times 875 = \$69,128$$

■ Case Study Analysis ■

The Most Likely Sales Price calculation in the model neither adds nor subtracts the value of $5.00 to the Price per Square Foot cell in the Comp Averages section. It is simply the product of the Average Price per Square Foot and the Square Feet. Take a moment to review the calculation.

Most Likely Sales Price

Avg. Price/Sq Ft × Subject Property Sq Ft

= Most Likely Sales Price

$74.00 × 877 = $64,753

For the Worst Case Sales Price, the model subtracts $5.00 from the Price per Square Foot cell in the Comp Averages section, and then multiplies the difference of the two by the square feet of the subject property. Take a minute to study the calculation.

Worst Case Sales Price

(Avg. Price/Sq Ft − Adj to Comps) × Subject Property Sq Ft

= Worst Case Sales Price

($74.00 − $5.00) × 875 = $60,378

The purpose of creating three different scenarios in the model is to provide investors with a range for the estimated sales price. This allows you to evaluate the very minimum you might expect on the low end of the price range, and the very most you might expect on the high end of the price range. The Purchase Price, Improvements, Interest Charges, and Taxes remain constant across all three scenarios since these values are not affected by the Adjustment to Comps variable of $5.00. The value for Closing Costs, however, does not remain constant but is instead derived by multiplying 4 percent by the Estimated Sales Price. The Profit Margin is the dollar amount that can be expected from an investment after all costs have been accounted for. The Return on Investment is calculated as the ratio of the Profit Margin divided by the total cash invested in the property. It is calculated in this example for the Most Likely scenario as follows:

Return on Investment

$$\frac{\text{Profit Margin}}{\text{Primary Down Payment} + \text{Secondary Down Payment}} = \text{ROI}$$

$$\frac{\$23,294}{\$2,295 + \$1,458)} = 620.75\%$$

Based on the assumptions used in our model, the expected return on the subject property is $23,294, which represents a 620 percent return on invested capital. How many stocks are you aware of that offer that kind of return? My guess is not very many, if any at all. Now let's take a look at the actual results and see how they compare to the original projections as calculated in the model. Take a moment to review Exhibit 15.2, the Job Profitability Detail Report for the subject property.

The actual purchase price of the house was $22,200, which was the same figure used in the Rehab Analyzer (excluding closing costs). The total cost for the project including the house, improvements, carrying costs, and closing costs was $44,529. This compares to a total cost of $41,459 in the model. The actual costs were higher than expected, primarily as a result of $4,955 in seller contributions. The sales price on this house was $65,000, which compares with the $64,753 used in the most likely scenario in the model. The actual net profit for this property was $20,471, which compares with the $23,294 in the model. Once again, the shortfall can be attributed to the seller contributions I agreed to pay for the buyer. Although the profit margin was slightly less than expected in the most likely scenario, it nevertheless fell within the range of profit margins calculated in the Rehab Analyzer.

In this example, I purchased a house that had already been foreclosed on for slightly more than $20,000, then put another $20,000 into it, and then sold it for a profit of $20,000. I think you would agree with me that a $20,000-plus profit margin on a house I only paid $22,200 for would certainly be an acceptable return by most standards. As you can see, using a dynamic model like the Value Play Rehab Analyzer can be extremely beneficial to an investor. All of the purchase, financing, and improvement assumptions for an investment property can be made quickly and easily in a matter of minutes. Buyers can then accurately assess the level of profitability in it before even a single dime is invested (see Appendix A for more information about the Value Play Rehab Analyzer).

This particular house sold the very first weekend I put it on the market. One of my sales agents held an open house on a Saturday and Sunday after advertising the property in the

Exhibit 15.2
Symphony Homes Job
Profitability Detail Actual Cost

Symphony Homes Job Profitability Detail Actual Costs	
Administrative	$ 55
Cabinets	1,448
Caulking	225
Cleaning	95
Countertops	445
Door Hardware	464
Dwelling	22,200
Electrical	335
Equipment Rental	250
Flooring	1,700
General Labor	540
Glass	112
HVAC	223
Insurance Premiums	351
Interest Expense	556
Landscaping	420
Lighting	177
Other	55
Painting	1,883
Plumbing	432
Roofing	2,445
Sales Agents	1,877
Seller Contributions	4,955
Settlement Charges	2,622
Superintendent	420
Utilities	244
Total Costs	**44,529**
Sales Price	**65,000**
Net Profit	**$ 20,471**

classified rent section of the newspaper as a "Rent to Own." The agent had about fifteen people all together who attended the open house. She took applications from each person who was interested in renting the house to own and then submitted them to a mortgage company the following Monday with the idea in mind that one of the applicants may very well qualify for a loan. As it turned out, I had more than one buyer to choose from as several people actually qualified to obtain a mortgage to buy the house. I was in and out of this particular deal in less than 90 days from the time I purchased it to the time I sold it. By following the principles and precepts described in this book, you, too, can go from zero to $20,000 in 90 days.

Chapter 16

The Three Principles of Power

In the concluding chapter of *The Complete Guide to Buying and Selling Apartment Buildings,* I wrote about the five keys to success as follows:

The central focus of this book is to arm you with the specific tools necessary to identify potential acquisition candidates, to acquire and manage those properties once identified, to implement sound techniques for creating value, and finally, to capture all of that value, or as much of it as possible, through various exit strategies. The process by which all of this can be accomplished rests, I believe, on five keys that are crucial to success. These keys do not deal with the mechanical processes involved in buying and selling apartment buildings, but are grounded in principles fundamental to life itself. These laws deal with the human psyche. They govern our thoughts, which in turn, direct our actions. The failure to understand these keys—which can provide the foundation of happiness, and ultimately of success—will almost certainly guarantee your defeat.

The Five Keys to Success

1. Understanding risk
2. Overcoming fear of failure
3. Accepting responsibility
4. Willingness to persevere
5. Defining your sense of purpose

Although the book was comprehensive in dealing with the subject of apartment buildings, I received more correspondence from individuals who were moved and inspired by this chapter than by any other material in the book, a factor which I believe has largely contributed to its success. One such reader, a Mr. David S. of West Hollywood, California, writes, "Your book has truly taught me about investing in apartment buildings, but more importantly it has taught me about life.... The words not only inspired this reader, but allowed me to see the importance of having a purpose."

This chapter is much like the concluding chapter in *The Complete Guide to Buying and Selling Apartment Buildings.* In this chapter, I discuss what I refer to as the three principles of power. These three principles have absolutely nothing to do with real estate in particular, yet everything to do with your success in it. For that matter, the three principles of power can be applied to any business or profession and are not just limited to real estate. These laws can furthermore be used in your personal life, and when properly applied, can be a source of great joy and happiness to you and to those with whom you associate.

Although I have a passion for investing in real estate, the things that I write in this chapter are far more important to me than finding the next house to buy or sell. These principles lie at the very core of my belief system. They are an integral part of who I am. They are what compel me each and every day to strive for that perfection which I know I will never achieve in this life. It is my hope to inspire you to incorporate these three principles of power into your belief system. Doing so will enable you to reach the highest level of achievement of which you are truly capable. You will be empowered to fulfill the measure of your creation, to reach your potential, and to enjoy the abundant gifts life has to offer. (See Exhibit 16.1.)

The three principles of power can best be illustrated by sharing with you an example of how one man I knew applied them in his life. The principle of vision, the principle of passion, and the principle of autonomy are all embodied within his story. Although this individual is relatively unknown in corporate America's public business circles, he has had a profound impact on the retailing industry. He is, in fact, directly responsible for creating the largest and most successful single retail store in America! You may be thinking of Sam Walton, the founder of Wal-Mart. This is not Sam's story, however. It is instead the story of Jim "Mattress Mack" McIngvale. "Who is he?" you ask. If you've ever lived in or visited Houston, Texas, in the last 20 to 25 years, chances are you know who Mattress Mack is. His 30-second commercials air on radio and television continuously, averaging one every seven minutes of every hour, or about 200 a day! Jim McIngvale is the creator and founder of the Houston-based Gallery Furniture store. With annual sales in excess of $200 million, his single site furniture store sells more furniture per square foot of retail space than any other store in the world!

Having lived in Houston for a number of years and being exposed to at least a portion of Gallery's 200-plus commercials a day, I was always impressed with the remarkable

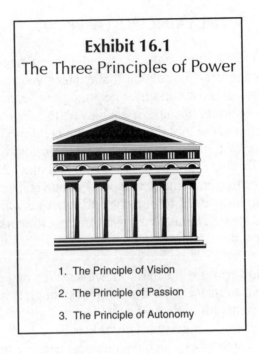

Exhibit 16.1
The Three Principles of Power

1. The Principle of Vision
2. The Principle of Passion
3. The Principle of Autonomy

success of Jim McIngvale. Although I didn't know Jim personally, his face was a familiar sight, as he did all of his own TV commercials. Jim's commercials, which were always the low-budget type with no paid actors, featured him jumping up and down with a wad of money in his hand and shouting, "Gallery Furniture really will save . . . you . . . money!!!" Jim is also a well-known community activist and participates in and supports many events in the Houston area. For example, Jim and Gallery Furniture are official sponsors of the Houston Rockets, and are also known for purchasing the grand champion steer each year at the Houston Livestock and Rodeo Show.

It wasn't until *Always Think Big* by Jim McIngvale was published (Dearborn Trade, 2002) that I was able to learn more about what made Mattress Mack so successful. *Always Think Big* is the story of Jim's life experiences as they relate to his business and the factors that contributed to his extraordinary accomplishments. The three principles of power—vision, passion, and autonomy—are exemplified in his story. Jim McIngvale personifies these three principles as he outlines his vision for what he intends to be the largest and most successful furniture store in Houston, then vigorously and passionately carries out that vision by acting autonomously through a series of independent-minded decisions acting against the advice of other professionals.

THE PRINCIPLE OF VISION

The principle of vision is a fundamental and essential component of the three principles of power, as it provides the very foundation that enables you to enjoy and exercise the other two precepts of passion and autonomy. The principle of vision is a priceless treasure for which there is no substitute, because it enables us to see where we are going long before we get there. Vision is the tool that gives us the power to create our own destiny.

Jim McIngvale's story of building the world's most productive retail furniture store began with a vision. At the age of about 22, Jim, who had played football in high school and college, yearned to be like his father, "independent and self-reliant." In *Always Think Big,* Jim's vision of who he wanted to become and what he wanted to do with his life had already begun. He states, "The 30-year plan of going to work for someone else was never a consideration for me. I'm an entrepreneur. I knew that I was going to start and run my own business."

Before going into the furniture business, however, Jim had suffered a devastating setback in the health club industry. His love of sports coupled with his entrepreneurial spirit led him to open six health clubs in Dallas, Texas, within a five-year period. Jim recalls, "Some time after opening my third club, I realized I wasn't paying attention to my customers, couldn't watch or examine the business details, and failed to make many scheduled meetings." It wasn't long after that that the cash flow from the health clubs began to dry up and Jim knew that the stores were in trouble. He writes, "Finally, when the cash could no longer be shuffled from club to club, and from club to creditors at a satisfactory rate, I had to file for bankruptcy protection. I was devastated." To make matters even worse, Jim was served with divorce papers by his wife's attorney shortly thereafter. The financial stress and pressure had not only ruined him financially, but it had also ruined his family.

Jim McIngvale sold his car, broke the lease on his luxury apartment, and moved back in with his parents, stripped not only of all his worldly possessions, but also of his pride and self-esteem. He began to sink into a dark state of despair and depression. He had lost all hope and sense of purpose. His life became meaningless. In his despondent state, Jim's battered spirit suffered greater and greater emotional trauma with each passing day. His love of life, his dreams of success, his hope for a brighter future were all but lost. Jim writes,

I spent days at a time without leaving my parents' house. I felt like a failure. When I looked in the mirror, I thought to myself that I even looked like a failure. A mostly shy and private person already, I was now becoming even more withdrawn. Talking became a burden. My depression began to feed on itself. The more depressed I got, the less functional I became. The less functional I became, the more depressed I got. It became a vicious cycle that anyone who has suffered from depression knows all too well. I had always had something to lift my spirits when things weren't going well—football, weight lifting, business. Now I wasn't sure what to do. (p. 12)

After several months of moping around his parents' house, Jim's dad had finally had enough. Although he had tried to be understanding of what Jim was going through, he decided that in order for Jim to climb out of the hole of self-pity, he was going to need a good kick in the pants. Actually, what he gave Jim was a kick right out of the front door. That's right. Just like a mother bird, Jim's dad pushed him right out of the nest to force him to fly, or in this case, to get back on his feet. He gave him exactly one week to find a place and get out.

The nudge Jim's father gave him turned out to be just what he needed. With very little money, Jim decided to approach his sister, who was married and had a family to care for, about staying with her for a few days until he could figure out what he wanted to do with his life. The following Sunday morning while watching TV, Oral Roberts happened to come on. Although Jim didn't much care for television evangelism, something was different on this day. It seemed as though Oral Roberts was speaking directly to him,

Are you feeling as if you don't have the power to change? Do you feel as though you've lost control of your life? What should you do about it? Many people feel this way. The problem is, most people think small, and small results are what they get. The solution is to always think big. Think big and believe good things will happen. Think big and strive to achieve greater things each day. You have the choice. Think small and keep on getting small results, or think big and strive for goals that stretch your limits. (p. 19)

Oral Roberts's message was exactly what Jim needed to hear at that moment in his life. Jim had always been in the habit of thinking big, or of having a vision, just as he did with his health clubs. He had just suffered a minor and temporary setback. That was all. It was now time to get back on track. By the following Tuesday morning, he had already made up his mind about what he wanted to do. From the time he was a small boy, Jim had always been fascinated with furniture. He wasn't sure where that fascination stemmed from, but thought it probably had something to do with his mother. She constantly rearranged the furniture in the house, and from time to time, bought new and unusual pieces to decorate the house with. Jim determined right away that if he were going to open his own furniture store, he would first need to learn something about the business. He got a job at one of the local furniture stores in Dallas as a salesman and began to immediately apply himself by studying and learning everything he could about the business. After only five months, Jim McIngvale became the top sales producer in the store and was already planning his next move, which was to open his own store.

Jim had firmly believed in the message Oral Roberts delivered on that dark and lonely Sunday morning, the message of thinking big. Jim had a plan. He had a vision of opening the most successful furniture store in the city. The only problem was, he just wasn't sure which city to open his new store in. He didn't want to compete against his employer who had given him an opportunity to prove himself, and if he was going to fulfill his dream of owning the most successful furniture store in the city, that meant that it would have to be in a different city. Jim had heard that Houston was experiencing strong growth, so that's where he decided he would have the best chance of becoming the furniture king of the city.

One of my all-time favorite quotes is by Zig Ziglar. He says, "Go as far as you can see, and when you get there, you can always see farther." Think about Zig's statement for a moment. While it is simplistic in structure, it is profound in meaning. Imagine traveling on a ship across the ocean and looking out across the vast expanse of water to the point where the sky meets the ocean. It's the horizon. In this case, if you "go as far as you can see," you will travel on the ship to the point where you first saw the horizon. As you travel closer to that specific point, however, you realize that the horizon is now at a point beyond where you first saw it; hence, "when you get there, you can always see farther."

Zig Ziglar's quote aptly applies to having a vision of what you want to become or of what level you want to grow your real estate business to. You will naturally not have all of the answers when you first start out. Your vision begins as a tiny seed. As you water it and nourish it, it will begin to grow. Just like the seed, your vision needs food and nourishment too. This means that in addition to being a dreamer or a visionary, you must be a doer as well. You must take action upon your vision or it will never bear fruit. The more you act upon achieving your dreams, the clearer they will become to you. As you take steps toward fulfilling your vision, the vision will begin to crystallize and become more well-defined with each passing day. "Go as far as you can see, and when you get there, you can always see farther."

That is exactly what Jim McIngvale did. He had a vision of owning and operating the largest and most successful furniture store in Houston. When Jim first started out, he didn't have all of the answers. His vision was but a tiny seed. It was through his continued efforts to nourish the seed that he was able to successfully achieve his dream. With each passing day, Jim's dream became more and more vivid. It was beginning to take shape. It was beginning to become crystal clear exactly what steps he needed to take to solidify and fulfill his dream. Jim's approach was that he wanted to do absolutely everything he could to "delight" the customer. His customers told him over and over that they didn't like having to wait four to six weeks to get their furniture like they did at other furniture stores. In *Always Think Big,* Jim describes this important aspect of his vision by stating

> The trickle of customers started to pick up over time, and I learned immediately that delivering furniture when the customer wants it had to become a Gallery promise. I wanted Gallery to be totally committed to same-day delivery. This was an important anchor in my plan and vision of how to succeed in the furniture business. (p. 36)

As Jim listened intently each and every day to what his customers were telling him, he became absolutely convinced that the same-day approach to delivering furniture was the key to his success. Not only did Jim listen to his customers for information that would help fuel the growth of his business, he had also formed the habit of observing other successful businesses and what steps they had taken to achieve success. One such example is Southwest Airlines. Jim notes,

> I had observed carefully and occasionally firsthand one particular segment of Southwest Airlines' approach to customers and how they repeatedly turned around and cleaned planes to meet schedules. I believed that Southwest's approach to meeting schedules could be applied to the furniture business. Even today, the practice of most furniture stores is to take a customer's order and deliver it in about six, ten, or fifteen weeks. I knew that this gap between purchase and delivery was disappointing and frustrating to customers. Southwest Airlines cut out all the frills and provided passengers with better, faster, and cheaper service. Why not better, faster, and cheaper delivery of furniture? (pp. 36–37)

And that is exactly what Jim "Mattress Mack" McIngvale did. He had a vision of becoming the most successful store in Houston. He didn't start out with all of the answers, but by going as far as he could see, he was always able to go farther when he got there. Jim watered and nourished his vision by acting upon the feedback his customers were giving him, and by observing other successful businesses. Jim's vision is no longer a dream. It has become a reality. By acting upon his intense vision, Gallery Furniture of Houston, Texas, now delivers furniture "better, faster, and cheaper" than any other furniture store in the world. The first principle of power, the principle of vision, enabled Jim McIngvale to achieve remarkable heights in the furniture business. This principle can no doubt empower you to achieve extraordinary success in the real estate business as well. To those who would dare to dream, and dream big, Jim offers this wise counsel:

> Dreams can be powerful motivators for taking action. . . . Before you start to assemble your own plan and lessons to follow, think about what you want. . . . Don't hold back. Let your dream evolve. Most people have to learn how to dream again. When you were young, dreams were a natural process. Try to reestablish your ability to dream. Practice, practice, practice dreaming each day. (p. 215)

THE PRINCIPLE OF PASSION

Although having a vision is a good place to start, it is simply not enough. You must be absolutely *passionate* about that vision. To be passionate about a vision, an idea, or a cause means that you feel very strongly about it. You believe in that idea or vision with every fiber of your soul. In fact, you feel so strongly about your vision or your dream that you are compelled to act upon it. It is that level of enthusiastic belief in a principle or idea that will enable you to be successful.

A vision often starts as an idea or strong belief in something. Over time it begins to take shape. The vision becomes more distinct and pronounced, and as it does, your feelings about it begin to intensify. They become so strong, in fact, that you begin to pursue your dream with a passionate and zealous fervor. Jim "Mattress Mack" McIngvale is a perfect example of one who pursued his dreams with great passion. In his book *Always Think Big*, Jim asserts,

> My plan and dedication to success was burning and passionate. I would sell furniture, move furniture around, help deliver furniture, treat customers

like royalty, and think up ways to outsell the competition.... I spent every minute selling, selling, selling. Each day required 100 percent focus on and attention to customers.... I had a powerful desire and determination to succeed. What I possessed was deeper than a goal or destination. I had a determination to be successful. (pp. 35–39)

One of the benefits of being passionate about your vision is that the enthusiasm you exert is often contagious. If you believe with all your heart and soul in what you are trying to accomplish, that belief will begin to be shared by others. When you are passionate about your dreams, your actions tend to reflect a level of zeal and fervor that others can't help but notice. Although many of your associates will share your beliefs, there are those who will have no interest whatsoever in your ideas. While it is okay to share your vision with others, be careful not to impose it upon them. Writing of his own personal experience, Jim affirms,

One thing I learned through reading and observation is that there is a degree of fanaticism in some individuals that allows passion to actively destroy them in the long run.... Over the years I have learned to back off when others are smothered by my passion and determination.... I finally learned that not everyone can work at my pace. So what? As long as they treat customers right, delight them, and give Gallery their best, I can live with it. It took me years to learn the lesson that everyone is different and to respect these differences. (p. 40)

I encourage you to adapt the second principle of power, the principle of passion, in your pursuit of success. Believe with all of your heart, might, mind, and soul in the principles for which you stand. Transform your enthusiasm into determination and focused action, tempered with respect for others. The fervent application of this principle has propelled many individuals to success. The principle of passion can help you to achieve your dreams as well.

THE PRINCIPLE OF AUTONOMY

The principle of autonomy is a crucial component of the three principles of power and is necessary to carry out and implement the first two principles, the principle of vision and the principle of passion. Autonomy has to do with your ability to think, and *act,* independently of what others may think of you or your ideas. While it is imperative that you have a vision and are passionate about that vision, you must be confident enough within yourself to carry out that vision regardless what others may say.

There are, and will always be, the naysayers of the world. They will tell you that what you are trying to achieve simply cannot be done. And they know, because they have tried to do the same thing and have failed. This is not to suggest that you completely disregard what other people have to say. You should always be open-minded and welcome the input of others. To be autonomous, however, means that you are capable of making up your own mind. You listen to the suggestions of others, objectively evaluate the information, and then determine what course of action best fits your needs. In *Always Think Big,* Jim McIngvale describes the traditional furniture establishments' approach to delivering furniture, and how he was told time after time that his vision of "buy it today and we'll deliver it tonight" would never work. Jim writes,

> Our competitors doubted that we could stick with the same-day delivery approach. Gallery did, and we continue to prove them wrong. We enjoy being able to occasionally beat the customer to their home with their new furniture. Even today, the Gallery delivery truck is waiting for some of our customers as they pull up to their homes. What a treat! (p. 36)

So there you have it. Time after time, Jim McIngvale's competitors told him that it just couldn't be done. No one had succeeded in doing it before, and Gallery Furniture wouldn't be able to do it now. If Jim had listened to all of the well-respected and so-called experts in the furniture industry, he never would have succeeded in his dream to build the largest and most successful furniture store in Houston. As it turns out, Jim was able to far surpass his original goal by building the most successful furniture store in the world!

The third principle of power, the principle of autonomy, is vital to your success in real estate. You must be able to think and act independently of what others may advise. Don't be afraid to stand up for what you so passionately believe in—your visions, your dreams, your aspirations. Business acquaintances, friends, and even family members will tell you that it "just simply can't be done." I encourage you to politely ignore their pessimistic remarks and exercise your own free will. The ability to act autonomously is what distinguishes a leader from a follower. You already have the seed of leadership within you. Now you must water it and nourish it. You can do that by standing up for the principles you so firmly believe in. As you do, your leadership skills will grow enabling you to achieve your goals. Jim "Mattress Mack" McIngvale offers this sage advice to those who dare to pursue their dreams, in spite of what others may say.

> The principle of thinking big should be another part of your personal plan. ... If you believe that your body is what it is fed, so is your mind. If your mind only thinks small or is uncertain, then you will act accordingly. In addition to doing the necessary small things, you should also think big and think bold. Telling me that it was impossible to adhere to my promise of same-day delivery was like a jumpstart to me. Instead of accepting the naysayers' views about furniture delivery, I made up my mind to prove the doubters wrong. I never doubted that Gallery could be the business that brings same-day delivery into the furniture industry. I refused to accept the noise coming at me for being "foolish," a "huckster," and "crazy dreamer."
>
> Surrendering to the doubters and naysayers would have been easy. Surrendering or changing my big dream was never an option. The pessimistic, negative, can't-do-it thinking of others required me to focus, pay attention to details, and to work around the clock. To me, pessimism, small thinking, and ridicule are poisons to be avoided. (pp. 229, 230)

In summary, adapting the three principles of power into your real estate investment strategy can mean the difference between success and failure. First, you must have a clear and distinct vision of what it is you want to achieve. While your vision may lack clarity and detail initially, remember that as you work toward fulfilling it, the vision will eventually become crystal clear as you draw closer to accomplishing it. Once again, in the words of Zig Ziglar, "Go as far as you can see, and when you get there, you can always see farther." Second, you must be passionate about your dreams and aspirations to be successful. Your passion and enthusiasm for your dreams demonstrates to others your level of commitment. Pursuing your vision with passion and zeal is a manifestation to them that you are indeed determined to succeed. Finally, you must be able to act autonomously. You must break the shackles of dependence that so easily bind the commoners. You have the power to set yourself free! By incorporating the three principles of power—vision, passion, and autonomy—into your life, you will not only be able to achieve your goals, but you will be able to far surpass them. Implementing these principles will enable you to attain the highest level of achievement of which you are capable. You will be empowered to fulfill the measure of your creation, to reach your true potential, and to enjoy the generous gifts life has to offer. Your capacity to soar to magnificent heights that are far beyond the reach of the general masses shall become infinite in scope, unlimited in magnitude, and vastly immeasurable by ordinary standards. You have the power within you to create your destiny. I encourage you to apply these principles in your life, for by doing so, you will not only be able to create your destiny, but you will also be able to fulfill it.

> **The soul is dyed in the color of its thoughts. Think only on those things that are in line with your principles and can bear the full light of day. The content of your character is your choice. Day by day, what you choose, what you think, and what you do, is who you become. Your integrity is your destiny. It is the light that guides your way.**
> *—Heraclitus, Greek poet and philosopher*

Chapter 17 (Bonus!)

S.M.A.R.T. Goals

Setting goals for yourself is fundamental to achieving success and is undeniably one of the most important steps you can take in the process of accumulating wealth. Setting goals applies not only to achieving financial success, but to achieving success in all realms of life. Whether you want to excel in educational, spiritual, or physical areas of your life, you must be willing to set goals. I know, I know. You don't have time to set goals, right? The kids are keeping you up at night, the boss is over-demanding, and it's all you can do to keep up with everything else going on. My response to that is that if you don't *have* the time to set goals, then you need to *make* the time to set goals. If you don't have a plan of action in place, then you'll end up exactly where you started, which is at the beginning. Before you know it, 20 years will have gone by and you still won't have made the kind of progress that you had hoped to. If you don't know where you are going, how will you know when you get there?

I like to think of the process of wealth accumulation as more of a lifelong journey than as something that happens overnight. As stated in Chapter 1, this is not a get-rich-quick book. It is, however, a get-rich book. A successful real estate investor is also a patient real estate investor. I am not suggesting that it will take 50 years to amass a sizable fortune, although it certainly could for some people. The average investor should begin to see results on the very first transaction and from there, it is a matter of how well and how quickly one is able to duplicate those efforts. You can build a phenomenal real estate portfolio one house at a time. The person who invests in one house a year will obviously not achieve the level of results as the person who invests in one house a month. It is not so much the rate or the speed that counts in the pursuit of wealth as it is the consistent and diligent application of the efforts required to achieve it. Remember the story of the tortoise and the hare? Mr. Hare was much faster than Mr. Tortoise. He was so fast, in fact, that he thought he would surely beat Mr. Tortoise to the finish line. It didn't take long, however, for Mr. Hare to get sidetracked with one thing or another and before he knew it, Mr. Tortoise had passed him by and won the race. While Mr. Speedy O. Hare was much faster, he had lost his focus. Mr. Slow N. Steady Tortoise, on the other hand, did not. He continued to plod along, slowly but surely, in the race against the hare. It was Mr. Tortoise's ability to stay focused and to consistently stay on the path without getting sidetracked that allowed him to win the race. Speed had nothing to do with it.

Like the tortoise, we also must be willing to apply ourselves on a consistent and ongoing basis. Accumulating wealth is not about who can get to the finish line first, but just simply getting to the finish line. It's more like running a marathon than running a 100-yard dash. Everyone who finishes the race is considered a winner. Like the hare, it's easy to get sidetracked by the many distractions of the world. These distractions often become excuses that are used to justify our inability to achieve the success we desire, and therein lies the necessity of establishing S.M.A.R.T. Goals.

Okay, enough of the small talk. So what exactly are S.M.A.R.T. goals anyway? S.M.A.R.T. is an acronym that can help us to effectively set goals. It stands for *specific, measurable, attainable, reasonable,* and *time-oriented.* Just as following a compass keeps us from getting lost, adhering to these five precepts enables us to stay on the path that will ultimately lead to our success. Setting goals the S.M.A.R.T way is not just limited to achieving financial success, but can help you achieve success in any and all areas of life, including educational, spiritual, and physical goals. (See Exhibit 17.1.)

Now let's break the S.M.A.R.T acronym down and take it one step at a time. The first letter of the acronym is *S.* This letter stands for *specific.* The goals you set must be specific in nature and not just generalized. For example, you can't just say "I want to be rich," or "I want to lose weight." You must be specific. Your definition of rich, or losing weight, is most likely different from other people's definition. Being rich to one person might mean having $1 million in the bank, while being rich to another person might mean having just $100,000 in the bank. It could also be defined as your overall net worth, or how much equity you have in your real estate portfolio. Being rich has many meanings, and chances are, your definition of rich is different from your neighbor's. The same principle holds true for losing weight. You must be very specific with the amount of weight you want to lose. Do you want to lose 5 pounds, 10 pounds, or perhaps as much as 50 or 100 pounds? Whatever the answer is, it must be a well-defined and specific amount.

Okay, by now I think you get the picture of what it means to set specific goals. Let's move on to the next letter of the acronym, which is *M.* The letter M stands for *measurable.* The goals you establish must be able to be measured. For example, it is relatively easy to measure your financial progress by looking at your bank statements or investment

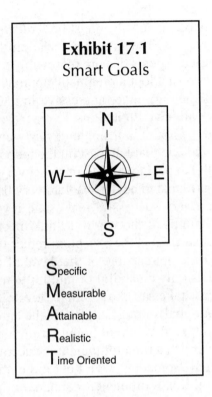

Exhibit 17.1
Smart Goals

Specific
Measurable
Attainable
Realistic
Time Oriented

account statements. You get a printout each month or each quarter that measures your progress. Whether the account goes up or down, forward or backward, the statement is a tool or an instrument that helps measure the progress you have made toward achieving your financial goals. Likewise, a scale is used to measure one's progress toward the goal of losing weight. Once every few days, we pull the scale out of the closet and stand on it to determine how well we are doing toward achieving our goal of shedding those few unwanted pounds. We may not like what we see, but the scale nevertheless measures our progress, whether it be good or bad, up or down.

The next letter of the acronym in our S.M.A.R.T formula for success is *A*. The letter A stands for *attainable*. Very simply put, the goals you set must be attainable. For example, if a person is 50 years old and sets the goal of becoming an astronaut and is just now getting started, chances are slim to none that the goal will be attained. On the other hand, if a person is in her twenties and wants to become an astronaut, the opportunity to attain this goal is much greater.

In addition to being attainable, goals also must be *realistic,* which is the next step in the S.M.A.R.T formula for success. The term *realistic* is similar to the term *attainable* in that both terms are used to refer to goals that are reasonably achievable. To set goals that are realistic implies that you must adopt a pragmatic approach. This suggests that while it is appropriate to set goals that are rather aggressive in nature, we must nevertheless recognize that as humans we all have limitations. In other words, there is only so much we can do given the number of hours in a single day. My approach over the years has been to shoot for the stars and hope that I at least hit the moon. My cautiously optimistic approach has served me well. I expect to do well in most everything I set my mind to, but don't necessarily believe that I have to be the absolute very best in a particular category. In other words, while I am a very successful real estate investor, my success pales in comparison to the Donald Trumps of the world. I think most people would agree with me that his level of financial success is the exception rather than the rule. That is not to say, however, that you and I are not capable of that level of achievement, but rather to say that in general there exists only a handful of multibillionaires in the world and that to achieve that level of success takes an extraordinary level of commitment.

Finally, the last letter of our goal-setting acronym is the letter *T,* which stands for *time oriented.* If you are going to take the time of going through the process of establishing goals, then you also must establish a time for them to be accomplished by. For example, to say that you want to be rich "someday" won't cut it. On the other hand, if the stated objective was to build a $1 million retirement account over the next five years, the goal then meets the criterion for being time oriented. My suggestion would be to break that goal down even further by annual and even quarterly increments. To do so in this example means increasing the account by an average of $200,000 per year and $50,000 per quarter.

Now that we have examined all of the components of the S.M.A.R.T formula individually, let's put them all together to see more clearly how this works. Let's assume that your goal as a real estate investor is to increase your wealth by a minimum of $1 million through the process of flipping properties over the next 10 years. Now let's apply this goal to our S.M.AR.T formula to determine whether or not it contains all of the necessary components.

Specific—yes, $1 million
Measurable—yes, by measuring the profits of each transaction
Attainable—yes, requires a diligent individual with a persistent attitude
Realistic—yes, $1 million is very realistic and if anything, is a conservative goal
Time Oriented—yes, wealth is accumulated over a 10-year period

After applying our stated goal to the S.M.A.R.T formula, it appears that it does, in fact, contain all of the necessary components called for in the formula. We can therefore conclude that an investor who diligently applies the techniques contained in this book can achieve the goal of building a $1 million retirement portfolio over a 10-year period. Whether the stated goal is 3 years, 5 years, or 10 years is up to you. You also may set your sights higher than $1 million. Perhaps that's just the tip of the iceberg of your real estate portfolio. It is up to you to determine where you want to be 5 or 10 years from now. The point is that you must have a plan in place because if you don't, there's a good chance you'll still be right where you are today if you do not.

Take a moment to review Exhibit 17.2, Seven Keys to Our Success. I attribute much of our success to these seven very important keys. I have included this exhibit for two reasons. First, it is an example of the S.M.A.R.T formula of setting goals and includes all of its key components, and second, to illustrate that I practice what I preach. Yes, believe it or not, I do set goals for our company. I furthermore require the managers who work for me to set goals as well. We then follow up by taking time to review them each quarter. I have adapted what I refer to as a return-and-report philosophy. In other words, I expect my managers to be accountable by periodically reporting to me. If all we did was just set goals, and then never take the time to review them, we might as well not bother to set them to begin with. My managers know in advance that when they set their goals, they will be expected to provide me with progress reports from time to time. If they never had to report their progress, it would be a waste of time for me and for them to set their goals.

Exhibit 17.2
Seven Keys to Our Success

1. Professional Leadership

2. The QVS Product Equation

3. Aggressive Marketing Initiatives

4. Access to Capital to Fuel Growth

5. Continued Market Expansion

6. Formation of Alliance with Market Leaders

7. Development of Large Well Trained Sales Force

Another principle that will help you attain your goals is the principle of *inertia*. Recall from one of your early grade school science classes that inertia is defined as "a property of matter whereby it remains at rest, or continues in uniform motion unless acted upon by some outside force." By now you must be asking, "What in the world does inertia have to do with setting goals?" The best way to answer that is to look at a couple of examples. Let's first examine the property of inertia as it applies to launching and flying one of the NASA space shuttles. I'm sure you've seen the impressive video footage of a space shuttle as it is first launched into orbit. Smoke billows upward and outward as the shuttle rumbles on the launching pad, and flames of fire shoot out hundreds of feet as all of its rockets are engaged. It takes literally thousands of pounds of thrust to get the space shuttle up off the launching pad into the atmosphere and finally into space where it settles into a perfect orbit over the earth. The principle of inertia requires that the shuttle "remain at rest" until it is "acted upon by some outside force." In this example, it took the tremendous power and thrust created by the rocket engines to get the shuttle off the launching pad and into space. Once the shuttle is in orbit, however, it no longer requires the energy created by its rockets that it once needed in the earth's atmosphere. The shuttle can continue in orbit indefinitely, flying at approximately 25,000 miles per hour with only minor adjustments needed occasionally to keep it on track. It will "continue in uniform motion until acted upon by some outside force."

Before I explain how this relates to setting goals, let's look at one more quick example. How many of you have a difficult time getting out of bed in the morning? If you're like most people, there's a good chance that waking up and crawling out of bed is often a challenge. Your body is "at rest" all night long. When it's time to wake up in the morning, a "force" is required to get your body out of bed and moving. Once you wake up, however, have a bite of breakfast, and take a shower, your body seems to move a little more easily. Before you know it, you're wide awake, full of energy, and ready for the new day. It just took a little "force" to get you up and moving around.

Now let's tie these examples back to using real estate as a vehicle to accumulate wealth along with the process of setting goals. In order to create wealth by flipping properties, an outside force is going to be needed to get you started. The outside force is in reality a force that must come from *within* you. Only you can apply the tools and concepts outlined in this book to get you started. No one else is going to do it for you. Yes, building a respectable retirement portfolio will require effort on your part. The good news, however, is that once you get started, you will discover that flipping properties becomes easier and easier. You gain more knowledge and experience with every transaction, you become a little more efficient each time you buy and sell, and before you know it, you're well on your way to becoming the next Donald Trump! Remember also that the principle of inertia applies not just to creating wealth, but to almost any goal you set. It requires effort to get started, but once you get going, you're well on your way to accomplishing that goal.

One final point that I suggest you keep in mind when setting goals is this—*half of the battle is just showing up*. I know, that sounds like common sense and everyone should already know that, so why bother to state the obvious? I need to state the obvious because sometimes the answer is right in front of us and for one reason or another, we don't recognize it as such. Let me share a personal example with you. I set a goal several years ago to lose weight, get in shape, and earn the rank of Black Belt in the style of martial arts known as Tang Soo Do. There were many, many times I absolutely did not feel like going to work out and to train, for one reason or another. The excuses were endless. I had a busy day at work, I was too tired, my wife needed help with the kids at home, and the list went on and on and on. Although I did succumb to those feelings every now and then, for the most part I was very diligent (and still am) about going to work out and train. I accomplished all three of the goals I set. I lost weight, got in shape, and earned a Black Belt in Tang Soo Do. I should mention also that my oldest son, Philip, earned his Black Belt right along with me at the ripe old age of 10 (yes, I did say *10!*). I can honestly say that I am in better shape today than at any other time in my life. The key to my success was *showing up!* Once I got to the gym, the rest was easy. I enjoyed the workouts, I enjoyed the training, and by the end of each session I genuinely felt better. Although my body had just been put through intense training, it was nevertheless quite invigorating. Little by little, the training became easier, my endurance increased, and my skills improved. So the next time you don't feel like working toward your goals, remember this very simple principle—*half the battle is just showing up!*

Author Steve Berges Achieving Black Belt Along with His Son Philip

Appendix A

Property Inspection Checklist

Date_____

Property Information: Seller's Name
                               Address
                               Phone Number

For the Project: Project Name
                               Address
                               Other Information

INSTRUCTIONS: Inspect the project and carefully check whether all items meet the project specifications. Initial in the space marked "Satisfactory" if the item meets with your approval. If an item is not satisfactory, describe the problem in the "Comments" field. Add additional information where necessary. Modify the list to fit your finish schedule. After work on the noted items has been completed, you will need to make a second inspection and initial in the last box for final approval.

Item	Satisfactory	Comments	Est Cost
Foyer			
Floors			
Ceilings			
Walls			
Light Fixtures			
Windows			
Doors			
Trim Moldings			
Other			
Dining Room			
Floors			
Ceilings			
Walls			
Light Fixtures			
Windows			
Doors			
Trim Moldings			
Other			
Living Room			
Floors			
Ceilings			
Walls			
Woodwork			
Light Fixtures			
Windows			
Doors			

Initialed by: Buyer___ Seller___

Item	Satisfactory	Comments	Est Cost
Trim Moldings			
Fireplace			
Other			
Kitchen			
Floors			
Ceilings			
Walls			
Light Fixtures			
Windows			
Doors			
Trim Moldings			
Cabinets			
Countertop			
Sink			
Oven and range			
Hood and exhaust fan			
Microwave			
Dishwasher			
Disposal			
Trash Compactor			
Other			
Breakfast Room			
Floors			
Ceilings			
Walls			
Light Fixtures			
Windows			

Initialed by: Buyer___ Seller___

Item	Satisfactory	Comments	Est Cost
Doors			
Trim Moldings			
Other			
Family Room			
Floors			
Ceilings			
Walls			
Light Fixtures			
Windows			
Doors			
Trim Moldings			
Woodwork			
Other			
Powder Room			
Floors			
Ceilings			
Walls			
Light Fixtures			
Windows			
Doors			
Trim Moldings			
Vanity			
Toilet			
Towel Bar			
Paper Holder			
Other			

Initialed by: Buyer___ Seller___

Item	Satisfactory	Comments	Est Cost
Utility Room			
Floors			
Ceilings			
Walls			
Light Fixtures			
Windows			
Doors			
Trim Moldings			
Hot Water Heater			
Furnace/Heat Pump			
Washer Hookup			
Dryer Hookup			
Other			
Master Bedroom			
Floors			
Ceilings			
Walls			
Light Fixtures			
Windows			
Doors			
Trim Moldings			
Other			
Master Bath			
Floors			
Ceilings			

Initialed by: Buyer___ Seller___

Item	Satisfactory	Comments	Est Cost
Walls			
Light Fixtures			
Windows			
Doors			
Trim Moldings			
Vanity			
Toilet			
Whirlpool/Garden Tub			
Shower			
Shower door			
Towel Bar			
Paper Holder			
Other			
Bedroom Two			
Floors			
Ceilings			
Walls			
Light Fixtures			
Windows			
Doors			
Trim Moldings			
Other			
Bedroom Three			
Floors			
Ceilings			
Walls			
Light Fixtures			

Initialed by: Buyer___ Seller___

Item	Satisfactory	Comments	Est Cost
Windows			
Doors			
Trim Moldings			
Other			
Bedroom Four			
Floors			
Ceilings			
Walls			
Light Fixtures			
Windows			
Doors			
Trim Moldings			
Other			
Bedroom Five			
Floors			
Ceilings			
Walls			
Light Fixtures			
Windows			
Doors			
Trim Moldings			
Other			
Bath Two			
Floors			

Initialed by: Buyer___ Seller___

■ Appendix A ■

Item	Satisfactory	Comments	Est Cost
Ceilings			
Walls			
Light Fixtures			
Windows			
Doors			
Trim Moldings			
Vanity			
Toilet			
Shower			
Shower door			
Towel Bar			
Paper Holder			
Other			
Bath Three			
Floors			
Ceilings			
Walls			
Light Fixtures			
Windows			
Doors			
Trim Moldings			
Vanity			
Toilet			
Whirlpool/Garden Tub			
Shower			
Shower door			
Towel Bar			
Paper Holder			
Other			

Initialed by: Buyer___ Seller___

Item	Satisfactory	Comments	Est Cost
Bath Four			
Floors			
Ceilings			
Walls			
Light Fixtures			
Windows			
Doors			
Trim Moldings			
Vanity			
Toilet			
Whirlpool/Garden Tub			
Shower			
Shower door			
Towel Bar			
Paper Holder			
Other			
Hallway			
Floors			
Ceilings			
Walls			
Light Fixtures			
Windows			
Doors			
Trim Moldings			
Other			

Initialed by: Buyer___ Seller___

Item	Satisfactory	Comments	Est Cost
Garage			
Floors			
Ceilings			
Walls			
Light Fixtures			
Windows			
Doors			
Trim Moldings			
Garage Door			
Garage Door Opener			
Storage Area			
Other			
Study/Library			
Floors			
Ceilings			
Walls			
Light Fixtures			
Windows			
Doors			
Trim Moldings			
Other			
Additional Room			
Floors			
Ceilings			
Walls			
Light Fixtures			
Windows			

Initialed by: Buyer___ Seller___

Item	Satisfactory	Comments	Est Cost
Doors			
Trim Moldings			
Other			
Exterior			
Paint			
Exterior Veneer			
Chimney			
Roof			
Doors			
Walkways			
Driveway			
Light Fixtures			
Outlets			
Vents, dryer, fans, etc.			
Deck			
Porches			
Brick			
Siding			
Other			
HVAC Equipment			
Furnace			
Air Conditioner			
Filters			
Ducts and Vents			
Other			
Electrical			
Outlets			

Initialed by: Buyer___ Seller___

Item	Satisfactory	Comments	Est Cost
Wall Switches			
Wiring			
Breaker Panel			
Circuit Breakers			
Other			
Foundation			
Concrete Slab			
Basement			
Cracks			
Settling			
Evidence of Leaks			
Mold or Mildew			
Other			

First Inspection

Having inspected the project listed herein, except for those specific items listed above, the Buyer accepts the project as is, in satisfactory condition and understands the Buyer will not have a claim against the Seller for any overlooked items not listed above that could have been seen in the Buyer's inspection. The Buyer has discussed the specific items with the Seller and understands that the Seller makes no other guarantees or warranties other than those that are stated in the contract documents.

_____   _____

Seller's Signature   **Date**

_____   _____

Buyer's Signature   **Date**

Appendix B

Owner and Subcontractor Agreement

THIS AGREEMENT, Made as of January 2, in the Year of 2004.

Between the Owner: Mr. H. A. Stephens
                            1234 N. Main St.
                            (555) 555–5555

And the Subcontractor: Cool's Air Conditioning Service
                            License #123456
                            1234 S. Main St.
                            (555) 555–4444

For the Project: Sample A/C Project
                            4321 E. Main St.

ARTICLE 1. SCOPE OF WORK

1.1 Subcontractor has heretofore entered into a contract with said Owner to furnish all labor, materials, and equipment to perform all work described below according to the construction documents.

ARTICLE 2. PAYMENT TERMS

2.1   The Owner agrees to pay the Subcontractor within 14 days after the completion of the work and payment by the owner for such work.

2.2   Subcontractor understands and agrees that progress payment requests shall be written and given to the owner before Wednesday for payment on the following Friday. All work for the portion requested must be completed prior to the request for payment. The Owner will request a draw and payment will be made to the Subcontractor after the draw is received. Please note that a certificate of Workmen's Compensation Insurance must be received before the first payment is made or the Owner will hold a percentage needed to cover the labor portion of the job.

2.3   The Total Contract Amount shall be $3,687.00

ARTICLE 3. TIME OF COMPLETION

3.1   Subcontractor shall keep both an adequate size and properly trained crew on the job site so as to complete the project within 30 days and work within the project schedule.

ARTICLE 4. CHANGE ORDERS

4.1   Subcontractor understands and agrees that no change orders or contract additions will be made unless agreed to in writing by Owner. If any additional work is performed and not covered in this contract, the Subcontractor proceeds at his own risk and expense. No alterations, additions, or small changes can be made in the work or method of the performance, without the written change order signed by the owner and Subcontractor.

ARTICLE 5. CLEANUP

5.1   Subcontractor will be responsible for cleaning up the job on a daily basis, including all generated construction debris, drink cans, food wrappers, and/or other trash. If it becomes necessary, the Subcontractor will be back-charged for appropriate cleanup by deducting cleanup costs from payments.

ARTICLE 6. TAXES AND PERMITS

6.1 The Subcontractor understands and agrees to be responsible for all taxes, fees, and expenses imposed directly or indirectly for its work, labor, material, and services required to fulfill this contract. The Subcontractor is responsible for all permits pertaining to the law, ordinances, and regulations where the work is performed.

ARTICLE 7. INSURANCE

7.1 The Subcontractor shall maintain, at his own expense, full and complete insurance on its work until final approval of the work described in the contract. The Subcontractor shall not hold the Owner liable for any and all costs, damages, fees, and expenses from any claims arising on the project. Failure of the Subcontractor to maintain appropriate insurance coverage may deem a material breach, allowing the Owner to terminate this contract or to provide insurance at the Subcontractor's expense.

ARTICLE 8. LIQUIDATED DAMAGES

8.1 If the project is not substantially completed on the stated completion date, the Subcontractor shall pay to the Owner the sum of $100 per day for each calendar day of inexcusable delay until the work is substantially completed, as liquidated damages.

ARTICLE 9. WARRANTY

9.1 Subcontractor shall warranty all labor, materials, and equipment furnished on the project for one year against defects in workmanship or materials utilized. The manufacturer's warranty will prevail. No legal action of any kind relating to the project, project performance, or this contract shall be initiated by either party against the other party after five years beyond the completion of the project or cessation of work.

ARTICLE 10. HAZARDOUS MATERIALS, WASTE, AND ASBESTOS

10.1   Both parties agree that dealing with hazardous materials, waste, or asbestos requires specialized training, processes, precautions, and licenses. Therefore, unless the scope of this agreement includes the specific handling, disturbance, removal, or transportation of hazardous materials, waste, or asbestos, upon discovery of such hazardous materials the Subcontractor shall notify the Owner immediately and allow the Owner to contract with a properly licensed and qualified hazardous material owner.

ARTICLE 11. ARBITRATION OF DISPUTES

11.1   Any controversy or claim arising out of or relating to this contract, or the breach thereof, shall be settled by arbitration administered by the American Arbitration Association under its Construction Industry Arbitration Rules, and judgment on the award rendered by the arbitrator(s) may be entered in any court having jurisdiction thereof.

ARTICLE 12. ATTORNEY FEES

12.1   In the event of any arbitration or litigation relating to the project, project performance or this contract, the prevailing party shall be entitled to reasonable attorney fees, costs, and expenses.

ARTICLE 13. ACCEPTANCE

WITNESS our hand and seal on this ____ day of ____, 20 ____.

Signed in the presence of:

_____   _____
Owner's Name   **Date**

_____   _____
Subcontractor's Name   **Date**

Appendix C

Sample Real Estate Forms

■ Appendix C ■

SELLER'S DISCLOSURE OF PROPERTY CONDITION

(SECTION 5.008, TEXAS PROPERTY CODE)

CONCERNING THE PROPERTY AT _____
                                              (Street Address and City)

THIS NOTICE IS A DISCLOSURE OF SELLER'S KNOWLEDGE OF THE CONDITION OF THE PROPERTY AS OF THE DATE SIGNED BY SELLER AND IS NOT A SUBSTITUTE FOR ANY INSPECTIONS OR WARRANTIES THE PURCHASER MAY WISH TO OBTAIN. IT IS NOT A WARRANTY OF ANY KIND BY SELLER OR SELLER'S AGENTS.

Seller ☐ is ☐ is not occupying the Property. If unoccupied, how long since Seller has occupied the Property? _____

1. The Property has the items checked below [Write Yes (Y), No (N), or Unknown (U)]:

___Range	___Oven	___Microwave
___Dishwasher	___Trash Compactor	___Disposal
___Washer/Dryer Hookups	___Window Screens	___Rain Gutters
___Security System	___Fire Detection Equipment	___Intercom System
___TV Antenna	___Cable TV Wiring	___Satellite Dish
___Ceiling Fan(s)	___Attic Fan(s)	___Exhaust Fan(s)
___Central A/C	___Central Heating	___Wall/Window Air Conditioning
___Plumbing System	___Septic System	___Public Sewer System
___Patio/Decking	___Outdoor Grill	___Fences
___Pool	___Sauna	___Spa ___Hot Tub
___Pool Equipment	___Pool Heater	___Automatic Lawn Sprinkler System
___Fireplace(s) & Chimney(Woodburning)	___Fireplace(s) & Chimney (Mock)	___Gas Lines (Nat./LP)
___Gas Fixtures	Garage: ___Attached	___Carport
	___Not Attached	
Garage Door Opener(s):	___Electronic	___Control(s)
Water Heater:	___Gas	___Electric
Water Supply: ___City	___Well ___MUD	___Co-op

Roof Type: _____ Age: _____ (approx)

Are you (Seller) aware of any of the above items that are not in working condition, that have known defects, or that are in need of repair? ☐ Yes ☐ No ☐ Unknown. If yes, then describe. (Attach additional sheets if necessary): _____
_____

2. Are you (Seller) aware of any known defects/malfunctions in any of the following? Write Yes (Y) if you are aware, write No (N) if you are not aware.

___Interior Walls	___Ceilings	___Floors
___Exterior Walls	___Doors	___Windows
___Roof	___Foundation/Slab(s)	___Basement
___Walls/Fences	___Driveways	___Sidewalks
___Plumbing/Sewers/Septics	___Electrical Systems	___Lighting Fixtures
___Other Structural Components (Describe)		

_____
_____

01A   TREC No. OP-H

■ Appendix C ■

Seller's Disclosure Notice Concerning the Property at_____
(Street Address and City)

If the answer to any of the above is yes, explain. (Attach additional sheets if necessary): _____
_____
_____

3. Are you (Seller) aware of any of the following conditions? Write Yes (Y) if you are aware, write No (N) if you are not aware.

__Active Termites (includes wood-destroying insects)	__Termite or Wood Rot Damage Needing Repair	__Previous Termite Damage
__Previous Termite Treatment	__Previous Flooding	__Improper Drainage
__Water Penetration	__Located in 100-Year Floodplain	__Present Flood Insurance Coverage
__Previous Structural or Roof Repair	__Hazardous or Toxic Waste	__Asbestos Components
__Urea-formaldehyde Insulation	__Radon Gas	__Lead Based Paint
__Aluminum Wiring	__Previous Fires	__Unplatted Easements
__Landfill, Settling, Soil Movement, Fault Lines	__Subsurface Structure or Pits	

If the answer to any of the above is yes, explain. (Attach additional sheets if necessary): _____
_____
_____

4. Are you (Seller) aware of any item, equipment, or system in or on the Property that is in need of repair? ☐ Yes (if you are aware) ☐ No (if you are not aware). If yes, explain (attach additional sheets as necessary). _____
_____
_____

5. Are you (Seller) aware of any of the following? Write Yes (Y) if you are aware, write No (N) if you are not aware.

___ Room additions, structural modifications, or other alterations or repairs made without necessary permits or not in compliance with building codes in effect at that time.

___ Homeowners' Association or maintenance fees or assessments.

___ Any "common area" (facilities such as pools, tennis courts, walkways, or other areas) co-owned in undivided interest with others.

___ Any notices of violations of deed restrictions or governmental ordinances affecting the condition or use of the Property.

___ Any lawsuits directly or indirectly affecting the Property.

___ Any condition on the Property which materially affects the physical health or safety of an individual.

If the answer to any of the above is yes, explain. (Attach additional sheets if necessary): _____
_____
_____

_____   _____   _____   _____
Date   Signature of Seller   Date   Signature of Seller

The undersigned purchaser hereby acknowledges receipt of the foregoing notice.

_____   _____   _____   _____
Date   Signature of Purchaser   Date   Signature of Purchaser

01A   TREC No. OP-H

■ Appendix C ■

PROMULGATED BY THE TEXAS REAL ESTATE COMMISSION (TREC)

9-22-97

ONE TO FOUR FAMILY RESIDENTIAL CONTRACT (RESALE)
ALL CASH, ASSUMPTION, THIRD PARTY CONVENTIONAL OR SELLER FINANCING

NOTICE: Not For Use For Condominium Transactions

1. **PARTIES:** _____ (Seller) agrees
   to sell and convey to _____(Buyer) and Buyer
   agrees to buy from Seller the property described below.

2. **PROPERTY:** Lot _____, Block _____, _____
   Addition, City of _____, _____ County,
   Texas, known as _____
   (Address/Zip Code), or as described on attached exhibit, together with the following items, if any: curtains and rods, draperies and rods, valances, blinds, window shades, screens, shutters, awnings, wall-to-wall carpeting, mirrors fixed in place, ceiling fans, attic fans, mail boxes, television antennas and satellite dish system with controls and equipment, permanently installed heating and air-conditioning units, window air-conditioning units, built-in security and fire detection equipment, plumbing and lighting fixtures including chandeliers, water softener, stove, built-in kitchen equipment, garage door openers with controls, built-in cleaning equipment, all swimming pool equipment and maintenance accessories, shrubbery, landscaping, permanently installed outdoor cooking equipment, built-in fireplace screens, artificial fireplace logs and all other property owned by Seller and attached to the above described real property except the following property which is not included: _____

   _____

   _____.
   All property sold by this contract is called the "Property." The Property ❑ is ❑ is not subject to mandatory membership in an owners' association. The TREC Addendum For Property Subject To Mandatory Membership In An Owners' Association ❑ is ❑ is not attached.

3. **SALES PRICE:**
   A. Cash portion of Sales Price payable by Buyer at closing .... $_____
   B. Sum of all financing described below
      (excluding any private mortgage insurance [PMI] premium) .... $_____
   C. Sales Price (Sum of A and B) .... $_____

4. **FINANCING:** Within _____ days after the effective date of this contract Buyer shall apply for all third party financing or noteholder's approval of any assumption and make every reasonable effort to obtain financing or assumption approval. Financing or assumption approval will be deemed to have been obtained when the lender determines that Buyer has satisfied all of lender's financial requirements (those items relating to Buyer's net worth, income and creditworthiness). If financing (including any financed PMI premium) or assumption approval is not obtained within _____ days after the effective date hereof, this contract will terminate and the earnest money will be refunded to Buyer. Each note to be executed hereunder must be secured by vendor's and deed of trust liens.
   The portion of Sales Price not payable in cash will be paid as follows: (Check applicable boxes below)
   ❑ A. THIRD PARTY FINANCING:
      ❑ (1) This contract is subject to approval for Buyer of a third party first mortgage loan having a loan-to-value ratio not to exceed _____ % as established by such third party (excluding any financed PMI premium), due in full in _____ year(s), with interest not to exceed _____ % per annum for the first _____ year(s) of the loan. The loan will be ❑ with ❑ without PMI.

Initialed for identification by Buyer_____ and Seller_____   **01A**   TREC NO. 20-3

▪ Appendix C ▪

One to Four Family Residential Contract Concerning_____ Page Two   9-22-97
(Address of Property)

❑ (2) This contract is subject to approval for Buyer of a third party second mortgage loan having a loan-to-value ratio not to exceed _____ % as established by such third party (excluding any financed PMI premium), due in full in _____ year(s), with interest not to exceed _____ % per annum for the first _____ year(s) of the loan. The loan will be ❑ with ❑ without PMI.

❑ B. TEXAS VETERANS' HOUSING ASSISTANCE PROGRAM LOAN: This contract is subject to approval for Buyer of a Texas Veterans' Housing Assistance Program Loan (the Program Loan) of $_____ for a period of at least _____ years at the interest rate established by the Texas Veterans' Land Board at the time of closing.

❑ C. SELLER FINANCING: A promissory note from Buyer to Seller of $_____, bearing _____ % interest per annum, secured by vendor's and deed of trust liens, in accordance with the terms and conditions set forth in the attached TREC Seller Financing Addendum. If an owner policy of title insurance is furnished, Buyer shall furnish Seller with a mortgagee policy of title insurance.

❑ D. ASSUMPTION:

❑ (1) Buyer shall assume the unpaid principal balance of a first lien promissory note payable to _____ which unpaid balance at closing will be $ _____ . The total current monthly payment including principal, interest and any reserve deposits is $ _____ . Buyer's initial payment will be the first payment due after closing.

❑ (2) Buyer shall assume the unpaid principal balance of a second lien promissory note payable to _____ which unpaid balance at closing will be $ _____ . The total current monthly payment including principal, interest and any reserve deposits is $ _____ . Buyer's initial payment will be the first payment due after closing.

Buyer's assumption of an existing note includes all obligations imposed by the deed of trust securing the note.

If the unpaid principal balance(s) of any assumed loan(s) as of the Closing Date varies from the loan balance(s) stated above, the ❑ cash payable at closing ❑ Sales Price will be adjusted by the amount of any variance; provided, if the total principal balance of all assumed loans varies in an amount greater than $350.00 at closing, either party may terminate this contract and the earnest money will be refunded to Buyer unless the other party elects to eliminate the excess in the variance by an appropriate adjustment at closing. If the noteholder requires (a) payment of an assumption fee in excess of $ _____ in D(1) above or $ _____ in D(2) above and Seller declines to pay such excess, or (b) an increase in the interest rate to more than _____ % in D(1) above, or _____ % in D(2) above, or (c) any other modification of the loan documents, Buyer may terminate this contract and the earnest money will be refunded to Buyer. A vendor's lien and deed of trust to secure assumption will be required which shall automatically be released on execution and delivery of a release by noteholder. If Seller is released from liability on any assumed note, the vendor's lien and deed of trust to secure assumption will not be required.

NOTICE TO BUYER: The monthly payments, interest rates or other terms of some loans may be adjusted by the lender at or after closing. If you are concerned about the possibility of future adjustments, do not sign the contract without examining the notes and deeds of trust.

NOTICE TO SELLER: Your liability to pay the note assumed by Buyer will continue unless you obtain a release of liability from the lender. If you are concerned about future liability, you should use the TREC Release of Liability Addendum.

❑ E. CREDIT APPROVAL ON ASSUMPTION OR SELLER FINANCING: Within _____ days after the effective date of this contract, Buyer shall deliver to Seller ❑ credit report ❑ verification of employment, including salary ❑ verification of funds on deposit in financial institutions ❑ current financial statement to establish Buyer's creditworthiness for assumption approval or seller financing and ❑ _____ .

If Buyer's documentation is not delivered within the specified time, Seller may terminate this contract by notice to Buyer within 7 days after expiration of the time for delivery, and the earnest money will

Initialed for identification by Buyer_____and Seller_____   **01A**   TREC NO. 20-3

▪ 241 ▪

■ Appendix C ■

(Address of Property)

be paid to Seller. If this contract is not so terminated, Seller will be deemed to have accepted Buyer's credit. If the documentation is timely delivered, and Seller determines in Seller's sole discretion that Buyer's credit is unacceptable, Seller may terminate this contract by notice to Buyer within 7 days after expiration of the time for delivery and the earnest money will be refunded to Buyer. If Seller does not so terminate this contract, Seller will be deemed to have accepted Buyer's credit. Buyer hereby authorizes any credit reporting agency to furnish to Seller at Buyer's sole expense copies of Buyer's credit reports.

5. **EARNEST MONEY:** Buyer shall deposit $_____ as earnest money with _____ _____ at _____ (Address), as escrow agent, upon execution of this contract by both parties. Additional earnest money of $_____ must be deposited by Buyer with escrow agent on or before _____, 19____. If Buyer fails to deposit the earnest money as required by this contract, Buyer will be in default.

6. **TITLE POLICY AND SURVEY:**
   ❑ A. TITLE POLICY: Seller shall furnish to Buyer at ❑ Seller's ❑ Buyer's expense an owner policy of title insurance (the Title Policy) issued by _____(the Title Company) in the amount of the Sales Price, dated at or after closing, insuring Buyer against loss under the provisions of the Title Policy, subject to the promulgated exclusions (including existing building and zoning ordinances) and the following exceptions:
   (1) Restrictive covenants common to the platted subdivision in which the Property is located.
   (2) The standard printed exception for standby fees, taxes and assessments.
   (3) Liens created as part of the financing described in Paragraph 4.
   (4) Utility easements created by the dedication deed or plat of the subdivision in which the Property is located.
   (5) Reservations or exceptions otherwise permitted by this contract or as may be approved by Buyer in writing.
   (6) The standard printed exception as to discrepancies, conflicts, shortages in area or boundary lines, encroachments or protrusions, or overlapping improvements.
   (7) The standard printed exception as to marital rights.
   (8) The standard printed exception as to waters, tidelands, beaches, streams, and related matters.
   Within 20 days after the Title Company receives a copy of this contract, Seller shall furnish to Buyer a commitment for title insurance (the Commitment) and, at Buyer's expense, legible copies of restrictive covenants and documents evidencing exceptions in the Commitment other than the standard printed exceptions. Seller authorizes the Title Company to mail or hand deliver the Commitment and related documents to Buyer at Buyer's address shown below. If the Commitment is not delivered to Buyer within the specified time, the time for delivery will be automatically extended up to 15 days. Buyer will have 7 days after the receipt of the Commitment to object in writing to matters disclosed in the Commitment.
   ❑ B. SURVEY: (Check one box only)
      ❑ (1) Within_____ days after Buyer's receipt of a survey furnished to a third-party lender at ❑ Seller's ❑ Buyer's expense, Buyer may object in writing to any matter shown on the survey which constitutes a defect or encumbrance to title.
      ❑ (2) Within_____ days after the effective date of this contract, Buyer may object in writing to any matter which constitutes a defect or encumbrance to title shown on a survey obtained by Buyer at Buyer's expense.
   The survey must be made by a Registered Professional Land Surveyor acceptable to the Title Company and any lender. Utility easements created by the dedication deed and plat of the subdivision in which the Property is located will not be a basis for objection.
   Buyer may object to existing building and zoning ordinances, items 6A(1) through (8) above and matters shown on the survey if Buyer determines that any such ordinance, items or matters prohibits the following use or activity: _____
   _____

Initialed for identification by Buyer_____ and Seller_____   **01A**   TREC NO. 20-3

■ Appendix C ■

Buyer's failure to object under Paragraph 6A or 6B within the time allowed will constitute a waiver of Buyer's right to object; except that the requirements in Schedule C of the Commitment will not be deemed to have been waived. Seller shall cure the timely objections of Buyer or any third party lender within 15 days from the date Seller receives the objections and the Closing Date will be extended as necessary. If objections are not cured by the extended Closing Date, this contract will terminate and the earnest money will be refunded to Buyer unless Buyer elects to waive the objections.

NOTICE TO SELLER AND BUYER:

(1) Broker advises Buyer to have an abstract of title covering the Property examined by an attorney of Buyer's selection, or Buyer should be furnished with or obtain a Title Policy. If a Title Policy is furnished, the Commitment should be promptly reviewed by an attorney of Buyer's choice due to the time limitations on Buyer's right to object.

(2) If the Property is situated in a utility or other statutorily created district providing water, sewer, drainage, or flood control facilities and services, Chapter 49 of the Texas Water Code requires Seller to deliver and Buyer to sign the statutory notice relating to the tax rate, bonded indebtedness, or standby fee of the district prior to final execution of this contract.

(3) If the Property abuts the tidally influenced waters of the state, Section 33.135, Texas Natural Resources Code, requires a notice regarding coastal area property to be included in the contract. An addendum either promulgated by TREC or required by the parties should be used.

(4) Buyer is advised that the presence of wetlands, toxic substances, including asbestos and wastes or other environmental hazards or the presence of a threatened or endangered species or its habitat may affect Buyer's intended use of the Property. If Buyer is concerned about these matters, an addendum either promulgated by TREC or required by the parties should be used.

(5) Unless expressly prohibited in writing by the parties, Seller may continue to show the Property for sale and to receive, negotiate and accept back up offers.

(6) Any residential service contract that is purchased in connection with this transaction should be reviewed for the scope of coverage, exclusions and limitations. **The purchase of a residential service contract is optional. Similar coverage may be purchased from various companies authorized to do business in Texas.**

7. PROPERTY CONDITION:

A. INSPECTIONS, ACCESS AND UTILITIES: Buyer may have the Property inspected by an inspector selected by Buyer, licensed by TREC or otherwise permitted by law to make such inspections. Seller shall permit access to the Property at reasonable times for inspection, repairs and treatment and for reinspection after repairs and treatment have been completed. Seller shall pay for turning on utilities for inspection and reinspection.

B. SELLER'S DISCLOSURE NOTICE PURSUANT TO SECTION 5.008, TEXAS PROPERTY CODE (Notice) (check one box only):

☐ (1) Buyer has received the Notice.

☐ (2) Buyer has not received the Notice. Within _____ days after the effective date of this contract, Seller shall deliver the Notice to Buyer. If Buyer does not receive the Notice, Buyer may terminate this contract at any time prior to the closing. If Seller delivers the Notice, Buyer may terminate this contract for any reason within 7 days after Buyer receives the Notice or prior to the closing, whichever first occurs.

☐ (3) The Texas Property Code does not require this Seller to furnish the Notice.

C. SELLER'S DISCLOSURE OF LEAD-BASED PAINT AND LEAD-BASED PAINT HAZARDS is required by Federal law for a residential dwelling constructed prior to 1978. An addendum providing such disclosure ☐ is ☐ is not attached.

D. ACCEPTANCE OF PROPERTY CONDITION: (check one box only):

☐ (1) In addition to any earnest money deposited with escrow agent, Buyer has paid Seller $_____ (the "Option Fee") for the unrestricted right to terminate this contract by giving notice of termination to Seller within _____ days after the effective date of this contract. If Buyer gives notice of termination within the time specified, the Option Fee will not be refunded, however, any earnest money will be refunded to Buyer. If Buyer does not give notice of

Initialed for identification by Buyer_____ and Seller_____   **01A**   TREC NO. 20-3

■ Appendix C ■

(Address of Property)

termination within the time specified, Buyer will be deemed to have accepted the Property in its current condition and the Option Fee ❑ will ❑ will not be credited to the Sales Price at closing.

❑ (2) Buyer accepts the Property in its present condition; provided Seller, at Seller's expense, shall complete the following repairs and treatment: _____

_____.

E. LENDER REQUIRED REPAIRS AND TREATMENTS (REPAIRS): Unless otherwise agreed in writing, neither party is obligated to pay for lender required repairs or treatments for wood destroying insects. If the cost of lender required repairs exceeds 5% of the Sales Price, Buyer may terminate this contract.

F. COMPLETION OF REPAIRS AND TREATMENT. Unless otherwise agreed by the parties in writing, Seller shall complete all agreed repairs and treatment prior to the Closing Date. Repairs and treatments must be performed by persons who regularly provide such repairs or treatments. At Buyer's election, any transferable warranties received by Seller with respect to the repairs will be transferred to Buyer at Buyer's expense. If Seller fails to complete any agreed repairs and treatment prior to the Closing Date, Buyer may do so and the Closing Date will be extended up to 15 days, if necessary, to complete repairs and treatment or treatments for wood destroying insects.

8. **BROKERS' FEES:** All obligations of the parties for payment of brokers' fees are contained in separate written agreements.

9. **CLOSING:** The closing of the sale will be on or before _____, 19____, or within 7 days after objections to matters disclosed in the Commitment or by the survey have been cured, whichever date is later (the Closing Date). *If financing or assumption approval has been obtained pursuant to Paragraph 4,* the Closing Date will be extended up to 15 days if necessary to comply with lender's closing requirements (for example, appraisal, survey, insurance policies, lender-required repairs, closing documents). If either party fails to close this sale by the Closing Date, the non-defaulting party will be entitled to exercise the remedies contained in Paragraph 15. At closing Seller shall furnish tax statements or certificates showing no delinquent taxes and a general warranty deed conveying good and indefeasible title showing no additional exceptions to those permitted in Paragraph 6.

10. **POSSESSION:** Seller shall deliver possession of the Property to Buyer on _____ in its present or required repaired condition, ordinary wear and tear excepted. Any possession by Buyer prior to closing or by Seller after closing which is not authorized by a temporary lease form promulgated by TREC or required by the parties will establish a tenancy at sufferance relationship between the parties. *Consult your insurance agent prior to change of ownership or possession as insurance coverage may be limited or terminated. The absence of a written lease or appropriate insurance coverage may expose the parties to economic loss.*

11. **SPECIAL PROVISIONS:** (Insert only factual statements and business details applicable to this sale. TREC rules prohibit licensees from adding factual statements or business details for which a contract addendum, lease or other form has been promulgated by TREC for mandatory use.)

Initialed for identification by Buyer_____ and Seller_____   **01A**   TREC NO. 20-3

One to Four Family Residential Contract Concerning_____Page Six   9-22-97
                                        (Address of Property)

12. SETTLEMENT AND OTHER EXPENSES:

   A. The following expenses must be paid at or prior to closing:

   (1) Appraisal fees will be paid by _____.

   (2) The total of loan discount fees (including any Texas Veterans' Housing Assistance Program Participation Fee) may not exceed _____% of the loan of which Seller shall pay _____ and Buyer shall pay the remainder. The total of any buydown fees may not exceed _____ which will be paid by _____.

   (3) Seller's Expenses: Releases of existing liens, including prepayment penalties and recording fees; release of Seller's loan liability; tax statements or certificates; preparation of deed; one-half of escrow fee; and other expenses stipulated to be paid by Seller under other provisions of this contract.

   (4) Buyer's Expenses: Loan application, origination and commitment fees; loan assumption costs; preparation and recording of deed of trust to secure assumption; lender required expenses incident to new loans, including PMI premium, preparation of loan documents, loan related inspection fee, recording fees, tax service and research fees, warehouse or underwriting fees, copies of restrictions and easements, amortization schedule, premiums for mortgagee title policies and endorsements required by lender, credit reports, photos; required premiums for flood and hazard insurance; required reserve deposit for insurance premiums and ad valorem taxes; interest on all monthly installment notes from date of disbursements to one month prior to dates of first monthly payments; customary Program Loan costs for Buyer; one-half of escrow fee; and other expenses stipulated to be paid by Buyer under other provisions of this contract.

   B.   If any expense exceeds an amount expressly stated in this contract for such expense to be paid by a party, that party may terminate this contract unless the other party agrees to pay such excess. In no event will Buyer pay charges and fees expressly prohibited by the Texas Veterans' Housing Assistance Program or other governmental loan program regulations.

13. PRORATIONS: Taxes for the current year, interest, maintenance fees, assessments, dues and rents will be prorated through the Closing Date. If taxes for the current year vary from the amount prorated at closing, the parties shall adjust the prorations when tax statements for the current year are available. *If a loan is assumed* and the lender maintains an escrow account, the escrow account must be transferred to Buyer without any deficiency. Buyer shall reimburse Seller for the amount in the transferred account. Buyer shall pay the premium for a new insurance policy. If taxes are not paid at or prior to closing, Buyer will be obligated to pay taxes for the current year.

14. CASUALTY LOSS: If any part of the Property is damaged or destroyed by fire or other casualty loss after the effective date of the contract, Seller shall restore the Property to its previous condition as soon as reasonably possible, but in any event by the Closing Date. If Seller fails to do so due to factors beyond Seller's control, Buyer may either (a) terminate this contract and the earnest money will be refunded to Buyer (b) extend the time for performance up to 15 days and the Closing Date will be extended as necessary or (c) accept the Property in its damaged condition and accept an assignment of insurance proceeds.   Seller's obligations under this paragraph are independent of any obligations of Seller under Paragraph 7.

15. DEFAULT: If Buyer fails to comply with this contract, Buyer will be in default, and Seller may either (a) enforce specific performance, seek such other relief as may be provided by law, or both, or (b) terminate this contract and receive the earnest money as liquidated damages, thereby releasing both parties from this contract. If, due to factors beyond Seller's control, Seller fails within the time allowed to make any non-casualty repairs or deliver the Commitment, Buyer may either (a) extend the time for performance up to 15 days and the Closing Date will be extended as necessary or (b) terminate this contract as the sole remedy and receive the earnest money. If Seller fails to comply with this contract for any other reason, Seller will be in default and Buyer may either (a) enforce specific performance, seek such other relief as may be provided by law, or both, or (b) terminate this contract and receive the earnest money, thereby releasing both parties from this contract.

Initialed for identification by Buyer_____ and Seller_____   **01A**   TREC NO. 20-3

■ Appendix C ■

One to Four Family Residential Contract Concerning_____Page Seven   9-22-97
(Address of Property)

16. DISPUTE RESOLUTION: It is the policy of the State of Texas to encourage the peaceable resolution of disputes through alternative dispute resolution procedures. The parties are encouraged to use an addendum approved by TREC to submit to mediation disputes which cannot be resolved in good faith through informal discussion.

17. ATTORNEY'S FEES: The prevailing party in any legal proceeding brought under or with respect to the transaction described in this contract is entitled to recover from the non-prevailing party all costs of such proceeding and reasonable attorney's fees.

18. ESCROW: The earnest money is deposited with escrow agent with the understanding that escrow agent is not (a) a party to this contract and does not have any liability for the performance or nonperformance of any party to this contract, (b) liable for interest on the earnest money and (c) liable for any loss of earnest money caused by the failure of any financial institution in which the earnest money has been deposited unless the financial institution is acting as escrow agent. At closing, the earnest money must be applied first to any cash down payment, then to Buyer's closing costs and any excess refunded to Buyer. If both parties make written demand for the earnest money, escrow agent may require payment of unpaid expenses incurred on behalf of the parties and a written release of liability of escrow agent from all parties. If one party makes written demand for the earnest money, escrow agent shall give notice of the demand by providing to the other party a copy of the demand. If escrow agent does not receive written objection to the demand from the other party within 30 days after notice to the other party, escrow agent may disburse the earnest money to the party making demand reduced by the amount of unpaid expenses incurred on behalf of the party receiving the earnest money and escrow agent may pay the same to the creditors. If escrow agent complies with the provisions of this paragraph, each party hereby releases escrow agent from all adverse claims related to the disbursal of the earnest money. Escrow agent's notice to the other party will be effective when deposited in the U. S. Mail, postage prepaid, certified mail, return receipt requested, addressed to the other party at such party's address shown below. Notice of objection to the demand will be deemed effective upon receipt by escrow agent.

19. REPRESENTATIONS: Seller represents that as of the Closing Date (a) there will be no liens, assessments, or security interests against the Property which will not be satisfied out of the sales proceeds unless securing payment of any loans assumed by Buyer and (b) assumed loans will not be in default. If any representation in this contract is untrue on the Closing Date, this contract may be terminated by Buyer and the earnest money will be refunded to Buyer. All representations contained in this contract will survive closing.

20. FEDERAL TAX REQUIREMENT: If Seller is a "foreign person," as defined by applicable law, or if Seller fails to deliver an affidavit that Seller is not a "foreign person," then Buyer shall withhold from the sales proceeds an amount sufficient to comply with applicable tax law and deliver the same to the Internal Revenue Service together with appropriate tax forms. IRS regulations require filing written reports if cash in excess of specified amounts is received in the transaction.

21. AGREEMENT OF PARTIES: This contract contains the entire agreement of the parties and cannot be changed except by their written agreement. Addenda which are a part of this contract are (list): _____
_____
_____
_____
_____
_____.

22. CONSULT YOUR ATTORNEY: Real estate licensees cannot give legal advice. This contract is intended to be legally binding. READ IT CAREFULLY. If you do not understand the effect of this contract, consult your attorney BEFORE signing.

Buyer's
Attorney is:_____   Seller's
Attorney is:_____

Initialed for identification by Buyer_____ and Seller_____   **01A**   TREC NO. 20-3

■ 246 ■

One to Four Family Residential Contract Concerning_____Page Eight 9-22-97
                                                              (Address of Property)

23. NOTICES: All notices from one party to the other must be in writing and are effective when mailed to, hand-delivered at, or transmitted by facsimile machine as follows:

To Buyer at: **To Seller at:**

_____   _____

_____   _____

_____   _____

Telephone:(   )_____   Telephone:(   )_____

Facsimile:(   )_____   Facsimile:(   )_____

EXECUTED the_____day of _____, 19___ (THE EFFECTIVE DATE). (BROKER: FILL IN THE DATE OF FINAL ACCEPTANCE.)

_____   _____
Buyer   Seller

_____   _____
Buyer   Seller

> The form of this contract has been approved by the Texas Real Estate Commission. Such approval relates to this contract form only. No representation is made as to the legal validity or adequacy of any provision in any specific transaction. It is not suitable for complex transactions. Extensive riders or additions are not to be used. Texas Real Estate Commission, P.O. Box 12188, Austin, TX 78711-2188, 1-800-250-8732 or (512) 459-6544 (http://www.trec.state.tx.us) TREC NO. 20-3. This form replaces TREC NO. 20-2.

BROKER INFORMATION AND RATIFICATION OF FEE

Listing Broker has agreed to pay Other Broker _____ of the total sales price when Listing Broker's fee is received. Escrow Agent is authorized and directed to pay Other Broker from Listing Broker's fee at closing.

Other Broker _____ License No. ____   Listing Broker _____ License No. ____
represents ☐ Seller as Listing Broker's subagent   represents ☐ Seller and Buyer as an intermediary
            ☐ Buyer only as Buyer's agent   ☐ Seller only as Seller's agent

                                                            Listing Associate _____ Telephone ____

                                                            Selling Associate _____ Telephone ____

Associate _____ Telephone ____   Broker Address _____

Broker Address _____   Telephone _____ Facsimile ____

Telephone _____ Facsimile ____

RECEIPT

Receipt of ☐ Contract and ☐ $_____ Earnest Money in the form of_____is acknowledged.

Escrow Agent: _____   Date: _____, 19___

By:_____

Address _____   Telephone: (   )_____

City _____ State ____ Zip Code ____   Facsimile: (   )_____

01A   TREC NO. 20-3

■ Appendix C ■

10-29-01

PROMULGATED BY THE TEXAS REAL ESTATE COMMISSION (TREC)

THIRD PARTY FINANCING CONDITION ADDENDUM

TO CONTRACT CONCERNING THE PROPERTY AT

_____

(Street Address and City)

Buyer shall apply promptly for all financing described below and make every reasonable effort to obtain financing approval. Financing approval will be deemed to have been obtained when the lender determines that Buyer has satisfied all of lender's financial requirements (those items relating to Buyer's assets, income and credit history). If financing (including any financed PMI premium) approval is not obtained within _____ days after the effective date, this contract will terminate and the earnest money will be refunded to Buyer. Each note must be secured by vendor's and deed of trust liens.

CHECK APPLICABLE BOXES:

❑ A. CONVENTIONAL FINANCING:

    ❑ (1) A first mortgage loan in the principal amount of $ _____ (excluding any financed PMI premium), due in full in _____ year(s), with interest not to exceed _____% per annum for the first _____year(s) of the loan with Loan Fees not to exceed _____ % of the loan. The loan will be ❑ with ❑ without PMI.

    ❑ (2) A second mortgage loan in the principal amount of $_____(excluding any financed PMI premium), due in full in _____year(s), with interest not to exceed _____% per annum for the first _____year(s) of the loan with Loan Fees not to exceed _____ % of the loan. The loan will be ❑ with ❑ without PMI.

❑ B. TEXAS VETERANS' HOUSING ASSISTANCE PROGRAM LOAN: A Texas Veteran's Housing Assistance Program Loan of $_____ for a period of at least _____years at the interest rate established by the Texas Veteran's Land Board at the time of closing.

❑ C. FHA INSURED FINANCING: A Section _____ FHA insured loan of not less than $_____ (excluding any financed MIP), amortizable monthly for not less than _____years, with interest not to exceed _____% per annum for the first _____year(s) of the loan with Loan Fees not to exceed _____ % of the loan. As required by HUD-FHA, if FHA valuation is unknown, "_It is expressly agreed that, notwithstanding any other provision of this contract, the purchaser (Buyer) shall not be obligated to complete the purchase of the Property described herein or to incur any penalty by forfeiture of earnest money deposits or otherwise unless the purchaser (Buyer) has been given in accordance with HUD/FHA or VA requirements a written statement issued by the Federal Housing Commissioner, Department of Veterans Affairs, or a Direct Endorsement Lender setting forth the appraised value of the Property of not less than $_____. The purchaser (Buyer) shall have the privilege and option of proceeding with consummation of the contract without regard to the amount of the appraised valuation. The appraised valuation is arrived at to determine the maximum mortgage the Department of Housing and Urban Development will insure. HUD does not warrant the value or the condition of the Property. The purchaser (Buyer) should satisfy himself/herself that the price and the condition of the Property are acceptable._"

If the FHA appraised value of the Property (excluding closing costs and MIP) is less than the Sales Price, Seller may reduce the Sales Price to an amount equal to the FHA appraised value (excluding closing costs and MIP) and the sale will be closed at the lower Sales Price with proportionate adjustments to the down payment and loan amount.

Initialed for identification by Buyer_____ and Seller_____   01A

Third Party Financing Condition Addendum Concerning

_____

(Address of Property)

❑ D. VA GUARANTEED FINANCING: A VA guaranteed loan of not less than $_____
(excluding any financed Funding Fee), amortizable monthly for not less than_____years,
with interest not to exceed_____% per annum for the first _____year(s) of the loan
with Loan Fees not to exceed _____ % of the loan.

VA NOTICE TO BUYER: "*It is expressly agreed that, notwithstanding any other provisions of
this contract, the Buyer shall not incur any penalty by forfeiture of earnest money or
otherwise or be obligated to complete the purchase of the Property described herein, if the
contract purchase price or cost exceeds the reasonable value of the Property established by
the Department of Veterans Affairs. The Buyer shall, however, have the privilege and
option of proceeding with the consummation of this contract without regard to the amount
of the reasonable value established by the Department of Veterans Affairs.*"

If Buyer elects to complete the purchase at an amount in excess of the reasonable value
established by VA, Buyer shall pay such excess amount in cash from a source which Buyer
agrees to disclose to the VA and which Buyer represents will not be from borrowed funds
except as approved by VA. If VA reasonable value of the Property is less than the Sales
Price, Seller may reduce the Sales Price to an amount equal to the VA reasonable value and
the sale will be closed at the lower Sales Price with proportionate adjustments to the down
payment and the loan amount.

_____   _____
Buyer   Seller

_____   _____
Buyer   Seller

01A

■ Appendix C ■

SELLER FINANCING ADDENDUM
TO CONTRACT CONCERNING THE PROPERTY AT

_____
(Street Address and City)

A. CREDIT DOCUMENTATION. Within_____days after the effective date of this contract, Buyer shall deliver to Seller ❏ credit report ❏ verification of employment, including salary ❏ verification of funds on deposit in financial institutions ❏ current financial statement to establish Buyer's creditworthiness and ❏ _____
_____.

Buyer hereby authorizes any credit reporting agency to furnish to Seller at Buyer's sole expense copies of Buyer's credit reports.

B. CREDIT APPROVAL. If Buyer's documentation is not delivered within the specified time, Seller may terminate this contract by notice to Buyer within 7 days after expiration of the time for delivery, and the earnest money will be paid to Seller. If the documentation is timely delivered, and Seller determines in Seller's sole discretion that Buyer's credit is unacceptable, Seller may terminate this contract by notice to Buyer within 7 days after expiration of the time for delivery and the earnest money will be refunded to Buyer. If Seller does not terminate this contract, Seller will be deemed to have accepted Buyer's credit.

C. PROMISSORY NOTE. The promissory note (Note) described in Paragraph 4 of this contract payable by Buyer to the order of Seller will be payable at the place designated by Seller. Buyer may prepay the Note in whole or in part at any time without penalty. Any prepayments are to be applied to the payment of the installments of principal last maturing and interest will immediately cease on the prepaid principal. The Note will contain a provision for payment of a late fee of 5% of any installment not paid within 10 days of the due date. The Note will be payable as follows:

❏ (1) In one payment due _____ after the date of the Note
with interest payable_____.

❏ (2) In _____ installments of $ _____ ❏ including interest
❏ plus interest beginning _____ after the date of the
Note and continuing at _____ intervals thereafter for _____when
the balance of the Note will be due and payable.

❏ (3) Interest only in _____ installments for the first _____ month(s)
and thereafter in installments of $_____ ❏ including interest ❏ plus
interest beginning _____ after the date of the Note and
continuing at _____ intervals thereafter for _____ when the
balance of the Note will be due and payable.

D. DEED OF TRUST. The deed of trust securing the Note will provide for the following:

(1) PROPERTY TRANSFERS: (check only one)

❏　(a) Consent Not Required: The Property may be sold, conveyed or leased without the consent of Seller, provided any subsequent buyer assumes the Note.

❏　(b) Consent Required: If all or any part of the Property is sold, conveyed, leased for a period longer than 3 years, leased with an option to purchase, or otherwise sold (including any contract for deed), without the prior written consent of Seller, Seller may declare the

Initialed for identification by Buyer_____ and Seller_____　　　01A

◾ Appendix C ◾

_____
(Address of Property)

balance of the Note, to be immediately due and payable. The creation of a subordinate lien, any conveyance under threat or order of condemnation, any deed solely between buyers, the passage of title by reason of the death of a buyer or by operation of law will not entitle Seller to exercise the remedies provided in this paragraph.

(2) TAX AND INSURANCE ESCROW: (check only one)

❑ (a) Escrow Not Required: Buyer shall furnish Seller annually, before the taxes become delinquent, evidence that all taxes on the Property have been paid. Buyer shall furnish Seller annually evidence of paid-up casualty insurance naming Seller as an additional loss payee.

❑ (b) Escrow Required: With each installment Buyer shall deposit with Seller in escrow a pro rata part of the estimated annual ad valorem taxes and casualty insurance premiums for the Property. Buyer shall pay any deficiency within 30 days after notice from Seller. Buyer's failure to pay the deficiency constitutes a default under the deed of trust. Buyer is not required to deposit any escrow payments for taxes and insurance that are deposited with a superior lienholder. The casualty insurance must name Seller as an additional loss payee.

(3) PRIOR LIENS: Any default under any lien superior to the lien securing the Note constitutes default under the deed of trust securing the Note.

_____   _____
Buyer   Seller

_____   _____
Buyer   Seller

01A

PROMULGATED BY THE TEXAS REAL ESTATE COMMISSION (TREC)   10-29-01

LOAN ASSUMPTION ADDENDUM
TO CONTRACT CONCERNING THE PROPERTY AT

_____

(Street Address and City)

A. CREDIT DOCUMENTATION. Within_____days after the effective date of this contract, Buyer shall deliver to Seller ❑ credit report ❑ verification of employment, including salary ❑ verification of funds on deposit in financial institutions ❑ current financial statement to establish Buyer's creditworthiness and ❑ _____ _____.
Buyer hereby authorizes any credit reporting agency to furnish to Seller at Buyer's sole expense copies of Buyer's credit reports.

B. CREDIT APPROVAL. If Buyer's documentation is not delivered within the specified time, Seller may terminate this contract by notice to Buyer within 7 days after expiration of the time for delivery, and the earnest money will be paid to Seller. If the documentation is timely delivered, and Seller determines in Seller's sole discretion that Buyer's credit is unacceptable, Seller may terminate this contract by notice to Buyer within 7 days after expiration of the time for delivery and the earnest money will be refunded to Buyer. If Seller does not terminate this contract, Seller will be deemed to have accepted Buyer's credit.

C. ASSUMPTION.

❑ (1) The unpaid principal balance of a first lien promissory note payable to _____ _____ which unpaid balance at closing will be $ _____. The total current monthly payment including principal, interest and any reserve deposits is $ _____. Buyer's initial payment will be the first payment due after closing.

❑ (2) The unpaid principal balance of a second lien promissory note payable to _____ _____which unpaid balance at closing will be $ _____. The total current monthly payment including principal, interest and any reserve deposits is $ _____. Buyer's initial payment will be the first payment due after closing.

Buyer's assumption of an existing note includes all obligations imposed by the deed of trust securing the note. If the unpaid principal balance(s) of any assumed loan(s) as of the Closing Date varies from the loan balance(s) stated above, the ❑ cash payable at closing ❑ Sales Price will be adjusted by the amount of any variance; provided, if the total principal balance of all assumed loans varies in an amount greater than $350.00 at closing, either party may terminate this contract and the earnest money will be refunded to Buyer unless the other party elects to eliminate the excess in the variance by an appropriate adjustment at closing. Buyer may terminate this contract and the earnest money will be refunded to Buyer if the noteholder requires (a) payment of an assumption fee in excess of $ _____ in (1) above or $ _____ in (2) above and Seller declines to pay such excess, (b) an increase in the interest rate to more than _____% in (1) above, or _____% in (2) above, (c) any other modification of the loan documents, or (d) consent to the assumption of the loan and fails to consent. A vendor's lien and deed of trust to secure assumption will be required which will automatically be released on execution and delivery of a release by noteholder. If Seller is released from liability on any assumed note, the vendor's lien and deed of trust to secure assumption will not be required. If noteholder maintains an escrow account, the escrow account must be transferred to Buyer without any deficiency. Buyer shall reimburse Seller for the amount in the transferred accounts.

NOTICE TO BUYER: The monthly payments, interest rates or other terms of some loans may be adjusted by the noteholder at or after closing. If you are concerned about the possibility of future adjustments, do not sign the contract without examining the notes and deeds of trust.

NOTICE TO SELLER: Your liability to pay the note assumed by Buyer will continue unless you obtain a release of liability from the noteholder. If you are concerned about future liability, you should use the TREC Release of Liability Addendum.

Buyer _____   Seller _____

Buyer _____   Seller _____

01A

■ Appendix C ■

PROMULGATED BY THE TEXAS REAL ESTATE COMMISSION (TREC)

NOTICE OF TERMINATION OF CONTRACT

To: Seller(s)

In accordance with the unrestricted right of Buyer to terminate the contract between

_____

as Seller and _____

as Buyer dated _____, 20_____ for the Property located at _____

_____,

Buyer notifies Seller that the contract is terminated.

_____   _____
Buyer   Date   Buyer   Date

01A

Appendix D

Sample Personal Financial Statement

■ Appendix D ■

SECTION 3: SCHEDULES

SCHEDULE 1: CASH IN BANKS AND OTHER INSTITUTIONS

Name and Location	Type of Account	Current Balance
ABC Federal Credit Union	Checking	4,500
My Favorite Bank	Money Market	210,000
E Bank	Savings	98,500
	TOTAL	313,000

SCHEDULE 2A: MARKETABLE SECURITIES/LIQUID ASSETS

Number of Shares	Description of Security	Cost	If Pledged, To Whom	Current Market Value
2,500	GOLD	12,500		28,000
5,000	DROOY	5,700		22,000
10,000	SSRI	18,900		29,800
4,500	Mutual Fund	45,000		48,500
	Precious Metals	125,000		147,000
			TOTAL	275,300

SCHEDULE 2B: NONMARKETABLE SECURITIES

Number of Shares	Description of Security	Cost	If Pledged, To Whom	Current Market Value
50% ownership	Symphony Homes, L.L.C.			485,000
			TOTAL	485,000

SCHEDULE 3: NOTES AND ACCOUNTS RECEIVABLE

Name and Address of Debtor	Is Debtor a Relative?	Origination Date	Nature or Description of Debt	Collateral Held	Final Payment Date	Current Balance
J.P. Smithers	No	02/01/2002	real estate loan	land	N/A	50,000
					TOTAL	50,000

SCHEDULE 4: REAL ESTATE, Legal & equitable title to real estate listed is solely in the name of undersigned unless otherwise noted.

Legal Description Or Street Address	Date Acquired	Type of Property	Mortgage or Lien Holder	Monthly Payments	Purchase Price	Remaining Loan Balance	Current Market Value
1234 Milcrest	06/01/1995	residence	Wells Fargo	800	147,500	70,000	265,000
5678 Angels Cove	07/01/1985	rental	None-1/2 interest	0	76,000	41,000	140,000
1234 Milcrest	12/10/2001	residence	Ntl City - HELOC	150		87,000	0
					TOTAL	198,000	405,000

SCHEDULE 5: NOTES PAYABLE

Holder's Name and Address	Original Amount	Date Opened	Collateral	Maturity Date	Monthly Payments	Current Balance
Larry Peabody	100,000	01/01/1998	unsecured line of credi	Open	742	44,265
GMAC	12,500	03/01/2000	GM auto	03/01/2004	245	10,155
SLAS - student loan	35,000	07/25/1992	none	07/25/2012	375	28,400
				TOTAL	1,362	82,820

SCHEDULE 6: CREDIT CARDS

Company's Name and Address	Credit Limit	Date Opened	Type (MC, Visa, Discover)	Maturity Date	Monthly Payments	Current Balance
Wells Fargo	2,500	04/08/1995	MC	Open	255	3,600
Citibank	15,000	09/09/1999	MC	Open	300	8,400
				TOTAL	555	12,000

PERSONAL FINANCIAL STATEMENT

SECTION 1A: INDIVIDUAL INFORMATION		SECTION 1B: SPOUSAL INFORMATION	
Name:	Benjamin Investor	Name:	Barbara Investor
Residence:	123 North 2nd Street	Residence:	123 North 2nd Street
City, State, and Zip:	Anywhere, PA 12345	City, State, and Zip:	Anywhere, PA 12345
Position or Occupation	Real Estate Investments	Position or Occupation	Real Estate Investments
Business Name:	Benjamin Real Estate Group	Business Name:	Benjamin Real Estate Group
Business Address:	456 East Main	Business Address:	456 East Main
City, State, and Zip:	Anywhere, PA 12345	City, State, and Zip:	Anywhere, PA 12345
Residence Phone: (212) 396-1234 Bus. Phone: (212) 396-1235		Residence Phone: (212) 396-1234 Bus. Phone: (212) 396-1235	
SSN:	123-45-6789 Date of Birth: 08/06/1959	SSN:	987-65-4321 Date of Birth: 08/06/1959
Driver's License #:	082812477	Driver's License #:	082812478

SECTION 2: BALANCE SHEET

ASSETS			LIABILITIES		
Cash (from Schedule 1)		313,000			
Securities (from Schedule 2)	Marketable	275,300	Notes Payable to Banks (Sched 5)	Secured	10,155
	Nonmarketable	485,000		Unsecured	72,665
Notes and Accounts Receivable (Schedule 3)		50,000	Other Accounts and Notes Payable	To Relatives	3,200
Professional Accounts Receivable		42,000		To Others	0
Real Estate (from Schedule 4)		405,000	Outstanding Credit Card Balances (Sched 6)		12,000
Cash Surrender Value Life Insurance		2,500	Real Estate (from Schedule 4)		198,000
Autos	Year: '96 Make: GM	11,500	Taxes Owed	Income Taxes	0
	Year: 2000 Make: Toy	16,000		Other Taxes	0
	Year: Make:				
Oil Interests/Production Leases		4,200			
Personal Property/Household, etc.		145,000	Other Liabilities (Itemize)		
Other Assets (Itemize)	Computer Equipment	14,800			
	Software & Peripherals	3,600			
	Jewelry	8,500			
			Total Liabilities		296,020
			Net Worth		1,480,380
TOTAL ASSETS		1,776,400	TOTAL LIABILITIES AND NET WORTH		1,776,400

CURRENT ANNUAL INCOME		CONTINGENT LIABILITIES	
Gross Annual Salary	82,000	As Endorser	
Bonuses and Commissions	16,000	As Guarantor	
Dividends and Interest	13,000	On Leases or Contracts	
Real Estate Income	145,000	Legal Claims or Judgments	
Oil Income	0	Provision for Federal Income Tax	
Other Income	1,500	Other (Itemize)	
TOTAL INCOME	257,500		

COMPARISON OF MONTHLY INCOME TO EXPENSES				
Net Monthly Income	21,458			
Rent or Home Payment	3,475	Have you ever declared bankruptcy?		
Food and Utilities	850	Yes	No	X
Incidentals, Travel, Insurance, etc.	1,400	If yes, please explain.		
Credit Cards and Loans	1,917			
TOTAL EXPENSES	7,642			
DISCRETIONARY INCOME	13,816			

The information contained in this statement is provided for the purpose of obtaining or maintaining credit on behalf of the undersigned or for the guarantee of debt by the undersigned. Each undersigned understands that the Bank is relying on the information provided herein (including the designation made as to the ownership of property) in deciding to grant or continue credit. Each undersigned represents and warrants that the information provided is true and complete and that the Bank may consider this statement as continuing to be true and correct until a written notice of a change is given to the Bank by the undersigned. I/we authorize the Bank to make all inquiries deemed necessary to verify the accuracy of the statements made herein, and to determine my/our credit worthiness. I/we authorize the Bank to answer questions about the Bank's credit experience with me/us.

Signature (Individual) _____

Date _____

Signature (Spouse) _____

Date _____

Appendix E

thevalueplay.com

Current ordering information for the Value Play Rehab Analyzer can be found at the web site address located at **thevalueplay.com**.

Appendix F

symphony-homes.com

Symphony Homes is one of Michigan's premier builders of high quality new homes. We maintain a tradition of excellence by ensuring that each and every home we build meets our strict standards of quality. Symphony Homes is built on a foundation of three principles — quality, value, and service. From start to finish, we take care to ensure that only the best materials and the finest craftsmanship are used throughout the construction process. By partnering with key suppliers and efficiently managing our resources, we can effectively create value for homebuyers by offering superior homes at competitive prices. Offering personal service to homebuyers and fulfilling commitments to them allows us to provide each and every customer with an enjoyable building experience.

As a custom builder, Symphony Homes builds on home sites owned by individuals, or those owned by the company. We offer new home construction services in all of Genesee County, Lapeer County, and North Oakland County. For information regarding Symphony Homes, one of Michigan's premier builders, please log on to **symphony-homes.com.**

Glossary

Real estate investors will find the Glossary helpful for understanding words and terms used in real estate transactions. There are, however, some factors that may affect these definitions. Terms are defined as they are commonly understood in the mortgage and real estate industry. The same terms may have different meanings in another context. The definitions are intentionally general, nontechnical, and short. They do not encompass all possible meanings or nuances that a term may acquire in legal use. State laws, as well as custom and use in various states or regions of the country, may in fact modify or completely change the meanings of certain terms defined. Before signing any documents or depositing any money before entering into a real estate contract, the purchaser should consult with a lawyer to ensure that her rights are properly protected.

Abstract of Title   A summary of the public records relating to the title to a particular piece of land. An attorney or title insurance company reviews an abstract of title to determine whether there are any title defects that must be cleared before a buyer can purchase clear, marketable, and insurable title.

Acceleration Clause   Condition in a mortgage that may require the balance of the loan to become due immediately in the event regular mortgage payments are not made or for breach of other conditions of the mortgage.

Adjustable Rate Mortgage Loans (ARM)   Loans with interest rates that are adjusted periodically on the basis of changes in a preselected index. As a result, the interest rate on your loan and the monthly payment will rise and fall with increases and decreases in overall interest rates. These mortgage loans must specify how their interest rate changes, usually in terms of a relation to a national index such as (but not always) Treasury bill rates. If interest rates rise, your monthly payments will rise. An interest rate cap limits the amount by which the interest rate can change; look for this feature when you consider an ARM loan.

Ad Valorem   Designates an assessment of taxes against property in a literal sense according to its value.

Adverse Possession   A possession that is inconsistent with the right of possession and title of the true owner. It is the actual, open, notorious, exclusive, continuous, and hostile occupation and possession of the land of another under a claim of right or under color of title.

Agency   The relationship that exists by contract whereby one person is authorized to represent and act on behalf of another person in various business transactions.

Agreement of Sale   Known by various names, such as contract of purchase, purchase agreement, or sales agreement according to location or jurisdiction. A contract in which a seller agrees to sell and a buyer agrees to buy, under certain specific terms and conditions spelled out in writing and signed by both parties.

Amortization   A payment plan that enables the borrower to gradually reduce a debt through monthly payments of principal, thereby liquidating or extinguishing the obligation through a series of installments.

Annual Compounding   The arithmetic process of determining the final value of a cash flow or series of cash flows when interest is added once a year.

Annual Percentage Rate (APR)   The cost of credit expressed as a yearly rate. The annual percentage rate is often not the same as the interest rate. It is a percentage that results from an equation considering the amount financed, the finance charges, and the term of the loan.

Appraisal   An expert judgment or estimate of the quality or value of real estate as of a given date. The process through which conclusions of property value are obtained. It also refers to the formalized report that sets forth the estimate and conclusion of value.

Appurtenance   That which belongs to something else. In real estate law, an appurtenance is a right, privilege, or improvement that passes as an incident to the land, such as a right of way.

Assessed Value   An official valuation of property most often used for tax purposes.

Assignment   The method or manner by which a right, a specialty, or contract is transferred from one person to another.

Assumption of Mortgage   An obligation undertaken by the purchaser of property to be personally liable for payment of an existing mortgage. In an assumption, the purchaser is substituted for the original mortgagor in the mortgage instrument and the original mortgagor is to be released from further liability in the assumption. The mortgagee's consent is usually required.

The original mortgagor should always obtain a written release from further liability if he desires to be fully released under the assumption. Failure to obtain such a release renders the original mortgagor liable if the person assuming the mortgage fails to make the monthly payments.

An assumption of mortgage is often confused with purchasing subject to a mortgage. When one purchases subject to a mortgage, the purchaser agrees to make the monthly mortgage payments on an existing mortgage, but the original mortgagor remains personally liable if the purchaser fails to make the monthly payments. Since the original mortgagor remains liable in the event of default, the mortgagee's consent is not required to a sale subject to a mortgage.

Both assumption of mortgage and purchasing subject to a mortgage are used to finance the sale of property. They may also be used when a mortgagor is in financial difficulty and desires to sell the property to avoid foreclosure.

Balance Statement   A statement of the firm's financial position at a specific point in time.

Balloon Mortgage   Balloon mortgage loans are short-term fixed-rate loans with fixed monthly payments for a set number of years followed by one large final balloon payment (the balloon) for all of the remainder of the principal. Typically, the balloon payment may be due at the end of 5, 7, or 10 years. Borrowers with balloon loans may have the right to refinance the loan when the balloon payment is due, but the right to refinance is not guaranteed.

Bankruptcy   A proceeding in a federal court to relieve certain debts of a person or a business unable to pay its debts.

Bill of Sale   A written document or instrument that provides evidence of the transfer of right, title, and interest in personal property from one person to another.

Binder or Offer to Purchase   A preliminary agreement, secured by the payment of earnest money, between a buyer and seller as an offer to purchase real estate. A binder secures the right to purchase real estate upon agreed terms for a limited period of time.

If the buyer changes his mind or is unable to purchase, the earnest money is forfeited unless the binder expressly provides that it is to be refunded.

Blanket Mortgage   A single mortgage that covers more than one piece of real estate. It is often used to purchase a large tract of land that is later subdivided and sold as individual parcels.

Bona fide   Made in good faith; good, valid, without fraud; such as a *bona fide* offer.

Bond   Any obligation under seal. A real estate bond is a written obligation, usually issued on security of a mortgage or deed of trust.

Breach   The breaking of law, or failure of a duty, either by omission or commission; the failure to perform, without legal excuse, any promise that forms a part or the whole of a contract.

Broker   One who is engaged for others in a negotiation for contracts relative to property, with the custody of which they have no concern.

Broker, Real Estate   Any person, partnership, association, or corporation who, for a compensation or valuable consideration, sells or offers for sale, buys or offers to buy, or negotiates the purchase or sale or exchange of real estate, or rents or offers to rent, any real estate or the improvements thereon for others.

Capital   Accumulated wealth; a portion of wealth set aside for the production of additional wealth; specifically, the funds belonging to the partners or shareholders of a business, invested with the express purpose and intent of remaining in the business to generate profits.

Capital Expenditures   Investments of cash or other property, or the creation of a liability in exchange for property to remain permanently in the business; usually pertaining to land, buildings, machinery, and equipment.

Capitalization   The act or process of converting or obtaining the present value of future incomes into current equivalent capital value; also the amount so determined; commonly referring to the capital structure of a corporation or other such legal entity.

Cash Out   Any cash received when a new loan is obtained that is larger than the remaining balance of the current mortgage, based upon the equity already built up in the property. The cash-out amount is calculated by subtracting the sum of the old loan and fees from the new mortgage loan.

Caveat Emptor The phrase literally means "let the buyer beware." Under this doctrine, the buyer is duty bound to examine the property being purchased and assumes conditions that are readily ascertainable upon view.

Certificate of Title A certificate issued by a title company or a written opinion rendered by an attorney that the seller has good marketable and insurable title to the property that he is offering for sale. A certificate of title offers no protection against any hidden defects in the title that an examination of the records could not reveal. The issuer of a certificate of title is liable only for damages due to negligence. The protection offered a home owner under a certificate of title is not as great as that offered in a title insurance policy.

Chain of Title A history of conveyances and encumbrances affecting the title to a particular real property.

Chattels Items of movable personal property, such as animals, household furnishings, money, jewelry, motor vehicles, and all other items that are not permanently affixed to real property and can be transferred from one place to another.

Closing Costs The numerous expenses that buyers and sellers normally incur to complete a transaction in the transfer of ownership of real estate. These costs are in addition to the price of the property and are items prepaid at the closing day. The following is a common list of closing costs.

Buyer's Expenses:
- ☐ Documentary Stamps on Notes
- ☐ Recording Deed and Mortgage
- ☐ Escrow Fees
- ☐ Attorney's Fee
- ☐ Title Insurance
- ☐ Appraisal and Inspection
- ☐ Survey Charge

Seller's Expenses:
- ☐ Cost of Abstract
- ☐ Documentary Stamps on Deed
- ☐ Real Estate Commission
- ☐ Recording Mortgage

    ☐ Survey Charge
    ☐ Escrow Fees
    ☐ Attorney's Fee

The agreement of sale negotiated previously between the buyer and the seller may state in writing who will pay each of the above costs.

Closing Day   The day on which the formalities of a real estate sale are concluded. The certificate of title, abstract, and deed are generally prepared for the closing by an attorney and this cost charged to the buyer. The buyer signs the mortgage, and closing costs are paid. The final closing merely confirms the original agreement reached in the agreement of sale.

Cloud on Title   An outstanding claim or encumbrance that adversely affects the marketability of title.

Collateral Security   A separate obligation attached to a contract to guarantee its performance; the transfer of property or of other contracts or valuables to ensure the performance of a principal agreement or obligation.

Commission   Money paid to a real estate agent or broker by the seller as compensation for finding a buyer and completing the sale. Usually it is a percentage of the sale price ranging anywhere from 6 to 7 percent on single family houses and 10 percent on land.

Compound Interest   Interest paid on the original principal of an indebtedness and also on the accrued and unpaid interest that has accumulated over time.

Condominium   Individual ownership of a dwelling unit and an individual interest in the common areas and facilities that serve the multiunit project.

Consideration   Something of value, usually money, that is the inducement of a contract. Any right, interest, property, or benefit accruing to one party; any forbearance, detriment, loss or responsibility given, suffered or undertaken, may constitute a consideration that will sustain a contract.

Contract of Purchase   (See *agreement of sale.*)

Conventional Mortgage   A mortgage loan not insured by HUD or guaranteed by the Department of Veterans Affairs. It is subject to conditions established by the lending institution and state statutes. The mortgage rates may vary with different institutions and between states. (States have various interest limits.)

Cooperative Housing   An apartment building or a group of dwellings owned by a corporation, the stockholders of which are the residents of the dwellings. It is operated for their benefit by their elected board of directors. In a cooperative, the corporation or association owns title to the real estate. A resident purchases stock in the corporation, which entitles him to occupy a unit in the building or property owned by the cooperative. While the resident does not own his unit, he has an absolute right to occupy his unit for as long as he owns the stock.

Covenant   An agreement between two or more persons entered into by deed whereby one of the parties promises the performance of certain acts, or that a given state does or shall, or does not or shall not, exist.

Debt   An obligation to repay a specified amount at a specified time.

Debt Service   The portion of funds required to repay a financial obligation such as a mortgage, which includes interest and principal payments.

Deed   A formal written instrument by which title to real property is transferred from one owner to another. The deed should contain an accurate description of the property being conveyed, should be signed and witnessed according to the laws of the state where the property is located, and should be delivered to the purchaser on the day of closing. There are two parties to a deed—the grantor and the grantee. (See also *deed of trust, general warranty deed, quitclaim deed,* and *special warranty deed.*)

Deed of Trust   Like a mortgage, a security instrument whereby real property is given as security for a debt; in a deed of trust, however, there are three parties to the instrument—the borrower, the trustee, and the lender (or beneficiary). In such a transaction, the borrower transfers the legal title for the property to the trustee who holds the property in trust as security for the payment of the debt to the lender or beneficiary. If the borrower pays the debt as agreed, the deed of trust becomes void. If, however, he defaults in the payment of the debt, the trustee may sell the property at a public sale, under the terms of the deed of trust. In most jurisdictions where the deed of trust is in force, the borrower is subject to having his property sold without benefit of legal proceedings. A few states have begun in recent years to treat the deed of trust like a mortgage.

Default   Failure to make mortgage payments as agreed to in a commitment based on the terms and at the designated time set forth in the mortgage or deed of trust. It is the mortgagor's responsibility to remember the due date and make the payment before the due date, not after. Generally, 30 days after the due date if payment is not received, the mortgage is in default. In the event of default, the mortgage may give the lender the right to accelerate payments, take possession and receive rents, and start foreclosure. Defaults may also come about by the failure to observe other conditions in the mortgage or deed of trust.

Depreciation   Decline in value of a house due to wear and tear, adverse changes in the neighborhood, or any other reason. The term is most often applied to tax purposes.

Down Payment   The amount of money to be paid by the purchaser to the seller upon the signing of the agreement of sale. The agreement of sale will refer to the down payment amount and will acknowledge receipt of the down payment. Down payment is the difference between the sales price and maximum mortgage amount. The down payment may not be refundable if the purchaser fails to buy the property without good cause. If the purchaser wants the down payment to be refundable, there should be inserted into the agreement of sale a clause specifying the conditions under which the deposit will be refunded, if the agreement does not already contain such a clause. If the seller cannot deliver good title, the agreement of sale usually requires the seller to return the down payment and to pay interest and expenses incurred by the purchaser.

Duress   Unlawful constraint exercised upon a person, whereby the person is forced to perform some act, or to sign an instrument or document against his will.

Earnest Money   The deposit money given to the seller or his agent by the potential buyer upon the signing of the agreement of sale to show that he is serious about buying a house of any other type of real property. If the sale goes through, the earnest money is applied against the down payment. If the sale does not go through, the earnest money will be forfeited or lost unless the binder or offer to purchase expressly provides that it is refundable.

Easement Rights   A right-of-way granted to a person or company authorizing access to or over the owner's land. An electric company obtaining a right-of-way across private property is a common example.

Economic Life   The period over which a property may be profitably used or the period over which a property will yield a return on the investment, over and above the economic or ground rent due to its land.

Economic Obsolescence   Impairment of desirability or useful life arising from economic forces such as changes in optimum land use, legislative enactments that restrict or impair property rights, and changes in supply and demand relationships.

Eminent Domain   The superior right of property subsisting in every sovereign state to take private property for public use upon the payment of just compensation. This power is often conferred upon public service corporations that perform quasi-public functions, such as providing public utilities. In every case, the owner whose property is taken must be justly compensated according to fair market values in the prevailing area.

Encroachment   An obstruction, building, or part of a building that intrudes beyond a legal boundary onto neighboring private or public land, or a building extending beyond the building line.

Encumbrance   A legal right or interest in land that affects a good or clear title, and diminishes the land's value. It can take numerous forms, such as zoning ordinances, easement rights, claims, mortgages, liens, charges, a pending legal action, unpaid taxes, or restrictive covenants. An encumbrance does not legally prevent transfer of the property to another. A title search is all that is usually done to reveal the existence of such encumbrances, and it is up to the buyer to determine whether he wants to purchase with the encumbrance, or what can be done to remove it.

Equity   The value of a homeowner's unencumbered interest in real estate. Equity is computed by subtracting from the property's fair market value the total of the unpaid mortgage balance and any outstanding liens or other debts against the property. A homeowner's equity increases as he pays off his mortgage or as the property appreciates in value. When the mortgage and all other debts against the property are paid in full, the homeowner has 100 percent equity in the property.

Escheat   The reverting of property to the state by reason of failure of persons legally entitled to hold, or when heirs capable of inheriting are lacking the ability to do so.

Escrow   Funds paid by one party to another (the escrow agent) to hold until the occurrence of a specified event, after which the funds are released to a designated individual. In FHA mortgage transactions, an escrow account usually refers to the funds a mortgagor pays the lender at the time of the periodic mortgage payments. The money is held in a trust fund, provided by the lender for the buyer. Such funds should be adequate to cover yearly anticipated expenditures for mortgage insurance premiums, taxes, hazard insurance premiums, and special assessments.

Estate   The degree, quantum, nature, and extent of interest that one has in real property.

Execute   To perform what is required to give validity to a legal document. To execute a document, for example, means to sign it so that it becomes fully enforceable by law.

Fee Simple   The largest estate a person can have in real estate. Denotes totality of ownership, unlimited in point of time, as in perpetual.

Fiduciary   A person to whom property is entrusted; a trustee who holds, controls, or manages for another. A real estate agent is said to have a fiduciary responsibility and relationship with a client.

Foreclosure   A legal term applied to any of the various methods of enforcing payment of the debt secured by a mortgage, or deed of trust, by taking and selling the mortgaged property, and depriving the mortgagor of possession.

Forfeiture Clause   A clause in a lease enabling the landlord to terminate the lease and remove a tenant when the latter defaults in payment of rent or any other obligation under the lease.

Functional Obsolescence   An impairment of desirability of a property arising from its being out of date with respect to design and style, capacity and utility in relation to site, lack of modern facilities, and the like.

Generally Accepted Accounting Principles (GAAP)   A standardized set of accounting principles and concepts by which financial statements are prepared.

General Warranty Deed   A deed that conveys not only all the grantor's interests in and title to the property to the grantee, but also warrants that if the title is defective or has a cloud on it (such as mortgage claims, tax liens, title claims, judgments, or mechanic's liens against it) the grantee may hold the grantor liable.

Grantee   That party in the deed who is the buyer or recipient; the person to whom the real estate is conveyed.

Grantor   That party in the deed who is the seller or giver; the person who conveys the real estate.

Hazard Insurance   Protects against damages caused to property by fire, windstorms, and other common hazards.

Highest and Best Use   That use of, or program of utilization of, a site that will produce the maximum net land returns over the total period comprising the future; the optimum use for a site.

Implied Warranty or Covenant   A guarantee of assurance the law supplies in an agreement, even though the agreement itself does not express the guarantee or assurance.

Income Statement   The financial report that summarizes a business's performance over a specific period of time.

Injunction   A writ or order of the court to restrain one or more parties to a suit from committing an inequitable or unjust act in regard to the rights of some other party in the suit or proceeding.

Interest   A charge paid for borrowing money.

Internal Rate of Return (IRR) Method   A method of ranking investment proposals using the rate of return on an investment, calculated by finding the discount rate that equates the present value of future cash inflows to the project's cost.

Joint Tenancy   Property held by two or more persons together with the right of survivorship. While the doctrine of survivorship has been abolished with respect to most joint tenancies, the tenancy by the entirety retains the doctrine of survivorship in content.

Judgment   The decision or sentence of a court of law as the result of proceedings instituted therein for the redress of an injury. A judgment declaring that one individual is indebted to another individual when properly docketed; it creates a lien on the real property of the judgment debtor.

Lease   A species of contract, written or oral, between the owner of real estate, the landlord, and another person, the tenant, covering the conditions upon which the tenant may possess, occupy, and use the real estate.

Lessee   A person who leases property from another person, usually the landlord.

Lessor   The owner or person who rents or leases property to a tenant or lessee; the landlord.

Liabilities   The debts of a business or entity, which are in the form of financial claims on its assets.

LIBOR (London Interbank Offered Rate)   The interest rate charged among banks in the foreign market for short-term loans to one another. A common index for ARM loans.

Lien   A claim by one person on the property of another as security for money owed. Such claims may include obligations not met or satisfied, judgments, unpaid taxes, materials, or labor.

Limited Liability Partnership (Limited Liability Company)   A hybrid form of organization in which all partners enjoy limited liability for the business's debts. It combines the limited liability advantage of a corporation with the tax advantages of a partnership.

Limited Partnership   A hybrid form of organization consisting of general partners, who have unlimited liability for the partnership's debts, and limited partners, whose liability is limited to the amount of their investment.

Loan Application   An initial statement of personal and financial information required to apply for a loan.

Loan Application Fee   Fee charged by a lender to cover the initial costs of processing a loan application. The fee may include the cost of obtaining a property appraisal, a credit report, and a lock-in fee or other closing costs incurred during the process, or the fee may be in addition to these charges.

Loan Origination Fee   Fee charged by a lender to cover administrative costs of processing a loan.

Loan-to-Value Ratio (LTV)   The percentage of the loan amount to the appraised value (or the sales price, whichever is less) of the property.

Lock or Lock-In   A lender's guarantee of an interest rate for a set period of time. The time period is usually that between loan application approval and loan closing. The lock-in protects you against rate increases during that time.

Marketable Title   A title that is free and clear of objectionable liens, clouds, or other title defects. A title that enables an owner to sell his property freely to others and which others will accept without objection.

Market Value   The amount for which a property would sell if put upon the open market and sold in the manner which property is ordinarily sold in the community in which the property is situated. The highest price estimated in terms of money that a buyer would be warranted in paying and a seller would be justified in accepting, provided both parties were fully informed, acted intelligently and voluntarily, and furthermore that all the rights and benefits inherent in or attributable to the property were included in the transfer.

Meeting of Minds   A mutual intention of two or more persons to enter into a contract affecting their legal status based on agreed-upon terms.

Metes and Bounds   A term from the old English word *metes,* meaning measurements, and *bounds,* meaning boundaries. It is generally applied to any description of real estate; describes the boundaries by distance and angles.

Mortgage   A lien or claim against real property given by the buyer to the lender as security for money borrowed. Under government-insured or loan-guarantee provisions, the payments may include escrow amounts covering taxes, hazard insurance, water charges, and special assessments. Mortgages generally run from 10 to 30 years, during which the loan is to be paid off.

Mortgage Commitment   A written notice from the bank or other lending institution saying it will advance mortgage funds in a specified amount to enable a buyer to purchase a house.

Mortgage Note   A written agreement to repay a loan. The agreement is secured by a mortgage, serves as proof of an indebtedness, and states the manner in which it shall be paid. The note states the actual amount of the debt that the mortgage secures and renders the mortgagor personally responsible for repayment.

Mortgage (Open End)   A mortgage with a provision that permits borrowing additional money in the future without refinancing the loan or paying additional financing charges. Open-end provisions often limit such borrowing to no more than would raise the balance to the original loan figure.

Mortgagee   The lender in a mortgage agreement.

Mortgagor   The borrower in a mortgage agreement.

Net Cash Flow   The actual net cash, as opposed to accounting net income, that a firm generates during some specified period.

Net Income   In general, synonymous with net earnings, but considered a broader and better term; the balance remaining after deducting from the gross income all expenses, maintenance, taxes, and losses pertaining to operating properties except for interest or other financial charges on borrowed or other forms of capital.

Net Lease   A lease where, in addition to the rent stipulated, the lessee assumes payment of all property charges such as taxes, insurance, and maintenance.

Nonconforming Use   A use of land that predates zoning, but is not in accord with the uses prescribed for the area by the current zoning ordinance. Because the use was there first, it may be continued, subject to certain limitations.

Note   An instrument of credit given to attest a debt; a written promise to pay money that may or may not accompany a mortgage or other security agreement.

Offer   A proposal, oral or written, to buy a piece of property at a specified price with specified terms and conditions.

Option   The exclusive right to purchase or lease a property at a stipulated price or rent within a specified period of time.

Percentage Lease   A lease of commercial property in which the rent is computed as a percentage of the receipts, either gross or net, from the business being conducted by the lessee, sometimes with a guaranteed minimum rental.

Personal Property   Movable property that is not by definition real property and includes tangible property such as moneys, goods, chattels, and debts and claims.

Planned Unit Development (PUD)   Residential complex of mixed housing types. Offers greater design flexibility than traditional developments. PUDs permit clustering of homes, sometimes not allowed under standard zoning ordinances, use of open space, and a project harmonious with the natural topography of the land.

Points   Sometimes referred to as *discount points*. A point is one percent of the amount of the mortgage loan. For example, if a loan is for $250,000, one point is $2,500. Points are charged by a lender to raise the yield on a loan at a time when money is tight, interest rates are high, and there is a legal limit to the interest rate that can be charged on a mortgage. Buyers are prohibited from paying points on HUD or Department of Veterans Affairs–guaranteed loans (sellers can pay them, however). On a conventional mortgage, points may be paid by either buyer or seller or split between them.

Portfolio   The combined holdings of more than one stock, bond, real estate asset, or other asset by an investor.

Prepayment   Payment of mortgage loan, or part of it, before due date. Mortgage agreements often restrict the right of prepayment either by limiting the amount that can be prepaid in any one year or charging a penalty for prepayment. The Federal Housing Administration does not permit such restrictions in FHA-insured mortgages.

Principal   The basic element of the loan as distinguished from interest and mortgage insurance premium. In other words, principal is the amount upon which interest is paid. The word also means one who appoints an agent to act for and on behalf of; the person bound by an agent's authorized contract.

Property   The term used to describe the rights and interests a person has in lands, chattels, and other determinate things.

Purchase Agreement   An offer to purchase that has been accepted by the seller and has become a binding contract.

Quiet Enjoyment   The right of an owner of an interest in land, whether an owner or a tenant, to protection against disturbance or interference with his possession of the land.

Quitclaim Deed   A deed that transfers whatever interest the maker of the deed may have in the particular parcel of land. A quitclaim deed is often given to clear the title when the grantor's interest in a property is questionable. By accepting such a deed the buyer assumes all the risks. Such a deed makes no warranties as to the title, but simply transfers to the buyer whatever interest the grantor has. (See *deed*.)

Real Estate Agent   An intermediary who buys and sells real estate for a company, firm, or individual and is compensated on a commission basis. The agent does not have title to the property, but generally represents the owner.

Real Estate Investment Trust (REIT)   An entity that allows a very large number of investors to participate in the purchase of real estate, but as passive investors. The investors do not buy directly, but instead purchase shares in the REIT that owns the real estate investment. REITs are fairly common with the advent of mutual funds and can be invested in for as little as $10 per share, and sometimes less.

Real Property   Land and buildings and anything that may be permanently attached to them.

Recording   The placing of a copy of a document in the proper books in the office of the Register of Deeds so that a public record will be made of it.

Redemption   The right that an owner-mortgagor, or one claiming under him, has after execution of the mortgage to recover back his title to the mortgaged property by paying the mortgage debt, plus interest and any other costs or penalties imposed, prior to the occurrence of a valid foreclosure. The payment discharges the mortgage and places the title back as it was at the time the mortgage was executed.

Refinancing   The process of the same mortgagor paying off one loan with the proceeds from another loan.

Reformation   The correction of a deed or other instrument by reason of a mutual mistake of the parties involved or because of the mistake of one party caused by the fraud or inequitable conduct of the other party.

Release   The giving up or abandoning of a claim or right to the person against whom the claim exists or against whom the right is to be exercised or enforced.

Release of Lien   The discharge of certain property from the lien of a judgment, mortgage, or claim.

Renewal   Taking a new lease after an existing lease expires.

Rent   A compensation, either in money, provisions, chattels, or labor, received by the owner or real estate from a tenant for the occupancy of the premises.

Rescission of Contract   The abrogating or annulling of a contract; the revocation or repealing of contract by mutual consent of the parties to the contract, or for other causes as recognized by law.

Restrictive Covenants   Private restrictions limiting the use of real property. Restrictive covenants are created by deed and may run with the land, thereby binding all subsequent purchasers of the land, or may be deemed personal and binding only between the original seller and the buyer. The determination of whether a covenant runs with the land or is personal is governed by the language of the covenant, the intent of the parties, and the law in the state where the land is situated. Restrictive covenants that run with the land are encumbrances and may affect the value and marketability of title. Restrictive covenants may limit the density of buildings per acre, regulate size, the style or price range of buildings to be erected, or prevent particular businesses from operating or minority groups from owning or occupying homes in a given area. This latter discriminatory covenant is unconstitutional and has been declared unenforceable by the U.S. Supreme Court.

Retained Earnings   That portion of the firm's earnings that has been saved rather than paid out as dividends.

Return on Assets (ROA)   The ratio of net income to total assets.

Return on Equity (ROE)   The ratio of net income to equity; measures the rate of return on common stockholders' investment.

Revocation   The recall of a power or authority conferred, or the vacating of an instrument previously made.

Right of Survivorship   Granted to two joint owners who purchase using that particular buying method. Stipulates that one gets full rights and becomes the sole owner of the property upon the death of the other. Right of survivorship is the fundamental difference between acquiring property as joint owners and as tenants in common.

Sales Agreement   (See *agreement of sale*.)

Security Deposit   Money or things of value received by or for a property owner to ensure payment of rent and the satisfactory condition of the rented premises upon termination of the written or oral lease.

Security Interest   An interest in property that secures payment or performance of an obligation.

Special Assessment   A legal charge, or special tax, imposed on property, individual lots, or all property in the immediate area, by a public authority to pay the cost of public improvements, such as for the opening, grading, and guttering of streets, the construction of sidewalks and sewers, or the installation of street lights or other such items to be used for public purposes.

Special Lien   A lien that binds a specified piece of property, unlike a general lien, which is levied against all of one's assets. It creates a right to retain something of value belonging to another person as compensation for labor, material, or money expended in that person's behalf. In some localities, it is called a *particular* lien or *specific* lien. (See *lien*.)

Special Warranty Deed   A deed in which the grantor conveys title to the grantee and agrees to protect the grantee against title defects or claims asserted by the grantor and those persons whose right to assert a claim against the title arose during the period the grantor held title to the property. In a special warranty deed, the grantor guarantees to the grantee that he has done nothing during the time he held title to the property, or anything that might in the future, impair the grantee's title.

Specific Performance   A remedy in court of equity whereby the defendant may be compelled to do whatever he has agreed to do in a contract executed by him.

Statute   A law established by an act of the legislature; the written will of the legislature solemnly expressed according to the forms necessary to constitute it as provided by law.

Subdivision   A tract of land divided into smaller parcels of land, or lots, usually for the purpose of constructing new houses.

Sublease   An agreement whereby one person who has leased land from the owner rents out all or a portion of the premises for a period ending before the expiration of the original lease.

Subordination Clause   A clause in a mortgage or lease stating that one who has a prior claim or interest agrees that his interest or claim shall be secondary or subordinate to a subsequent claim, encumbrance, or interest.

Survey A map or plat made by a licensed surveyor showing the results of measuring the land with its elevations, improvements, boundaries, and its relationship to surrounding tracts of land. A survey is often required by the lender to assure that a building is actually sited on the land according to its legal description.

Survivorship The distinguishing feature of a tenancy by the entirety, by which on the death of one spouse, the surviving spouse acquires full ownership.

Tax As applied to real estate, an enforced charge imposed on persons, property, or income, to be used to support the government. The governing body in turn uses the funds in the best interest of the general public.

Tax Deed A deed given where property has been purchased at public sale because of the owner's nonpayment of taxes.

Tax Sale A sale of property for nonpayment of taxes assessed against it.

Tenancy at Will An arrangement under which a tenant occupies land with the consent of the owner, but without a definite termination date and without any definite agreement for the regular payment of rent.

Tenancy in Common Style of ownership in which two or more persons purchase a property jointly, but with no right of survivorship. Each tenant in common is the owner of an undivided fractional interest in the whole property. They are free to will their share to anyone they choose, a primary difference between that form of ownership and joint tenancy.

Tenant One who holds or possesses land or tenements by any kind of title, either in fee, for life, for years, or at will. The term is most commonly used as one who has under lease, the temporary use and occupation of real property that belongs to another person or persons. The tenant is the lessee.

Time Is of the Essence A phrase meaning that time is of crucial value and vital importance and that failure to fulfill deadlines will be considered to be a failure to perform the contract.

Title As generally used, the rights of ownership and possession of particular property. In real estate usage, title may refer to the instruments or documents by which a right of ownership is established (title documents), or it may refer to the ownership interest one has in the real estate.

Title Insurance   Protects lenders or home owners against loss of their interest in property due to legal defects in title. Title insurance may be issued to a mortgagee's title policy. Insurance benefits will be paid only to the named insured in the title policy, so it is important that an owner purchase an owner's title policy if he desires the protection of title insurance.

Title Search or Examination   A check of the title records, generally at the local courthouse, to make sure the buyer is purchasing a house from the legal owner and there are no liens, overdue special assessments, or other claims or outstanding restrictive covenants filed in the record, which would adversely affect the marketability or value of title.

Trust   A relationship under which one person, the trustee, holds legal title to property for the benefit of another person, the trust beneficiary.

Trustee   A party who is given legal responsibility to hold property in the best interest of or for the benefit of another. The trustee is one placed in a position of responsibility for another, a responsibility enforceable in a court of law. (See *deed of trust*.)

Truth-in-Lending Act   Federal law requiring written disclosure of the terms of a mortgage (including the APR and other charges) by a lender to a borrower after application. Also requires the right to rescission period.

Underwriting   In mortgage lending, the process of determining the risks involved in a particular loan and establishing suitable terms and conditions for the loan.

Unimproved   As it relates to land, vacant or lacking in essential appurtenant improvements required to serve a useful purpose.

Useful Life   The period of time over which a commercial property can be depreciated for tax purposes. A property's useful life is also referred to as its economic life.

Usury   Charging a higher rate of interest on a loan than is allowed by law.

Valid   Having force, or binding forces; legally sufficient and authorized by law.

Valuation   The act or process of estimating value; the amount of estimated value.

Value   Ability to command goods, including money, in exchange; the quantity of goods, including money, that should be commanded or received in exchange for the item valued. As applied to real estate, value is the present worth of all the rights to future benefits arising from ownership.

Variance   An exception to a zoning ordinance granted to meet certain specific needs, usually given on an individual case-by-case basis.

Void   That which is unenforceable; having no force or effect.

Waiver   Renunciation, disclaiming, or surrender of some claim, right, or prerogative.

Warranty Deed   A deed that transfers ownership of real property and in which the grantor guarantees that the title is free and clear of any and all encumbrances.

Zoning Ordinances   The acts of an authorized local government establishing building codes and setting forth regulations for property land usage.

INDEX

A

Average Monthly Rent, 85

B

Back door exits, 98–99
broadcast fax, 57
business plan, 2, 18, 19, 21, 105, 112–113, 114
buy and hold strategy, 5, 23, 24–25, 27
buy and sell strategy, 5

C

capital gains, 11, 12, 21, 111
capitalization rate, 26, 29, 83–85, 86, 88, 89
cash flow, 2, 3, 12, 84, 85, 86, 88–89, 105, 106, 144, 145, 146, 147, 162, 165, 204
cash flow analysis, 2, 3, 12, 60
classified ads, 39
classified advertising, 42–43
clearly defined objectives, 18–19
closing process, 2, 117–119
Concessions, 99–100
Conventional mortgages, 105–107
cost approach, 58–59, 178, 179, 183
credit score, 2, 105, 112, 113–115, 165

D

Dealer, 13, 14–16, 17, 18, 20, 41, 42, 44, 48, 121, 122, 126, 135, 136
direct mail, 48, 49

E

entry strategy, 19, 20
escape clauses, 98
exit strategy, 19, 21

F

financial statements, 2, 60
flipping, 1, 3, 4, 17, 18, 20, 23, 29, 30, 35, 41, 57, 71, 106, 111, 122, 136, 139, 162, 187, 188, 194, 195, 216, 218
for sale by owners, 39, 40, 43, 44, 45, 51–52
foreclosures, 16, 39, 40, 52, 53–54, 156, 165, 167, 168, 171

H

handyman, 42, 43, 124
HELOC, 5, 108, 109, 162

I

income capitalization approach, 58, 60–61, 71, 80, 178, 179, 183

intermediate term investors, 12, 18
internal rate of return, 85
IRR, 85

L
leverage, 5–6, 12, 18, 108, 146, 148, 149, 153, 162, 165, 167, 170, 171, 172
local bank, 15, 47, 72, 105, 106, 107–108, 109, 112, 117
Long term investors, 12

M
model, 2, 17, 65, 67, 68, 69, 70, 75, 83, 87, 113, 182, 188, 195, 196, 197, 198
money talks approach, 92, 101–102
Mortgage brokers, 106, 107, 112, 124
multifamily, 2, 3, 26, 44, 63, 70, 71, 72, 179
Multiple Listing Service, 29, 44, 135

O
O.P.M., 5–6
office manager, 122, 123, 139
options, 12, 17–18, 39, 148, 155, 171, 172, 176
other people's money, 5, 6
owner financing, 65, 106, 110–111

P
Partnerships, 14, 106, 111–112, 164
post-entry strategy, 19, 20, 74, 129, 130, 135, 137
Preplanning, 134, 135
profit margins, 11
Property Location, 29–30, 31
property's physical condition, 4, 29, 31–37, 57, 98
proprietary model, 2, 65, 188

R
real estate agents, 14, 15, 29, 39–42, 44, 45, 48, 49, 51, 67, 79, 92, 122, 126–127, 135, 156, 159, 195

real estate investment clubs, 39, 40, 45
real estate owned, 15, 16, 47
real estate portfolio, 2, 3, 11, 23, 25, 213, 214, 217
real estate publications, 39, 40, 44, 48, 49
red herring technique, 92, 100–101, 102
Refinance Analyzer, 85, 86, 87, 89
rehab manager, 122, 123–124
REO, 15, 16, 47–48, 194
Retailer, 11, 23, 24, 26, 29, 30, 41, 169
ROI, 83, 84, 90, 198

S
sales comparison approach, 58, 59, 61–62, 178
Scout, 13–14, 16, 17, 18, 20, 121–123, 158
settlement statements, 117
Short term investors, 12
single family, 2, 3, 17, 20, 23, 26, 29, 39, 41, 44, 57, 58, 62, 63, 77, 79, 80, 91, 94, 132
Symphony Homes, 18, 35, 37, 79, 94, 100, 139, 145, 149, 151, 157, 166, 177, 199

T
the value play, 17, 23–37, 70, 71, 77, 90
The Value Play Rehab Analyzer, 65, 66, 70, 78, 82, 188, 193, 198
time horizon, 4, 12
title company, 117, 118, 122, 123, 125–126, 130
transfer tax, 118

U
underwriting guidelines, 2, 77, 105, 110, 115–117

V
vacant properties, 39, 40, 52–53

W
web sites, 39, 40, 44–45